Understanding Society through a Systems Approach

Kim offers an accessible, interdisciplinary textbook using systems theory as a framework to stimulate discussion about how the social sciences develop an understanding of society and its evolution. It promotes an integrated view of the social sciences by proposing politics, economics, administration, and community as the core areas of society, and explains their characteristics, how they are moved by what kind of systems, and how they have evolved through their interrelationships.

This book explains how the major areas operate on certain structures and principles, and how they have developed while maintaining certain relationships with each other. The beauty of the entire field of social sciences lies in understanding society and social sciences as a whole and the relationships that intertwine it. It is unique in that it approaches social science from an Eastern perspective, using traditional Eastern thought and social phenomena as examples in its explanations and proposes a methodology for understanding society that's different to traditional social science textbooks, which use the application of natural science methodology and statistics to understand society.

Designed for a wide range of students in sociology, politics, and economics, encouraging interdisciplinary thinking and understanding. It is written with citations of classical writings by social scientists, including Locke, Rousseau, Hobbes, Mill, Marx, Engels, Proudhon, Smith, Weber, Durkheim, Buber, Myrdal, Habermas, Popper, Hayek, Putnam, and others. Through this book, readers can gain panoramic insights into how the works of these social scientists are interconnected.

Kim Dong-Hwan is Professor of Public Administration at Chung-Ang University, Seoul, South Korea. In his youth, he was involved in information and telecommunication policy in Korea. During his mid-career, he authored several books in Korean, including "System Dynamics" and "Systems Thinking." In his later years, he served as the president of two academic societies: the Korean System Dynamics Society and the Korean Association of Futures Studies.

Understanding Society through a Systems Approach

Interdisciplinary Perspectives from the Social Sciences

Kim Dong-Hwan

Routledge
Taylor & Francis Group
LONDON AND NEW YORK

First published 2025
by Routledge
605 Third Avenue, New York, NY 10158

and by Routledge
4 Park Square, Milton Park, Abingdon, Oxon, OX14 4RN

Routledge is an imprint of the Taylor & Francis Group, an informa business

ISBN: 9781032735474 (hbk)
ISBN: 9781032735450 (pbk)
ISBN: 9781003464730 (ebk)

DOI: 10.4324/9781003464730

Typeset in Times New Roman
by Deanta Global Publishing Services, Chennai, India

Contents

Preface

I had no intention of writing a book anymore. With about three years left until my retirement as a professor, I wanted to quietly wrap up my life as a scholar rather than writing a new book. I believed that I had already written enough books that fulfilled my role in the academic field during my life as a scholar. I once told Professor Yoon, my close friend since graduate student, that my aspiration as a scholar was to write a book that understands the world from the perspective of feedback. The book I published in 2004, titled *Systems Thinking*, was that book. Of course, I also wrote other books such as *System Simulation*, *System Dynamics*, *Mechanisms of Candlelight Movement*, and *Big Data Is a Bubble*. But the book that realized my dream from my youth was *Systems Thinking*. Besides academic books, I also published *Brothers Who Love the Lord*, documenting my church life in the United States, and *One hundred Patterns of Three-Cushion*, a book about the billiard game. Thus, I have published more books than I initially hoped for.

However, recently I felt the urge to write a new book. The primary reason was that I had free time. On December 27, 2021, my 92-year-old mother fell at home and fractured her hip joint, leading to the beginning of my caregiving journey. From 8 am to 6 pm, a caregiver looked after my mother, and from 6 pm to the next morning, it was my responsibility. As my caregiving life stabilized, I realized that there were many topics I hadn't included in my previous books. I often told my students, "I expect one of you to write a book based on my lectures." As a scholar reaching retirement age, I initially thought I didn't need to invest time and effort into writing a new book. Yet, I found myself repeating the same words to my students while spending my free time idly. Wasn't I being too irresponsible? Shouldn't I leave a record of my thoughts during this free time?

Unable to let go of these thoughts, I opened my laptop and began listing the contents that would go into the new book. These were the concepts that I had accumulated over the past 40 years from various sources, including readings, discussions, and personal experiences. They were mostly related to the broader field of social sciences. They were crucial concepts for understanding social sciences and necessary for comprehending the overall structure of societies. However, they were not explicitly addressed by social scientists. That's why it took me 40 years to understand and organize these concepts. I believed that compiling these concepts would be helpful for younger social scientists.

The reason I am writing this book is to enable people to appreciate the beauty of social sciences. By understanding the overall structure of social sciences, we can comprehend how different areas are interconnected. This understanding allows us to respect and discover wisdom in other branches of social sciences. Political scientists won't ignore scholars of public administration, and economists will show respect for political scientists. Only when social scientists understand the entire structures of societies can they truly grasp the beauty of social sciences. I hope this book can unfold the beauty of social sciences.

The backbone of this book was initially published as a booklet in 2022 in Korean (Kim 2022). Building upon this foundation, I integrate a systems approach and classical literature from social scientists, incorporating exemplary cases from both Eastern and Western cultures. Ms Lim Clarissa of Routledge provided encouragement for this work, while Mr Lee Chan-Gyu of BOOKOREA offered support. I am grateful to all my companions on this journey, especially my mother, who has been with me in this wonderful social world.

From my mother's house
March 1, 2024

Part I
Methodology of Social Science

The essence of social science methodology lies in understanding society. I believe that true methodology does not involve delving into impractical concepts of philosophy or demanding strict adherence to statistical procedures. The true methodology is grounded in a sincere desire to comprehend society, stemming from a humble recognition of our ignorance about it.

Society emerges as an invisible entity from the interactions of individuals, extending beyond human perceptions. Understanding these intangible societies is the essential challenge of social science. Emerging societies and their dynamic changes construct a social world in which individuals live. Although societies are intangible to human perception, all human beings experience them every day and night. Societies and individuals consistently interact, ranging from socialization to individualization. This part discusses how social scientists, as individual human beings, can understand and explain society.

DOI: 10.4324/9781003464730-1

1 Target of Social Science

Emergent Property

What is the target of social science? Interestingly, many social scientists themselves do not know what social science is. Simply put, social science is the study of society. It sounds straightforward and clear, so why do many people not know what social science is? It is because society is an abstract construct. For example, let's consider a company like Google. Where does the true essence of Google as a company reside? Is it in the building where the headquarters are located? Or is it defined by the legal regulations in its articles of incorporation? If not, does the essence of Google as a company only exist in the minds of people? We frequently mention Google, but its core essence remains intangible. The same applies to society.

Let's consider another example. We can take the concept of "family" as a representative example of society with a small scale but a solid existence. A family is a fundamental social unit within which individuals live and interact on a daily basis. However, no one can directly encounter the essence of a family. The house we live in is not the family itself. Nor can we consider the parents or children who constitute the family as the essence of the family. The family registry certificate stored at the local government office is not the essence of the family either. So, what truly defines the essence of a family?

Let's consider this on a broader scale. What defines the essence of a nation, like South Korea? Is it the territory? Is it the people residing within that territory? Is it the constitutional entity governing South Korea? None of these elements –territory, populace, or the governing entity alone – can fully capture the essence of a nation. Reflecting on this, we come to realize that even societies we assume to know well are not completely understood, and their essence cannot be directly apprehended.

Consequently, since society is intangible, the first task of social scientists is how they perceive society. Emile Durkheim, in exploring the methods of sociology, questioned what "social facts" are. He clearly recognized that the concept of society is neither tangible nor visible. However, he could not leave the target of sociology ambiguous. Durkheim stated that "social facts must be treated as things," sparking much debate. He regarded society as an entity external to the individual that exerts pressure on the individual. As a father and a citizen, one performs his duties and obligations. The wave of pity and indignation in a public gathering affects all participants, although it may not be present in any one individual. Durkheim defined such social phenomena as "social facts."

DOI: 10.4324/9781003464730-2

> A social fact is any way of acting, whether fixed or not, capable of exerting over the individual an external constraint, or which is general over the whole of a given society whilst having an existence of its own, independent of its individual manifestations.
>
> (Durkheim 1895, p. 59)

In contemporary times, many social scientists tend to designate their research subjects as individuals. They conduct surveys and perform statistical analyses based on the responses from individual people. Consequently, there is a tendency to perceive the study of society as an examination of people's thoughts and responses, thereby losing sight of the original purpose of studying society through people. Engaging in research in this manner, social scientists often grapple with the question of whether their research subject is society itself or the individuals forming that society. This phenomenon is reminiscent of a Buddhist analogy where, while a teacher points his finger at the moon, people become so fixated on his finger that they miss the moon.

The study of individuals falls under the purview of the humanities, whereas social science encompasses the examination of societies shaped by these individuals. Consequently, the research subjects of humanities scholars and social scientists are inherently distinct. However, as social scientists often rely on surveys of individuals, they may occasionally lose sight of their unique subjects. This reliance on surveys can blur the lines between the study of individual thoughts and the exploration of societies beyond individuals. If they persist in this blurring, they may find themselves aligning more closely with humanities scholars rather than social scientists.

The fundamental distinction between humanities and social science becomes clear through the concept of "emergent property." An emergent property is a

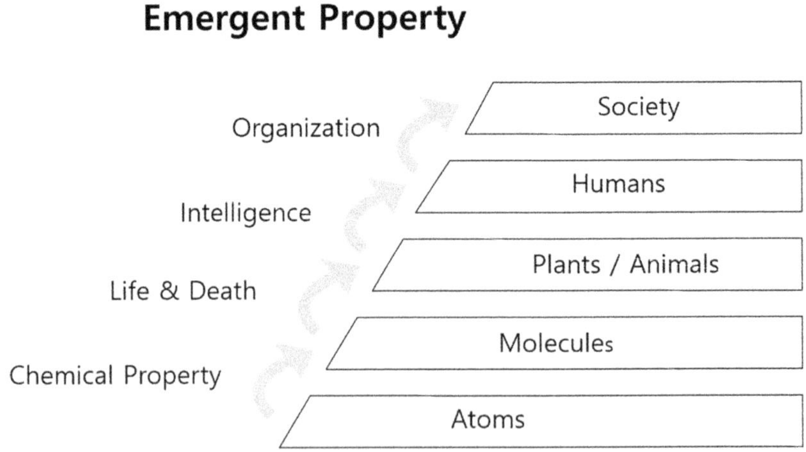

Figure 1.1 Society as an emerged entity from individual humans.

characteristic that is not present at the individual level but emerges at the level of the whole. Molecules, composed of atoms, exhibit properties that do not exist at the atomic level. For instance, certain molecules block electricity, while others conduct it, and some store electricity. Since molecules are composed of atoms, some people mistakenly assume that physicists studying atoms can comprehend all properties of molecules. However, focusing solely on atoms does not unveil the electrical properties of molecules. The exploration of emergent properties at the molecular level falls within the realm of chemistry.

In a similar vein, plants, composed of molecules, exhibit properties of life and death that are not present at the molecular level. Furthermore, animals form pairs, give birth to offspring, and propagate their species. These concepts of mates, offspring, and species do not exist at the molecular level. Likewise, society, comprised of individuals, manifests emergent properties that are not present at the individual level. While humanities scholars focus on studying the characteristics of individuals, social scientists delve into the emergent properties that arise at the level of society. Therefore, the research subjects of humanities and social science are fundamentally different.

Sawyer is a rare scholar who places a strong emphasis on emergence in social research. He defines emergence as "the processes whereby the global behavior of the system results from the actions and interactions of agents" (Sawyer 2005, p. 2). Given that social emergence is a central phenomenon in the social sciences, Sawyer highlights the importance for social scientists to focus on the concept of social emergence. He notes that in the mid-20th century, economic scholars developed their theories with a specific emphasis on the social emergence of the market, leading to the successful establishment of economic imperialism. Unfortunately, even today, many social scientists do not adequately address social emergence (Sawyer 2005, p. 189).

Diverse Social Emergences

When individuals unite to create a society, what emergent properties come into play? One of the most notable emergent properties is "organization." Individual humans gather to establish various forms of organizations. The most basic manifestation of organization is the "family." Once organizations are formed, they persist even when their members are gone. Even when family members are not physically present in the house, the family endures. Similarly, when all employees leave a company at the end of the workday, the company does not dissolve but continues to exist, just as it did during working hours. Even in the event of the passing of some family members, the family persists. Likewise, even if all employees in a company are replaced, the company does not vanish.

To affirm the existence of these organizations, people have developed the concept of a "legal entity." A "legal entity" treats an organization as a living entity in the legal world. Nearly all types of organizations, including companies, schools, religious groups, and academic societies, operate as legal entities. They function as if they are living entities, possessing the ability to own property and having various rights and obligations. Such an existence is not observable at the individual human level.

There is an entity that exceeds the scope of legal entities – it is the assembly of individuals known as a "nation." A nation possesses enigmatic attributes that transcend individuality. Not only does it have a life-like existence akin to humans, but it also holds the authority to sanction lethal force. Created by people, the "nation" now commands loyalty from its citizens, surpassing the significance of any individual human member within it.

Another emergent property that results from human interaction is "money." The essence of money is the promise and agreement among people. A ten-dollar bill, in its physical form, is merely paper, with an intrinsic value close to zero. However, it serves as a "certificate" symbolizing the agreed-upon value of ten dollars within a community. This agreement is underwritten by the state. Similarly, stocks and bonds also represent agreements among individuals in financial markets. Given that currencies, stocks, and bonds are fundamentally agreements among people, their practical values always experience slight fluctuations. Money holds no meaning for those living alone in mountains or islands.

Another emergent property that cannot be overlooked is "law," which constitutes an agreement among people. These are commitments made by the citizenry, with the understanding that there will be consequences if not adhered to. However, not all citizens participate in these agreements; they are established by those who claim to represent the citizens. Laws are enforced through punishments, even extending to sentencing people to death. As the Danish writer Piet Hein aptly put it, "Man is the animal that draws lines which he himself then stumbles over." While we create these agreements, they take on a life of their own, binding us. Laws do not exist at the individual level but emerge at the societal level. Therefore, legal studies belong to social science rather than humanities.

A person who does not abide by the law is called a criminal or sinner. Just as laws gain meaning at the societal level, the concepts of sin and crime also gain meaning at the societal level. Similarly, the concepts of good and evil are societal constructs. The notions of good and evil cannot be found at the individual level. The discussions of whether the nature of human being is good or evil are meaningless. The concepts of sin, good, and evil belong to the realm of social science.

Another significant emergent property that has become increasingly important in modern society is "standards." The width of railroad tracks is standardized, and trains are designed according to this standard. Similarly, the width of lanes on roads is standardized, and cars cannot exceed this standardized width. The voltage of electricity supplied to homes is standardized at 220 volts, and household appliances follow the standard voltage. In today's information and communication society, more and more standards are being established. Computers, internet protocols, Wi-Fi standards, mobile phones, electric chargers, and other electronic devices adhere to these standards. While there are standards defined by law, there are also de facto standards that practically dominate the market. The USB connector, widely used for data transfer and connecting devices to computers, is an example of a de facto standard that has been widely adopted without legal mandate.

Perhaps the earliest established standard in human history is language. The form of the language spoken in the capital city is often considered the standard dialect of the country. Without language standardization, communication becomes impossible, and societal activities are paralyzed. The existence of a standardized language among people allows for the existence of society. Conversely, because society exists, language exists. In a world where individuals live alone, language disappears. Robinson Crusoe, stranded on a deserted island, worried about forgetting his language.

In agricultural societies, a crucial standard was the calendar. By consulting the calendar, people could determine when to plant seeds and when the time for harvest would arrive. The more significant role of the calendar was its ability to facilitate cooperation with neighbors. When all neighbors shared the same standard calendar, they could discuss and decide together on days for planting and harvesting. In industrial societies, a crucial standard is the clock. All employees must arrive at the factory by the same time in the morning, for the factory to operate. It is only possible when all employees have clocks indicating the same time. Especially for soldiers who need to launch a coordinated attack on the enemy from different locations at a predetermined time, a standard clock is essential equipment.

In modern society, where numerous technologies emerge and disappear, silent wars often occur to gain recognition as a standard. This is referred to as "standard wars." The winner of the standard wars monopolizes the market and accumulates enormous wealth. This underscores the significance of standards as emergent properties in societies and emphasizes their importance in the study of social science.

Furthermore, culture also falls under a social emergence. Musicians play a composition created by someone, and the audience, witnessing and listening to it, becomes immersed in the joy of beauty. Music is created, played, and transmitted among individual humans who take their roles in musical society. The conductor of an orchestra orchestrates diverse melodies, rhythms, and breaths produced by members playing various instruments to unfold beautiful harmonies. The conductor of an orchestra is often likened to a political leader guiding a diverse and intricate society harmoniously. Music transcends the individual and becomes a societal experience.

Individuals who have spent a busy day in a business office find solace as they enter their small yet cozy homes. Houses and buildings externalize social relationships in various forms. A church aspiring to the heaven stands tall, while a tavern celebrating earthly pleasures positions itself in the darkness below ground. Schools, institutions for imparting societal knowledge, are constructed in an open manner accessible to all residents. Administrative offices, easily accessible to residents but constructed with a firm appearance that conveys authority and protects against intrusion from dissatisfied individuals, represent the power of law enforcement.

Rural houses, where self-sufficiency is crucial, often adopt the form of small, flat buildings. In contrast, urban houses, heavily dependent on market purchases for most necessities, tend to favor tall apartments situated along the streets. Furthermore, the most spacious and luxurious room in a house is typically reserved for the head of the household, while smaller, secluded rooms are inhabited by young children or maids. Buildings serve as tangible manifestations of societal culture.

When visiting a city, one can gain insights into its history simply by observing its buildings and roads. In old cities governed by powerful leaders, one can observe straight, wide roads stretching out from their central residences. In European cities, the presence of a church building in the center signifies the governing function of the church. In contrast, temples in China and Korea are typically situated on the outskirts of cities, reflecting a historical suppression of Buddhism by central governments over an extended period. Nevertheless, they persisted in cities because ordinary people held Buddhism dear to their hearts.

The extensive network of roads connecting buildings is also a social emergence, symbolizing the interactions among individuals. Society is essentially a network of individuals. As society expands, more and larger roads are constructed. Urban roads are often metaphorically compared to the veins in the human body. Just as blood flows through veins delivering oxygen and nutrients, roads supply energy and materials to the members of society.

Societies Emerging in Mirrors

Clothing goes beyond personal preference to signify social relationships. The attire worn by men and women differs in terms of form and color, reflecting societal roles and expectations. Some companies define the characteristics of clothing employees should wear when commuting, known as a dress code. In certain workplaces, wearing shorts may be prohibited, while in others, flashy clothing might be restricted. Dress codes that prohibit employees from wearing vibrant colors enforce uniformity and conformity. Furthermore, dress codes can be perceived as reflecting inequality and discrimination. Forcing female flight attendants to wear skirts instead of pants, for example, is indicative of gender discrimination.

A police officer's uniform is noticeably different from the attire of ordinary citizens, even from a distance. This distinction is essential due to the risky nature of their role, and citizens need to easily recognize their presence. Military uniforms also exhibit differences. To avoid easy detection and potential attacks from enemies, military uniforms typically blend in with the colors of the forest or desert sand. However, to prevent friendly fire incidents, they must be distinct from the uniforms of the opposing forces. Similarly, soccer players' uniforms follow a similar principle, where teammates wear identical uniforms, distinguishing them from the opposing team. This helps prevent mistakes in passing to opponents. Most importantly, wearing uniforms of different colors for each team contributes to reducing confusion for TV viewers.

Fragrance also emerges in social relationships. People cannot smell their own perfume. The perfume applied to oneself is not for one's own nose but for the noses of others. They apply perfume for others. Ultimately, perfume is oriented towards social relationships. Similarly, hairstyles also aim for social connections. I cannot see the shape and color of my hair; those who see my hair are the people I encounter. My hairstyle is not for my eyes but for the eyes of others.

Through the mirror, I see my reflection. The mirror is my society. The me reflected in the mirror and the I looking at the mirror form a small society.

Sometimes, I am startled by my reflection in the mirror. Occasionally, when I see my reflection in the mirror, it feels like a stranger. I engage in conversations with my reflection in the mirror. Through the dialogue between the "observing I" and the "observed me" in the mirror, social relationships are established. Most of the time, they share the same thoughts, but it's not always the case. When I close my eyes, the world turns dark, yet the me in the mirror stays in the light. With the help of the mirror, I and me engage in small talk and form a small society.

Even the concept of self is an emergent property shaped by society. Without you, there is no "I." In my youth, I read Martin Buber's book "*I and Thou*" and was deeply moved. I exist because "You" exist, and I am here because "It" is there. However, you and it are fundamentally different. Buber compares you and it as follows.

> The basic word I-You can only be spoken with one's whole being. The basic word I-It can never be spoken with one's whole being (p. 54). The world as experience belongs to the basic word I-It. The basic word I-You establishes the world of relation.
>
> (Buber 1923, p. 56)

The society discussed in this book is the world of I-You and I-It. In a world where I exist alone, there is neither You nor We, and ultimately, I cannot recognize myself. This is the paradox of society. Paradoxically, the individual is a social concept. This is why the humanities and social sciences are both separate and intertwined.

2 Statics vs. Dynamics of Social Sciences

Social phenomena are fundamentally emergent phenomena. "Emergent" means that they arise when people gather. Emergent phenomena that arise when people come together can undergo changes when people disperse. However, as mentioned earlier, the emergent properties do not disappear when people disperse. But their characteristics can change. A family that loses all its fortune remains fundamentally the same household, but its atmosphere inevitably changes. Similarly, a company losing a key executive is still the same corporation, but maintaining the same level of performance is a different story. Emphasizing its continuity as the same household or corporation underscores a stable order. Focusing on the changes in the household and corporation compared to the past highlights the dynamics of society.

Social science that emphasizes unchanging order is called "statics," while the one that focuses on change is termed "dynamics." The mainstream of social science is statics, with dynamics being the minority. Most social scientists prefer statics, which highlights social orders, including legal structures, governance systems, and principles of market equilibrium. Only a few social scientists delve into discussions about societal changes. As society undergoes transformations, new laws emerge while existing ones may be abolished. Ruling parties can lose elections, and unexpected figures may seize political power. In the market, businesses can either succeed or fail. In earlier times, John Locke observed as follows:

> Things of this world are in so constant a flux that nothing remains long in the same state. Thus people, riches, trade, power, change their stations; flourishing mighty cities come to ruin, and prove in time neglected desolate corners, whilst other unfrequented places grow into populous countries filled with wealth and inhabitants.
>
> (Locke 1689, Chapter XIII)

Scholars who perceive society as an unchanging order prefer nouns. However, scholars who constantly observe societal changes are inclined to use verbs rather than nouns. Hence, Karl Weick chose to use the present participle verb "organizing" instead of the noun "organization" (Weick 1979). Organizations are not fixed but continually undergo cycles of formation and dissolution. Even at this moment, political forces are collaborating and battling. Billions of households residing on

DOI: 10.4324/9781003464730-3

Table 2.1 Two approaches of social science: statics vs. dynamics

	Focus	*Popularity*	*Eastern culture*	*Modern age*
Statics	Order	Majority	Confucianism	Equilibrium economics
Dynamics	Change	Minority	I Ching	System dynamics

the Earth's surface are loving, fighting, and turning away. Taking Weick's perspective, the term "emerging property" might be more suitable for explaining society than "emergent property."

Many social scientists prefer order over change. This is partly because order is easier to study, but also because those in power in society prefer order. In the era of monarchies, it was forbidden to speak of the possibility of a change in the king. Whether in the East or West, an emphasis on statics was promoted, while dynamics were prohibited. Statics was acknowledged as a reputable discipline contributing to social order, while dynamics were perceived as a disruptive idea capable of destabilizing society.

In Eastern societies, Confucianism is considered the representative discipline of statics. In Western society, economics, which emphasizes the equilibrium of market prices, can be seen as the representative discipline of statics. In Confucianism, the relationship between the ruler and his subjects or the relationship between spouses is considered an unchanging order. Economics, particularly in its classical form, regards a market that maintains equilibrium prices as normal and good, while a market where prices are volatile is considered abnormal and bad. In the past, Confucianism was the mainstream discipline in Eastern societies, while equilibrium economics is the mainstream discipline in modern society.

Although social scientists who emphasize change are a minority, they do not disappear. Regardless of East or West, there have always been scholars studying dynamics. Why is that? In reality, society is constantly changing, and in order to understand and respond to such changes, dynamics was needed in the "field." In a battlefield where one must quickly respond to invading enemies to survive, dynamics is needed, not statics. While statics enjoys peace in the ivory tower, protected by the ruling class, dynamics engages in the field, relying on their own insights to navigate change.

In Eastern societies, the "I Ching" has been a representative text associated with the study of change and dynamics. Confucius summarized the core philosophy of "I Ching" as "Alternation of yin and yang is the truth." It means that one moment is dominated by yin and the next moment is dominated by yang, representing constant change. In Western society, system dynamics is the representative discipline of dynamics. System dynamics is a discipline developed by Professor Jay Forrester at MIT (Forrester 1961; Senge 1990; Sterman 2000), and it is a field of study that I found most interesting and dedicatedly studied when I was young (Kim et al. 1999).

Dynamics in Taijitu

"Taijitu (太極圖)" signifies the "diagram (圖)" of the "ultimate poles (太極)" encompassing yin and yang, the relationship of which generates all changes in the universe. Surprisingly, ancient Eastern Taijitu and modern Western system dynamics share three principles of change (Kim 2004). The first principle of dynamics acknowledges the continuous change in everything. System dynamics begins by observing changes in a system over time. The evident reality that all systems undergo change is a shared foundational principle for both Taijitu and system dynamics. The curve flowing through the center of the Taijitu symbolizes the moon's constant changes. This signifies that, much like the ever-changing appearance of the moon, society also undergoes continuous transformation. Although this principle may appear simple, it is not. Many philosophies and social sciences cherish unchanging elements as truth and tend to overlook change. Equilibrium economics perceives the concept of change as unnecessary. In their theory and mindset, no change is deemed worthy of attention.

The second principle of dynamics involves discovering structures that amplify change and structures that inhibit change. In Taijitu, the force that amplifies change is understood as yang (陽), while the force that inhibits change is understood as yin (陰). In terms of Chinese characters, yin (陰) represents a shaded area, and yang (陽) represents a sunlit area. In the shaded area, change is inhibited. Grass and trees cannot thrive. In the sunlit area, change is facilitated. Grass, flowers, and trees flourish, and bees and birds come, bringing about rapid transformations. Taijitu understands the change in the system through the interaction of the inhibiting force of yin and the facilitating force of yang.

The white section in the Taijitu signifies the force of yang, and the black section represents the force of yin. Taijitu illustrates a competitive relationship where the diminishing force of yin corresponds to the expanding force of yang. However, upon closer inspection, Taijitu reveals a mutual embrace between the forces of yin and yang. When the force of yin is insufficient, yang complements it, and when the force of yang is lacking, yin provides support. Taijitu symbolizes the continuous competition between yin and yang while representing the harmony of interdependence.

Figure 2.1 Taijitu with yin and yang to explain all changes in the universe.

On both sides of the Taijitu, small dots are marked – a white dot in the area of yin and a black dot in the area of yang. This signifies the seeds of change. It represents the birth of yang seeds from the center of yin area, and the growth of yin seeds from the center of yang area. This points to the idea that the force leading to the collapse of a nation exists not on the periphery but within the ruling class. Gorbachev, who dissolved the Soviet Union, was within the Grand Kremlin Palace. The one who dismantled the absolute power of the Roman Catholic Church was its priest, Martin Luther. Steve Jobs was dismissed by the board of directors of the company he had founded. The root cause of the downfall of a powerful entity lies not in external competitors but in the internal core members.

The attempt to comprehend the change from the perspectives of yin and yang is evident in system dynamics. In system dynamics, yin is associated with the term "negative" or the symbol "-", while yang corresponds to "positive" or the symbol "+". Within system dynamics, positive causation denotes causal relationships where the cause and effect move in the same direction, while negative causation refers to relationships where they move in opposite directions.

The third principle of dynamics is "circulation," symbolized by the circle forming the outer line of the Taijitu. While yin and yang are fundamental factors driving the system's change, circulation represents the overall structure of dynamics. System dynamics also emphasizes circulating causal relationships, referred to as feedback loops (Richardson 1991). Without circular causal relationships, all changes are nothing but onetime events. When causal relationships circulate, change occurs continuously. The persistence of change in a system indicates the presence of feedback loops.

Arnold Toynbee, who interpreted the history of human civilization as "challenges and responses," viewed history from a dynamic perspective. When a creative minority responds to the challenges of civilization, a new civilization is born. However, with the passage of time, the creative minority gradually loses its creativity and degrades into a dominant minority that rules through force. The civilization then degenerates into a static period. Toynbee explains the process of the emergence of a new civilization from this stagnation as follows:

> Against this static condition the secession of a proletariat is a dynamic reaction; and in this light we can see that, in the secession of a proletariat from a dominant minority, a new civilization is generated through the transition of a society from a static condition to a dynamic activity … In their pregnant imagery the sages of the Chinese Society described these alternations in terms of Yin and Yang - Yin the static and Yang the dynamic.
>
> (Toynbee 1946, p. 70)

Toynbee interpreted the history of human civilization from a dynamic perspective and interestingly applied the dynamics of Yin and Yang in Taijitu.

Dynamics Indispensable for Societies

We witness constant waves in nature: rivers flow incessantly, and the waves of the sea surge in and retreat. The human body also continuously generates waves, supplying blood to every nook and cranny. Even during sleep, the human body continues to produce waves without pause. Human existence relies on waves. Waves are not merely behavioral manifestations but also the fundamental basis of existence.

Moreover, beyond the realm of nature and the human body, society creates a rhythmic pattern of dynamic waves. Society not only exhibits dynamics but also cannot exist without them. Dynamic waves make society possible.

The market that sustains the capitalist world is the stock market. Stock prices never cease to change, even for a moment. Every stock price chart is a continuous series of waves, repeating cycles of rise and fall. What happens if stock prices maintain equilibrium? If stock prices remain in a steady state of equilibrium, it means one cannot profit by buying or selling stocks. This is because buying and selling at the same price yield no profit. In a stock market at equilibrium where no one can make a profit, everyone exits. Consequently, the stock market can no longer be sustained. Waves not only represent the dynamic behavior observed in the stock market but also serve as its foundation for existence. Without waves, there can be no stock market.

Similar to the stock market, there are numerous societal realms that rely on dynamics. The world of fashion, for instance, is premised on change. Without change, there would be no trends. There are contradicting forces constantly shaping trends. One driving force is the desire to conform and be like others. If people are wearing long pants, I also want to wear long pants. If I alone wear short pants and step out onto the street, I feel outdated. Another driving force is the desire to stand out and appear different from others. If many people wear jeans, suddenly jeans start to feel like a uniform. The ebb and flow of these two conflicting forces continually create and alter trends.

Sometimes, one can encounter fashions and fads in unexpected places. According to Eric Abrahamson's research, various management techniques spread and disappear based more on social trends than on their technical advantages or disadvantages. Certain management techniques have repeatedly gained and lost popularity since the turn of the century. Companies go through cycles of enthusiastic adoption of management techniques, including job enrichment, team organization, and quality circles (Abrahamson 1996). In the course of social trends, ineffective management techniques can proliferate throughout society. Conversely, management techniques with technical advantages may fade away if they fail to become trends. Abrahamson's discovery of management techniques as fashion can be applicable across a broad spectrum of social sciences.

Politics is a realm defined by dynamic waves. Without change in politics, the same ruling power persists, suggesting prolonged governance. Politics devoid of change is essentially stagnant. Similar to stagnant water in a puddle, politics without change tends to breed corruption. Ultimately, politics bereft of dynamic waves degrades from democracy to dictatorship. Politics thrives only in dynamics.

The public policy arena is also characterized by constant change. New societal issues emerge continuously, capturing the public's attention. However, as people realize the significant costs associated with addressing these issues, public attention often wanes. The environmental problem serves as a prime example. Anthony Downs termed this phenomenon the "issue-attention cycle," which dominates American public debates.

> American public attention rarely remains sharply focused upon any one domestic issue for very long – even if it involves a continuing problem of crucial importance to society. Instead, a systematic issue-attention cycle seems strongly to influence public attitudes and behavior concerning most key domestic problems. Each of these problems suddenly leaps into prominence, remains there for a short time, and then – though still largely unresolved – gradually fades from the center of public attention.
>
> (Downs 1972, p. 38)

I believe that the essence of social science lies in dynamics. However, this doesn't imply that statics is useless. If dynamics is the essence of social science, then statics represents its valuable order. Furthermore, statics is often esteemed by the elite majority. As a social scientist, one should not forget the essence of dynamics, but there is no need to forsake statics. With a dynamic perspective firmly in mind, a social scientist can maintain curiosity, interest, and awareness of societal issues. Additionally, by employing a static representation of society, he can capture the attention of the elite majority. Therefore, I encourage young scholars to study both dynamics and statics together. Ultimately, a comprehensive understanding of social sciences requires an appreciation of both the enduring roots reflected in statics and the fluid movements captured in dynamics.

3 Method of Testimony

Social phenomena are emergent and ever-changing. Like the wind, society is intangible and cannot be touched. However, we all experience society as we live within it every day. The mission of a social scientist is to discover and explain how and why societies undergo changes. Understanding and explaining these changes involves identifying constant patterns and structures within the dynamic nature of society. Therefore, social scientists seek to identify unchanging structures and patterns within the context of dynamic social changes.

Scholars refer to relatively stable institutions in society as "structures." A nation is composed of various sectors and institutions that interact with each other, including the military, government agencies, businesses, churches, and households. Individuals live and make choices within these structures. Social scientists aim to elucidate these social structures and explain their functioning. In this book, I use the term "frames" to describe the appearance of social structures, and the principles guiding the operation of these structures are referred to as "mechanisms."

Scholars endeavor to unveil the structures and mechanisms of their research subjects. Similar to how a botanist discerns the structure of a plant – comprising roots, stems, and leaves – and seeks to comprehend the plant's growth mechanism, social scientists follow a comparable approach. However, the challenge lies in the fact that social structures and mechanisms lack the visibility of plants. Because these structures and mechanisms are intangible, social scientists cannot directly demonstrate them in the way that is possible with physical entities. In essence, social scientists encounter difficulty in providing direct evidence for the structures and mechanisms they uncover. This represents the most significant and fundamental distinction between social science and natural science. Natural scientists can present and experimentally demonstrate the structures and mechanisms they discover, whereas social scientists cannot directly show the structures or experimentally prove the mechanisms they understand.

Everyone acknowledges that the most fundamental structure in society is the "family," and it is commonly understood that families operate based on love. However, the structure of a family cannot be physically demonstrated, and the mechanism that necessitates love for a family to function cannot be experimentally proven. While a plant biologist can experiment with how a plant withers when moisture is removed, experimenting on what happens when love is removed from a family is not feasible. At best, we can survey people about how important love is.

DOI: 10.4324/9781003464730-4

Does this mean we don't understand how love functions within a family? No, we do. Through our lived experiences within families, we comprehend the mechanism of how love operates within them. How can we study the structure of a family and the mechanism of love? It cannot be approached in the same way as natural sciences.

Social scientists do not need to strictly follow the methodology of natural scientists. It is not that they should not do it, but rather that they cannot do it even if they try. Social phenomena are emergent and continually evolving, devoid of tangible recordings. Instead, they are documented through testimonies of individuals. In this context, I consider "testimony" to be a paramount methodology in social science, akin to the significance Christianity places on testimonies. In Christianity, testimony is the act of testifying to the experience of encountering God, and it is recorded in the Old and New Testaments of the Bible.

Despite the crucial role of testimony in understanding social phenomena, most social scientists still do not recognize testimony as a valid methodology because it does not exist in the methodology of natural science. Social scientists who want to imitate natural scientists often obsess over the words "evidence" and "experiment" used by natural scientists. Notably, behaviorists within social science emphasize experimentation and evidence. However, what we can experiment on and gather evidence for is limited to individual responses and behaviors, not the emergent properties at the social level.

I have advocated for "testimony" as a methodology in social science, inspired by the teachings of my mentor, Professor Lee Moon-Young. He endured imprisonment three times during the democratization movement. Through his testimony of the prison experience, he exemplified his philosophy of social science. He recounted his experience in prison as follows.

> (In the cold prison) I once woke up with a smile. As I noticed the smile on my face, I lay facing the wall. I did so because if the guards patrolling the corridor saw me smiling, they would report to their superiors that Professor Lee had gone crazy. The guards were vigilant about reporting anything concerning me. Lying back and facing the wall, I pondered why I was smiling … From this experience in the prison, my approach to social science shifted towards a direction that incorporates deep humanities.
>
> (Lee Moon-Young 2008, pp. 300–301)

In the cold and lonely prison, he experienced overflowing joy from within. In this joy, he found a meaning that transcended personal suffering. What I learned from Professor Lee was that his testimony is persuasive and self-proving.

About a decade ago, there was a surging wave of enthusiasm for "big data" among intellectuals in Korea. Virtually all intellectuals, policymakers, and businessmen asserted that big data would offer opportunities for the survival and growth of South Korea. Witnessing an overly exaggerated fervor for this trend, I authored a book titled "*Big Data is a Bubble* (Kim 2016)." In a situation where most people were enchanted by the concept of big data, conventional methods such as surveys and interviews fell short of unveiling the hype around it. Faced with the limitations of applying conventional methodologies, the method that came to my mind was "testimony." In academic terms, it is referred to as "auto-ethnography." However, I prefer the term testimony for its clear meaning (Kim 2018). In Christianity, testimony involves recounting one's experience of encountering God. In social science, testimony entails sharing insights and observations by witnessing the society an individual has experienced.

Can testimony be recognized as a methodology in social science? Many social scientists have expressed doubts about this. In response, I pose a question: Who is closer to a social scientist – a natural scientist in a laboratory or a judge in a courtroom?

Think about the spectrum of judgments that spans across natural science, the judiciary, and religion. Natural science makes judgments about theoretical claims based on material evidence. Religion makes judgments about faith through the testimonies of individuals. In the courtroom, both material evidence and testimonies have legal validity as grounds for judgment. The evidence presented in court can be broadly divided into two categories: "physical evidence" and "human evidence." Fingerprints, bloodstains, and CCTV recordings are physical evidence, while testimonies of eyewitnesses or confessions by the accused are human evidence. Human evidence is essentially testimony. In the courtroom, testimonies are used as essential evidence for making judgments, alongside physical evidence.

Where does social science fit in this spectrum? Is it closer to natural science? Closer to the judiciary? Closer to religious judgments? It cannot be said that the judgments in social science are the same as religious judgments. Social science is more similar to judgments in the courtroom. This is because social scientists and judges deal with acts that occur in social relationships. In that case, the methodological position of social science would be somewhere between the judiciary and religion. Therefore, the primary foundation for judgments in social science should be testimony.

No one would argue that judgments in social science align with those in natural science. At best, social science finds its place somewhere between natural science and the judiciary. Even so, social scientists should acknowledge testimony as a valid methodology. There is no reason not to consider the testimonies of witnesses and confessions by actors as evidence. Many social scientists rely on survey methods, which essentially involve collecting numeric data representing people's opinions about society. In essence, these surveys serve as a collection of testimony

Table 3.1 Where does social science fall between natural science, the court of law, and religion?

	Location of social science?		
	Natural science	*Court of law*	*Religion*
Type of evidence	Material evidence	Material evidence + Human evidence	Testimony

provided by individual respondents. Researchers represent this information with numbers and statistical analysis, attempting to convey objectivity.

However, most social scientists fails to acknowledge the persuasive power of testimony. Those unable to liberate themselves from mimicking natural scientists finds themselves trapped in an intellectual obsession. They insists that academic work is only valid when employing statistical methods. It is in response to this mindset that I present and advocate the methodology of testimony.

The method of testimony originally had a religious context. Testimony began to be recognized as a tool of truth during the persecution period of Christianity. As Christianity formed, the disciples of Jesus were imprisoned, thrown to wild animals, and even burned alive. Despite the chance of release by renouncing Jesus as Savior, many people testified to their faith in Jesus. Their testimony was accepted as a reason for their deaths. The truthfulness of their testimony was widely acknowledged.

Paul Ricoeur is renowned for delving into testimony as a philosophical concept. He established the philosophy of testimony by identifying commonalities between legal witness and Christian testimony. Testimony is not merely a report; it takes sides in the context of debates about truth. Therefore, discussions about testimony focus on its truthfulness. Ricoeur suggests that the philosophy of testimony is inevitably hermeneutic. The hermeneutics of testimony connects the two axes of witness's confession of consciousness and the experience of historical events. On this point, he stated as follow:

> Such a philosophy of interpretation is an ellipse with two foci that meditation tends to conflate but which can never be reduced to a unified central point. What, in fact, is it to interpret testimony? It is a twofold act, an act of consciousness of itself and an act of historical understanding based on the signs that the absolute gives of itself.
>
> (Ricoeur 1980, p. 143)

The recent global spread of the MeToo movement has underscored the importance of testimony. Coined by Tarana Burke, MeToo became a movement for individuals to share their harrowing experiences by confessing to instances of sexual harassment and assault. This movement aimed to unite and heal powerless female victims who had experienced such traumas. Triggered by a tweet from American actress Alyssa Milano in 2017, the movement rapidly gained worldwide attention. Men in positions of power exploited women in lower positions, and these acts of sexual exploitation occurred discreetly yet publicly. Until now, such instances of sexual exploitation remained undisclosed. Even when brought into the open, victims faced more blame and suffering than the perpetrators. The MeToo movement exposed and accused male superiors of sexual harassment and assault against working women. It sheds new light on previously concealed instances of sexual misconduct by those in power.

In the unfolding of this movement, what we should pay attention to is that it was carried out through testimony. There were no physical evidences for the harassment and assault that occurred long ago. The victims' testimonies could not bring any benefit to them; instead, they often brought blame and harassment. The victims' testimonies added secondary social harm in addition to the sexual harm they suffered. Nevertheless, many women participated in the MeToo movement. Their testimonies were considered as a means to comfort the wounds of many victims. The truthfulness of their testimony was acknowledged by many people. As various social media outlets reported on their testimonies, the prosecution brought charges against the perpetrators. The MeToo movement demonstrated that testimony is an important tool for truth in 21st-century society.

Another example of testimony is confessing that one's job is pointless. In today's complex society, many people receive salaries for doing meaningless work. The problem is that those who hold such jobs know best that their work is meaningless. Nobody wants to admit that their job is pointless, fearing the possibility of losing it. David Graeber relies on the testimony method to expose such societal phenomena. The following is an interesting testimony he presents.

> A fairly typical testimony from within the IT industry: "I have often seen projects designed to obscure responsibility. For example, to evaluate an IT system. The purpose is not to affect the decision, which is taken somewhere in the corridors, but to claim that everyone was heard and all concerns were taken seriously. Since the project is only a pretense all work on the project is wasted, and people soon realize and stop taking it seriously." This kind of false consensus-seeking is common in ostensibly collegial institutions like universities or NGOs, but is quite common in the more hierarchical corporations as well.
>
> (Graeber 2018, p. 297)

From Testimony to Theory

Testimony provides important clues for social scientists. However, a single testimony is not sufficient to construct a theory reflecting the complexities of society. By expanding testimony experienced at the individual level to the societal dimension, we can construct social theory. Social theory does not objectively exist; rather, it involves extracting common patterns and mechanisms from multiple testimonies and experiences. Social theory is to be constructed by social scientists, not discovered objectively. For this work, social scientists need to take a more distant perspective. Only from a more distant perspective in which events and decisions are deliberately blurred into patterns of behavior and policy structure, social scientists can understand the patterns and structures behind social phenomena (Richardson 1991, p. 342). A methodology is needed to step away from complex and specific testimonies to see the overall framework.

If testimony and confession are considered primary methods in social science research, qualitative analysis is a secondary method. Recently "grounded theory" is widely accepted as a qualitative approach to social science. Grounded theory emerged around the middle of the 20th century when Anselm Strauss and Barney Glaser conducted joint research on patients' awareness of dying over six years.

They published "Awareness of Dying" in 1965, which is the first book that applied grounded theory. Later, they systematized the "grounded theory" method and published a book titled "*The Discovery of Grounded Theory: Strategies for Qualitative Research*" in 1967 (Glaser and Strauss 1967).

For Glaser and Strauss, the textual "data" obtained from observations and interviews with dying patients constituted the most crucial sources for their research. At that time, and even today, most social science research typically involves deducing hypotheses logically and deductively from theories by renowned scholars, followed by the collection of quantitative data to verify them. In this conventional approach, "data" is often perceived merely as a means for verification. However, for Glaser and Strauss, the data derived from "dying patients" carried a profound significance. To them, the data meant everything. Theories on the awareness of dying should emerge directly from the data they collected, not from the works of famous scholars. They firmly believed that authentic theories must "emerge" organically from the data. In this perspective, theories should be grounded in data, and they coined the term "grounded theory" to describe theories that are "formed" based on data (Glaser and Strauss 1967).

The data in grounded theory represents someone's confession and testimony. Glaser and Strauss tried to uncover theories hidden within textual data. However, their approach focuses on capturing simple conceptual relationships. I believe that grounded theory could further advance by concentrating on the circular relations embedded in text data. To achieve this, I proposed integrating system dynamics and grounded theory. What Richardson recommended – looking from a distance – is about discovering the feedback structures driving the system (Richardson 1991). Understanding the hidden circular relations behind the textual data will provide grounded theory scholars with profound insights into the social context.

Above all, social scientists must remain faithful to themselves and their data. They should not believe in or assert something just because a famous scholar said it. Those who feel ashamed of their own society and their own experiences cannot become genuine scholars of social science. Social scientists must be faithful to their own social experiences and confessions they have embraced deeply. That is the true methodology of social science.

4 Socialization vs. Individualization

The most crucial element constituting society is the individual. Individuals come together to form families, gather to create communities, and unite to establish businesses. In this way, society takes shape through the assembly of individuals. Every individual is born into this formed social structure, lives within it, and eventually passes away. There exists a mutual and interdependent relationship between individuals and society. The existence of society is made possible by the presence of individuals, and at the same time, individuals exist relying on society. An individual is not an independent entity but rather a social entity. The process of learning one's identity and role as an individual within society is referred to as "socialization."

Socialization

A family is composed of several individuals, including a mother, father, and children. In cases with multiple children, there may be siblings. Through life within the family, children learn about the roles of men and women. In the embrace of the mother, a young child experiences unilateral and absolute protection from the parents. The child has no choice but to trust the mother, who provides food, a place to sleep, and clothing. Through the relationship with the mother, a young child learns complete trust.

The most crucial socialization that occurs in the relationship with the mother is the learning of language. The language learned from birth is referred to as the native language or the mother tongue. Beyond facial expressions and gestures, the child learns a specific language for communication. They learn terms for food, expressions for wanting or refusing to eat, titles for the mother and father, and even lullabies. Above all, they learn terms that denote their own existence – baby, love, and their own name.

If we label socialization within the family as private socialization, socialization through educational institutions can be considered collective socialization. In contemporary society, the majority of people receive education in five institutions: kindergarten, elementary school, middle school, high school, and university. Some individuals may pass through only two or three of these institutions, while others may go through more. The shared characteristic of these educational institutions is

DOI: 10.4324/9781003464730-5

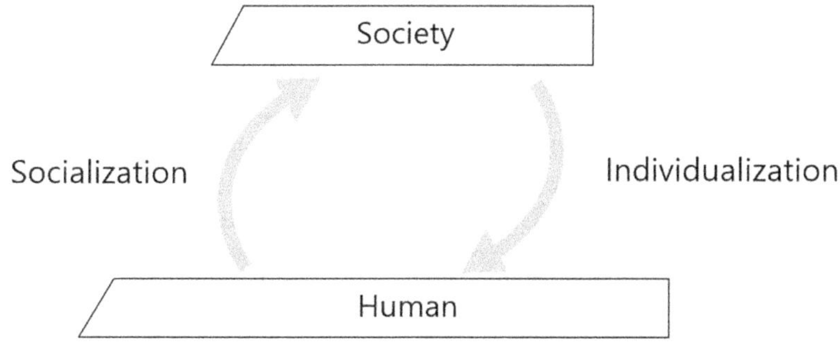

Figure 4.1 Socialization vs. individualization.

the method of collective education, where individual students gather in a physical classroom and listen to the lectures of the same teacher simultaneously.

Through educational institutions, individuals acquire the knowledge demanded by society. They learn both their native language and foreign languages, study the history of their society, and, most importantly, acquire scientific knowledge. However, education in institutions encompasses more than just knowledge; it includes etiquette as well. From a young age, students learn to adhere to a set schedule and attend school at specified times. While at school, they undergo training to resist laziness, endure sleepiness, and control impulses for play during class hours. Additionally, they learn the hierarchical relationship of listening attentively to their teachers. Consequently, students who acquire patience and obedience through educational institutions can be confidently employed in industrial settings, businesses, and bureaucratic structures in an industrial society.

Through educational institutions, students also learn to consider competition as a natural way of life. They engage in fierce competition, aiming to receive higher grades than other students, earning recognition from teachers, and receiving awards. Students who lag behind in the competition with their peers view the disadvantages they face in society as inevitable. The majority of students who fall behind in competition accept that they deserve these disadvantages due to their incompetence. In contrast, the few students who emerge as leaders in the competition believe in the blessings of competition and willingly enter into an even more intense competitive society.

As students consider competition as something natural, they are prepared to accept the capitalist society, where competition is deemed a vital virtue, as a matter of course. Marketplaces and businesses imbued with the logic of capitalist competition hire students who have demonstrated high performance in numerous competitions as corporate warriors. Their mission is to achieve better results than competing companies in the relentless arena of markets.

Socialization is strictly carried out based on the demands of society. If society requires warriors, socialization proceeds in a way that nurtures individuals to become warriors. If society needs technicians, socialization takes place in a manner that fosters the development of technicians. This is the visible aspect of socialization. The invisible aspect of socialization involves the process of degrading individuals whom society does not deem necessary. For instance, when society requires warriors, those lacking physical strength are socialized to accept a humble life as appropriate. Similarly, when society needs obedient individuals, creative minds are socialized to be regarded as abnormal and useless.

However, socialization is not only for the benefit of society. Socialization shapes individuals to live in society. This becomes evident when observing individuals lacking socialization. A child who grows up isolated from human society from an early age is referred to as a feral child. A notable case involves Amala and Kamala, discovered in India in the 1920s. These two girls were raised by wolves, deprived of family care and the experience of socialization. Children who do not undergo socialization appear more wolf-like than humans. They crawled like wolves, enjoyed raw meat, and had their tongues sticking out like wolves. Amala died after one year, and Kamala, despite the meticulous care of a missionary couple, passed away suddenly in 1929. Socialization is not only necessary for society but is also a crucial process for individual survival.

Peter Berger and Thomas Luckmann emphasize that human beings acquire meaning only when they exist within society. They stated as follows.

> Solitary human being is being on the animal level … Man's specific humanity and his sociality are inextricably intertwined. Homo sapiens is always, and in the same measure, homo socius.
>
> (Berger and Luckmann 1966, p. 69)

Many contemporary intellectuals tend to overly emphasize Homo sapiens. Yuval Harari's book S*apiens: A Brief History of Humankind* represents these intellectuals. He traces the origins of human civilization back to the cognitive revolution of Homo sapiens, arguing that society is merely an imagined order created by this revolution (Harari, 2015). Particularly with the rise of artificial intelligence, intellectuals often regard human intelligence as the pinnacle of civilization. However, stories of feral children suggest that the significance of civilized humans lies much more in Homo socius than in Homo sapiens.

Surely, not all socialization is beneficial. Excessive socialization suppresses an individual's unique personality, free will, and creativity. This is evident in the continued imposition of collective education in the 21st-century information society. Collective education involves gathering dozens of students in a confined space for an extended period, forcing them to listen to lectures and memorize the same text. Even in these days of the information society, with high-tech tools for personalized education, the outdated practice of collective education from the industrial age persists. Yuval Harari describes it as follows:

> The Industrial Revolution has bequeathed us the production-line theory of education. In the middle of town there is a large concrete building divided into many identical rooms, each room equipped with rows of desks and chairs. At the sound of a bell, you go to one of these rooms together with thirty other kids who were all born the same year as you. Every hour some

> grown-up walks in, and starts talking. They are all paid to do so by the government … But so far we haven't created a viable alternative.
>
> (Harari 2018, p. 272)

The global COVID-19 pandemic, which resulted in over eight million deaths worldwide, led to more than two years of comprehensive online education. This period demonstrated that traditional collective education is unnecessary. However, as the impact of COVID-19 waned, most educational institutions returned to collective education. In the 21st-century information age, personalized socialization, not collective education, is required.

Individualization

Individualization is the opposite process of socialization. It simplifies society into individuals. The most representative example of individualization was a famous declaration by Louis XIV of France, "L"État, c'est moi (The State, that is me)". Upon hearing the news of Louis XIV's death, the French citizens reportedly expressed profound gratitude and joy. Simplifying society into individuals is a form of arrogant idolization and dictatorship. However, such individualization can be easily observed in everyday life.

History textbooks taught in schools are filled with individualization. Rather than studying the Mongol Empire's society, students learn about the name of Genghis Khan. Instead of exploring social changes in France, they learn about Napoleon's revolution. Rather than delving into the social crises in Germany, they study Hitler's propaganda. The victory in World War II is remembered not as the triumph of the Allies but as Churchill, Roosevelt, and Stalin's victory. History education, which should focus on societal changes, easily devolves into stories about individual success and failure. While converting the history of society into personal narratives may help people's understanding, it falls short of providing a fundamental comprehension of societal changes.

On the opposite side of heroic individualization, there is scapegoat individualization, which attributes social problems to individuals. A notable example is the witch hunts in medieval Europe. The frenzy of witch hunts spread across most regions of medieval Europe, intensifying in the 15th and 16th centuries, leading to the execution of over 40,000 people. Witch hunts were characterized by collective hysteria, where various elements such as lies, greed, cunning, conspiracy, fear, and innocence intertwined, forming flames that burned the weakest individuals, often elderly women. While the witch hunts were a social phenomenon involving the mobilization of many people, they ultimately concluded with the individual execution of alleged witches, leaving the societal issues seemingly unresolved.

The witch hunts began with religious paranoia but persisted for various reasons over an extended period. On a personal level, witch hunts were carried out for private vendettas, personal animosities, or to accumulate illicit property. On a societal level, witch hunts were conducted to redirect the grievances of the discontented class toward individual witches. Simultaneously, they aimed to strengthen control over society through public execution and terrorization, such as witch burnings. The societal unrest and resulting turmoil were attributed to individual witches. The witch hunts were a process of individualization that shifted significant societal problems onto individual evils.

Another form of individualization is the transfer of social responsibility onto individuals. In a society marked by severe discrimination against black individuals, black children may lack motivation to study. A significant number of people attribute low employment rates among black people to their lower educational achievements. This effectively shifts societal failure onto individual failure. Criticizing black people becomes a convenient method of attributing societal failure to personal shortcomings.

In the past, it was believed that people with disabilities couldn't participate in social activities due to their personal shortcomings. Recently, there has been a shift in social awareness regarding this issue. Creating wheelchair-accessible paths for those who cannot walk is essential to enable their participation in society. The recognition is growing that the lack of such facilities and equipment is not the failure of individuals with disabilities but rather a failure of society. Individualization errors can also occur in judgments about criminals. When children, deprived of parental care at home, receive no support from any social institution, they inevitably wander and resort to stealing food. The crimes committed by these children are not individual transgressions but rather crimes of society.

Not all individualization is bad. It is sometimes inevitable to attribute societal problems to individual responsibility. The issue of drug addiction is fundamentally a societal problem. Society has facilitated the spread of drugs and has induced stress in individuals. Individuals become addicted to drugs provided by society as a means to cope with the stress received from society. The argument that society bears more responsibility for the issue of drug addiction seems plausible. However, refraining from holding individuals accountable for drug addiction might make it impossible to control the spread of drugs. In this way, there are situations where individualization is unavoidable.

Individual Religion vs. Social Religion

Is human religion oriented towards society or does it focus on the individual? There are religions that lean towards society, while others emphasize the individual. Confucianism and Christianity are religions that focus on society. In contrast, Buddhism and Taoism focus on the individual. Those who do not clearly understand society may fail to discern these differences.

Buddhism demands the severance of all social relationships, including family ties. It perceives all human suffering as originating from social connections. The goal is to detach from attachments to all kinds of social relationships and break free from their entanglements. To truly see oneself beyond human suffering, one must cut off social relationships and embark on meditation that introspects one's inner self. Sitting in meditation facing a wall for several years can lead to the discovery of one's true self. By freeing oneself from all social relationships, one enters the realm of enlightenment, often referred to as "non-self (無我)." In this state, there is no existence of any suffering or pain, referred to as "nirvana (寂寞 or 涅槃)." Those who attain such enlightenment are said to be liberated from the cycle of reincarnation, as mentioned in Hinduism. Buddhism asserts that true understanding can only be found by thoroughly liberating oneself from society. The ultimate stage of complete individualization in Buddhism is nirvana, where there is nothing.

Taoism follows the natural way (Tao 道) of the universe. Similar to Buddhism, Taoism also advocates for withdrawal from all social connections. It believes that by cutting off social relationships and retreating to the deep mountains, one can harmonize with nature and attain true freedom. The catchphrase of Taoism is "inaction (無爲)." Taoism asserts that human artificiality obscures the natural way of the Tao, the truth of the universe. Society, being the most representative form of artificiality, should be abandoned when returning to nature. Ultimately, when an individual becomes one with nature, there is hope for eternal life. People who witness the brutal exploitation by the ruling class and experience the horrors of unwanted battlefields begin to question the necessity of society. Some believe it is better to abandon all benefits offered by society, retreat to the deep mountains where no one lives, rely on the fruits and vegetables provided by nature, and preserve both physical and mental peace. Taoism, too, advocates for thorough individualization.

Confucianism regards society as a more significant existence than the individual. Confucius addresses fundamental social relationships such as the relationship between spouses, parents and children, rulers and subjects, elders and juniors, and friends, considering them as the foundation of society. The emphasized virtue in Confucianism, known as "仁 (Ren)," signifies love and devotion to others within these social relationships. Additionally, the emphasized principle in Confucianism, known as "禮 (Li)," denotes the attitude and manners through which individuals approach each other within these social relationships. In Confucianism, individual goodness ultimately serves the purpose of upholding society. The emphasized ancestral rites in Confucianism, a form of respect shown to ancestors, ultimately express reverence for society. It is believed that individuals, as integral parts of society, will never be forgotten. Confucius's teachings, emphasizing social relationships and social ethics, have become a form of religion for Asians.

Christianity is oriented towards society. The society that Christianity envisions goes beyond human society; it is the society of God. Among the Ten Commandments in the Old Testament, the first four commandments deal with the relationship between God and humans, while the remaining six commandments address human-to-human relationships. In Christianity, all sins stem from social relationships, and ultimately, sin is the rupture of the relationship between humans and God. The New Testament begins with the message of Jesus, "The kingdom of God is near; repent." It conveys the message of returning to the relationship with God and entering into His kingdom. The crucifixion of Jesus restores the relationship between humans and God through the forgiveness of sins. Here, sin is the transgression of the relationship between humans and God.

Having reached the pinnacle as a novelist, Leo Tolstoy found himself tormented by the lack of meaning in life. Eventually, he comes to realize the importance of relationships, particularly the relationship between the finite "I" and the infinite "God." In his own words,

> An answer can be obtained only by formulating the question differently, that is, only when the relationship between the finite and the infinite is introduced into the question. I also realized that no matter how irrational and unattractive the answers given by faith, they have the advantage of bringing to every reply a relationship between the finite and the infinite, without which there can be no reply.
>
> (Tolstoy 1882, p. 60)

Restoring the relationship through faith, Tolstoy finally finds meaning in life and manages to overcome the temptation of suicide. Subsequently, Tolstoy lives a religious life until his death.

The "nirvana" in Buddhism is the tranquility that can be attained in the silent spot where all relationships are severed. However, Christian shalom is the peaceful relationship with God and with neighbors. Peace in a solitary yet liberated state is sought after in Buddhism. Christian peace signifies a recovered relationship with God and eternal life in the kingdom of God. Christianity, as a social religion, believes in the divine society that transcends human society.

In this manner, religions are distinguished by two divergent orientations. One end is characterized by individual religion, while the other end is marked by social religion. Buddhism exemplifies individual religion, whereas Christianity exemplifies social religion. Numerous religions fall somewhere in between individual and social dimensions. Branches of Buddhism have emerged that emphasize teaching for the ignorant masses rather than transcending through individual enlightenment. Likewise, many Christian denominations emphasize individual peace of mind rather than the kingdom of God. Occasionally, Catholic priests engage with Buddhist monks regarding the pursuit of inner peace. Inner peace aligns more with the individual pole, while peace in relationships is closer to the social pole of religion.

Nowadays, there are many intellectuals who deny the existence of society. They believe that individual human beings are the only tangible entities, while society is nothing more than a fictional construct. They tend to regard Confucianism and Christianity as imaginary artifacts. They cannot accept the idea of transcending society and even the Kingdom of God. Instead, Buddhism and Taoism may be more appealing to them. Through personal meditation, they can approach the teachings of Buddhism, and by stepping away from social relationships, they can practice the inaction of Taoism. The understanding of society is closely tied to religious orientation, involving a choice between the transcendent socialization of Christianity and the serene individualization of Buddhism.

Society as Reality

We tend to believe that we have a clear understanding of individual human beings. However, do I really know my own individual entity? Let's consider it from the perspective of a cell. Can an individual cell perceive the existence of a human being? Cells can only perceive chemical elements that are lower than the level of the cell. From the standpoint of a cell, a human being is nothing but a potentially fictional entity. Similarly, from the perspective of an individual human being, society is beyond their senses. At the individual level, society cannot be experienced. However, just because an element does not perceive the whole does not mean the whole does not exist. Beyond the level of cells, human beings exist as tangible entities. What can be said about society beyond individual human beings?

Does society exist independently of humans? Or is it an illusion that disappears when humans depart? Is society merely a name attached to humans' repetitive gatherings? Or is it an entity that exists beyond humans? Burrell and Morgan describe the debate about this as a conflict between nominalism and realism in the ontological assumptions of the social sciences.

> The nominalist position revolves around the assumption that the social world external to individual cognition is made up of nothing more than names … Realism, on the other hand, postulates that the social world external to individual cognition is a real world made up of hard, tangible, and relatively immutable structures.
>
> (Burrell and Morgan, 1979, p. 4)

While nominalism and realism represent extreme positions on the concept of society, social constructionism offers a third way to understand the ontology of society. In 1966, Peter Berger and Thomas Luckmann co-authored a famous book titled *The Social Construction of Reality: A Treatise in the Sociology of Knowledge.* They acknowledge the "reality" of society while recognizing its human construction. The claim that humans construct society may seem incompatible with the idea that society exists independently of humans. However, they point out that these two seemingly exclusive claims coexist through a dialectical process. There are three stages of dialectical processes.

The first stage is externalization. Consider a group of hunters surrounding a deer to block its escape routes. What the deer experiences is a surrounding wall, a social entity resulting from the externalization of individual hunters. They state as follows:

> One may ask in what manner social order itself arises. The most general answer to this question is that social order is a human product, or, more precisely, an ongoing human production. It is produced by man in the course of his ongoing externalization.
>
> (Berger and Luckmann 1966, pp. 69–70)

The second stage is institutionalization or objectivation. When children go to school and sit at their desks, the teacher stands by the blackboard and teaches. Through the repetition of such reciprocal actions, school learning becomes institutionalized. Now, school learning has become an undeniable objective entity for the children. School learning existed before the children were born, and even after they grow up, school learning objectively persists.

> An institutional world, then, is experienced as an objective reality.
>
> (Berger and Luckmann 1966, p. 77)

The third stage is internalization. Internalization is the third process of dialectics, in which "the objectivated social world is retrojected into consciousness in the course of socialization" (Berger and Luckmann 1966, pp. 78–79). When school learning is internalized, the lessons learned in school continue to influence individuals even after they graduate and become adults. Actually, the school resides in their minds forever.

In this way, society emerges as an objective reality through three dialectical processes: externalization, objectivation, and internalization. Furthermore, along with the identity formed through internalization, society exists as an enduring subjective reality. They succinctly conclude as follows:

> Society is a human product. Society is an objective reality. Man is a social product.
>
> (Berger and Luckmann 1966, p. 79)

Part II

Frame of Social Science

Social scientists have the task of understanding and explaining the structure of society, which refers to how society is organized. The structure of society is shaped by the myriad interactions among individuals and the laws, institutions, and culture that sustain and guide these interactions. It is a complex process that evolves through various stages, thereby giving rise to institutions and the formation of culture. Consequently, objectively describing social structure is challenging. Thus, the term "frame," which underscores subjectivity, proves to be a more suitable choice than "structure."

The term frame draws its inspiration from the concept of a window frame. Just as individuals perceive the outside world through the frame of a window, the frame through which we view society shapes our perspective. If the frame through which we view the world is square, we are more likely to perceive things in a "square" manner; if it is circular, we are inclined to perceive them in a "circular" manner.

This book presents four realms of economy, community, politics, and administration as frames through which to view society. Each of these four domains that constitute society possesses unique institutions. They can be distinguished as public and private areas, as well as areas of fact and value. Furthermore, these realms may emphasize either competition or cooperation.

DOI: 10.4324/9781003464730-6

5 Four Realms of Society

Society is so diverse that it's difficult to identify consistent patterns. There are small and gentle societies, like families, as well as large and rigid ones, such as nations. Churches vary, ranging from small gatherings of a few dozen people to large congregations with thousands. Christian churches and Buddhist temples are distinct from each other. Businesses that create and sell products can be small enterprises formed by a couple of individuals or large corporations employing tens of thousands of workers. Schools around a town can be public schools established and operated by the government, privately owned schools created by individuals, and schools established by religious organizations. Society exhibits a wide range of scales and characteristics.

Due to the diversity within society, it is challenging to present a single framework for understanding it. However, a singular frame allows for understanding the inherent order within diversity. In this book, I aim to present a single framework composed of four domains, enabling the comparison of societal diversity and the comprehension of differences within it.

There are four realms that make up society: politics, administration, economy, and community. Although all these realms involve human gatherings, they vary in the values they pursue and the methods they employ.

In the realm of the economy, the primary focus is on money. Individuals come together to earn and spend money, where money holds a higher priority than individuals. People are essentially viewed as owners of money, categorized as capitalists, investors, entrepreneurs, consumers, and so on. Max Weber noted as follows.

> In a market economy, the striving for income is necessarily the ultimate driving force of all economic activity.
>
> (Weber 1922, p. 203)

The politics area is where people elect representatives or leaders. The most important element in the political domain is the ballot. The ability to gain votes determines the fate of politicians. The voting process varies depending on the political system. In a democratic system, citizens vote, while in a monarchy, the king or nobles with power decide the next king through voting. Politics ultimately revolves around obtaining votes.

DOI: 10.4324/9781003464730-7

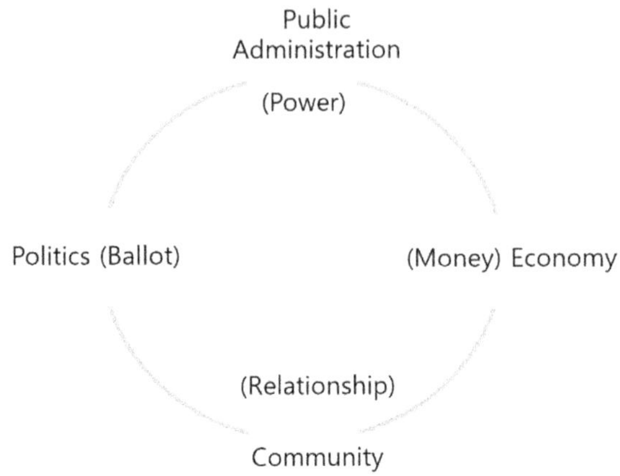

Figure 5.1 Four domains of society: economy, community, politics, and administration.

In the community realm, the most important aspect is the relationship that represents people's commonalities. In communities, relationships are highly valued, and members often prioritize the well-being of the group over individual interest. While the smallest-scale community is a household, we can think of larger communities such as religious groups like the Catholic Church. Communities can formally form organizations, but they can also maintain gatherings informally. What matters is recognizing and valuing relationships among people, providing support, and sometimes even making personal sacrifices.

The administration domain provides order to society. It requires institutions such as the military to defend against external threats, the police to apprehend criminals who disrupt social order, and the judiciary to judge them. Additionally, it involves the documentation of population information, including marriages and births, as well as the management of land ownership. The cornerstone for establishing and upholding societal order is force. It encompasses the physical violence employed by the police, such as guns and handcuffs, the power of judges in courts who sentence imprisonment or capital punishment, and the power of administrative agencies to grant or revoke public licenses. This is commonly referred to as public power. Thus, power holds great significance in the administrative domain. In modern societies, public administration alone has the legal power on physical forces. Max Weber stated as follows.

> The state claims for itself a monopoly on the legitimate use of physical force.
> (Weber 1919, p. 4)

These four realms of society place different values on what they consider important. Economy prioritizes money, community values relationship, politics revolves around the ballot, and administration relies on power. These values not only hold significance but also contribute to the formation of distinct cultures. The culture of the economy emphasizes the significance of money. It is not appropriate to blame individuals who openly express their pursuit of money in economic activities. Occasionally, there are business people who pretend to be uninterested in money. They claim to engage in business not to earn money but to help the weak. Such individuals deviate from the essence of the economy.

Politicians often engage in extensive efforts to gain support from a larger number of people. It is not uncommon to witness politicians bowing deeply and earnestly soliciting votes from residents, even when they do not genuinely respect them. These actions cannot be condemned as hypocritical since they are consistent with the essence of politics. Occasionally, there are politicians who do not prioritize the opinions of residents but dedicate themselves to proposing good policies based on their own thoughts. Such politicians are often praised as excellent politicians in the media. However, they could be viewed as politicians who have lost sight of the essence of politics. This is because they may easily advocate impractical policies that can be detrimental to society as a whole.

In a primitive society, the community is paramount. The mere inclusion in a community inherently provides protection for its members. Parents feed, shelter, and educate their children simply because they are family, irrespective of individual achievements. There are instances where people form close relationships as if they were family simply because they attend the same church. In such communities that place importance on human relationships, it is considered taboo to count money, solicit votes, or exert power. These actions deviate from the core culture of the community.

Axel Honneth, a contemporary philosopher of critical theory, emphasizes recognition as the fundamental relation of human beings. According to his philosophy, recognition takes precedence over cognition. Recognition can be broadly categorized into three forms: love, respect, and esteem (Honneth 1995). Love is the form of recognition that develops within the relationships of parents and children within the family. Respect is a form of recognition that acknowledges the universal rights shared by all individuals, such as human rights. Respect is particularly significant in relations close to the boundaries of politics within the community. Esteem is a form of recognition that acknowledges the uniqueness of individuals, such as their individual talent and wisdom. Esteem plays a crucial role in community areas that are closely related to the economic domain.

Civic organizations performing political functions within the community must respect each other's basic rights, while special teams serving economic functions within the community should recognize each other's strengths with esteem. Recognition is crucial in relationships within the community, while cognition is essential in other domains. This is because there are other factors more important than human relationships in other domains, such as money, ballots, and power, which are objects of cognition rather than recognition.

Intersection of Four Domains

There are cases where organizations with similar characteristics belong to different domains. An organization that produces electricity is typically classified as an entity in the economic domain when it is a private enterprise. However, if the government establishes a power company to supply electricity, it falls within the administrative domain. The provision of water for household use generally falls within the administrative domain, but selling bottled water in the market falls within the economic domain. A political party engaged in election campaigns falls within the political domain, but a user of social network service conducting the same campaign falls within the realm of communities. Nursing homes typically belong to the community, but profit-oriented nursing hospitals fall within the economic domain. Government-established schools are part of the community domain, but private academies offering similar education fall within the economic domain.

To educate young children, the government establishes schools and provides salaries to teachers. Government-established schools operate on a communal basis. They provide the same curriculum to all students, and it is prohibited to provide differentiated education based on the amount of money paid by students. School facilities such as playgrounds, auditoriums, and libraries are shared by all students. All students receive the same meals, and teachers must give equal attention to all students. Therefore, graduates from the same school create alumni associations, and these associations also operate on a communal basis throughout their lives.

However, unlike schools, private academies, while providing the same content of learning, operate not on a communal basis but rather in a market economic manner. Only those who pay tuition can attend classes, and students who pay counseling fees can engage in consultations with teachers. Academy facilities are accessible only to students who pay usage fees, and only students who pay for food can eat. Despite providing education to children, government-established schools belong to a community, while private academies in the market belong to the economic domain.

In this way, the boundaries of the four domains of society are not always clear-cut. There are organizations positioned at the boundaries of two domains. Private schools, newspapers, and hospitals exist at the intersection of the economic and communal domains. For these organizations to survive, they must pursue profit, yet they also need to maintain strong and trusting relationships with customers. A person operating an internet broadcasting station, advocating for a specific political position, exists at the intersection of politics, community, and economy.

The individuals belonging to the four domains of society are not distinct from one another; they are all the same people. Someone involved in the economic area during the day may be part of a household community in the evening. A person engaged in economic activities on weekdays might transition to the realm of politics on weekends and participate in a church community on Sundays. Does this mean that the distinction between the four domains is meaningless? Not at all. On the contrary, having a frame that distinguishes the four domains allows for a clearer understanding of the differences among similar organizations and a better observation of people's movements.

Differentiation from Community

It cannot be denied that the first society formed by humanity is a community. The foundation of society lies in the family, consisting of fathers, mothers, and children. As children marry, they form new families. There are also families of the parents' siblings and relatives. These kinship bonds come together to create a village or community.

As time passes, communities gradually differentiate. Differentiation can occur both vertically and horizontally. Vertical differentiation involves the division between ruling and subordinate classes. Tribes composed of kinship communities may experience conflicts with neighboring tribes over territory and resources. When disputes remain unresolved, inter-tribal wars may erupt, leading to one tribe prevailing and dominating the other. This results in the differentiation between the dominating and the dominated communities. The dominant community establishes armies and imposes taxes to solidify its control. In this process, the administrative domain emerges alongside the ruling class.

Horizontal differentiation can also occur within communities. Some communities focus on agriculture, while others specialize in animal husbandry. Agricultural communities enjoy abundance of food, while those engaged in animal husbandry have surplus milk and leather. Rather than plundering what is lacking in their community, they engage in exchanges of abundant goods with other communities. Horizontal differentiation is maintained not through war but through trade. The marketplace becomes the venue for these transactions. As more horizontal differentiation takes place, the market expands, and the exchange of goods eventually evolves into the exchange of currency, marking the emergence of the economic domain.

The political domain emerged only recently. During the era of monarchy, where a single kinship community passed down the governing power through generations, politics was not prominently visible. However, as monarchies declined and sovereignty shifted to the people, the political domain underwent rapid expansion. In the era of monarchy, politicians were eager to please the king, but now, success as a politician depends on how well one appeals to the citizens. The political arena has become a pivotal aspect of modern societies.

This process of differentiation is readily observable in everyday life. Students entering college form a community, sharing a wide range of information. They exchange details about nearby restaurants with delicious and affordable food, where to do laundry, locations of budget-friendly lodging places, among almost all other information. However, there are times when the community-based approach falls short. To advocate for students' rights against the college, representatives need to be appointed. Political differentiation emerges within the student community. Additionally, administrative organizations come into play, organizing student lists, collecting fees, and managing administrative tasks. As college life progresses, surplus items begin to emerge – textbooks from completed courses and unused sports equipment, for example. Graduating students must dispose of beds and furniture. To facilitate the exchange of such items, a student market is formed.

Thus, a society composed of students evolves from an initial information-sharing community, undergoing both vertical and horizontal differentiation, leading to the emergence of political, administrative, and economic domains.

Even among prisoners in a prison, such differentiation is observed. As various offenders enter the prison, communities are formed around shared rooms or areas. Food distribution is organized based on these communities. At first, these communities start out on equal footing, but they quickly diverge. The strongest individual within the community emerges as a leader. The leader's associates handle administration, assigning tasks such as food distribution, cleaning, and laundry to other prisoners. Over time, horizontal differentiation occurs. Some prisoners have a lot of cigarettes, others have plenty of soap, and yet others have an abundance of candy. They engage in exchanges among themselves, sometimes trading surplus items or offering bribes to the leaders among the prisoners. This creates a lively market within the prison.

The early community gave rise to administration through vertical differentiation, and with horizontal differentiation, the economy emerged. As dominant communities disintegrated, politics emerged to replace the ruling classes. Reflecting on this process of differentiation, it becomes evident that the community serves as the foundation for all societal domains. However, in contemporary society, communities are often regarded as less crucial. With the transition from agrarian to industrial societies, the significance of communities has diminished.

Community is the prototype and archetype of society. In the agricultural era, most societies belonged to a community realm. The cultivation of crops required many people for labor, and thus households were typically organized as extended families. Around extensive farmland, kinship communities were often formed. The ruling class was also essentially a kinship community. The king's child would become the next king, and the children of high-ranking officials mostly followed their parents into high positions. Communities were widespread throughout the societies of the agricultural era.

Since the 18th-century Industrial Revolution, the significance of communities has gradually diminished. Many people migrated from rural areas to cities to work in factories, leading to a transformation from an agrarian society, where the majority were peasants, to an industrial society with a predominant workforce of laborers. Urban workers found it a heavy burden to sustain large families. With limited wages, they were inclined to form small families. Over time, they adapted to an urban lifestyle, purchasing goods in the market. As industrial societies emerged, the realm of the market economy rapidly expanded and became the central aspect of people's lives.

The 21st century is an information society where the primary workplace is not a physical factory but cyberspace. Marketplaces for purchasing goods also exist in cyberspace, alongside workplaces. In cyberspace, one person can handle everything – working, shopping, studying, and enjoying hobbies. More and more people are choosing to live unmarried. In the information society, smaller households than nuclear families are increasing. With the emergence of single-person households, consumption patterns are undergoing rapid changes. Social Networking Services

(SNS), which drive the 21st-century information society, can be considered online communities. Many people use SNS to gather information, shop, and watch movies. They actually live on SNS, forming digital relationships with other members within the online community. The significance of communities, which had diminished since the industrial society, is on the rise these days.

6 Social Sciences of Four Realms

The economy focuses on money, community values relationships (networks), politics emphasizes votes, and administration relies on power as their core values. As a result, individuals who are interested in money tend to study economics or business, while those interested in human relationships tend to study sociology. Individuals aspiring to become leaders and seek the attention and support of others study political science, and those who admire the power to maintain order in the nation or society study public administration or law.

It is not uncommon to encounter students who lack a clear understanding of the academic characteristics of social sciences and make the wrong choice of major. Some students, intrigued by building relationships with diverse people, choose to major in business, assuming they will meet many people in corporate settings. However, after a while, they become disillusioned with the money-centric atmosphere of business studies and consider switching to public administration. They expect public administration to place less emphasis on money compared to business. However, once they enter the field of public administration, they find themselves frustrated as the discipline focuses more on rigid legal systems rather than delving deeply into human relationships. Such students are lost because they lack an understanding of the essence of economy, administration, and most importantly, the essence of communities. If these students had known in advance that sociology is the social science that explores human relationships in the community, they would have avoided such confusion.

Not only do students lack clarity, but there are also professors who are unsure. Many professors in social science departments are unaware of the essence of their own field. For instance, there are business professors in management who claim that the essence of business is not about making money but about serving customers. They even go as far as criticizing all profit-seeking businesses in the world. They perpetuate their own confusion by imparting false beliefs to their students, causing them to be lost.

Of course, pursuing money is not the sole focus in the field of economy, and valuing relationships is not the sole concern in the community domain. While ballots are crucial for politicians, and power is significant for administrators, they are simply the most important things within each respective domain. It is possible to argue that the value of money should be emphasized in the field of administration, or that customer relationships are crucial in making profits in the field of economy.

DOI: 10.4324/9781003464730-8

Figure 6.1 Fields of social sciences related to four domains of society.

Through such perspectives, new insights can be offered, and new aspects can be discovered. However, this can only be done under the premise of accepting the primary values of each realm. Otherwise, it could alter their essence. If a company claims that customer relationships are more important than making money, it is operating in the community domain rather than the economic domain. Similarly, if a religious organization, which is perceived as part of the community domain, emphasizes profitability, it is operating in the economic domain rather than the community domain.

Social scientists need a clear understanding of the realm in which their research is being conducted from the outset. When studying the economy, the focus should be on the profit-maximization perspective of individuals in business. In the case of public administration, the emphasis should be on understanding the forces at play. Scholars who fail to identify their realms accurately may become misguided in their research. The direction and content of research should be determined by the nature of the research subject rather than the personal inclination of the scholar.

One crucial point to note here is that the four domains do not exist in isolation, as emphasized by Myrdal in his study of the African American problem in the United States. As he highlighted, social issues are always interconnected with the entire society.

> The Negro problem is an integral part of, or a special phase of, the whole complex of problems in the larger American civilization. It cannot be treated in isolation.
>
> (Myrdal 1944, p. liii)

Social issues are simultaneously economic, political, administrative, and communal issues. The four domains of society are inherently closely linked. Above all, in a world where these domains overlap, human existence is shaped and social issues emerge.

For a long time, there has been a discipline studying social issues that span various societal domains. Political economy, connecting politics and economy, emerged in the 19th century. It explains politics from an economic perspective and, conversely, discusses the political background underlying economic actions. Moreover, it investigates social orders and changes where the outcomes of economic activities extend beyond the economic domain, leading to political changes.

Karl Marx's "*Das Kapital*," which prophesied the collapse of capitalism, is one of the most widely known works in political economy. He focuses on explaining how commodities, labor, and capital are socially interconnected. Labor creates commodities and forms capital, and capital pays wages to labor. However, as the process of capital accumulation progresses, the exploitation of labor worsens. Marx refers to this as the general law of capitalist accumulation.

> The law of capitalist accumulation, mystified by the economists into a supposed law of nature, in fact expresses the situation that the very nature of accumulation excludes every diminution in the degree of exploitation of labor, and every rise in the price of labor, which could seriously imperil the continual reproduction of the capital-relation … Just as man is governed, in religion, by the products of his own brain, so, in capitalist production, he is governed by the products of his own hand.
>
> (Marx 1867, pp. 771–772)

As the productivity of labor increases, capital accumulates more profits. Correspondingly, laborers face increased exploitation by the larger capitalists. This leads to the paradox of capitalism and its inevitable demise.

Max Weber studied the capitalist economy from the perspective of religion, within the realm of the community. In his 1904 publication, "*The Protestant Ethic and the Spirit of Capitalism*," he raised the question, "Why did capitalism develop in areas where Protestants resided?" Weber sought the answer in the differences between Protestants and Catholics. Unlike Catholics, who believed in salvation through good deeds and sacraments, Protestant leaders declared that good deeds and sacraments do not contribute to salvation. However, although Protestant leaders could gain the assurance of salvation through faith, known as "certitudo salutis (certainty of salvation)," most Protestant individuals did not share this conviction. The question of whether one was a chosen and saved saint by God became crucial for Protestants (Weber 1904, pp. 65–66). The solution to such a question was an ascetic life. While an ascetic life could not lead to salvation, it could serve as a sign of salvation (pp. 69–70). Furthermore, considering their secular labor and job as a sacred calling from God, hard work became another sign of being God's people (Weber 1904, p. 111). Due to hard work in their vocation, their income increased, and following the spirit of asceticism, most of their income was not wasted and accumulated as capital (Weber 1904, p. 116). The Protestant ethic became fertile ground for the development of capitalism.

Max Weber did not claim the superiority of Protestant ethics over Catholicism. He only emphasized that the ethics dominating the lives of Protestants contributed to the accumulation of capital. Later, Weber extended his research to the religions of China and India, discussing how the development of capitalism is influenced not by economic factors but by religion. Recently, scholars in religious studies have applied Weber's method in reverse. They adopt the perspective that individual religious choices are driven not by religious beliefs but by political and economic factors. Some scholars argue that understanding individual religious choices requires a market model for religion, similar to choosing products in the market. Thus, it is possible to understand economy from a religious perspective and, conversely, understand religion from an economic perspective.

The realms of society not only overlap but also circulate. In the 20th century, communication studies focused on newspapers, television broadcasting, and advertising in mass media, placing it within the economic domain as a massive business (Habermas 1964). However, in ancient Greece, communication studies centered on the rhetoric used by politicians to persuade audiences, falling within the realm of politics. During the medieval period, communication studies focused on how the king's orders were conveyed to the people, taking place within the administrative domain. In the 21st-century information society, the focus of communication studies is shifting toward social networks occurring on the internet and smartphones. It is transitioning into the realm of the community, sharing the same etymology as the word communication.

Economics and management, both falling within the realm of the economy, may seem similar but are distinct. While economics focuses on markets where voluntary transactions among people take place, management centers around hierarchical organizations. Williamson explained this coexistence of contrasting mechanisms in his book "*Market and Hierarchy*." It is absurd for a store owner to hire a cashier every morning for daily sales. Entering into a contract for a month or more is mutually advantageous. In this way, contracts and organizations emerge in the market. Williamson discusses several reasons why internal and hierarchical organizations are advantageous compared to transactions in the market (Williamson 1975, p. 40). Organizations can restrain opportunistic behavior and reduce uncertainty through supervision. Furthermore, organizations can embrace not only economic but also emotional factors. This signifies the communal nature of business organizations. Leaders of corporate organizations often emphasize to their employees that they are like a family. Business organizations play a role in implanting the mechanisms of community into the economic domain, softening the harshness of market competition with the warmth of community.

Political economy, which emerged in the 19th century, aimed to discuss various domains of society from a comprehensive perspective. However, throughout the 20th century, the path of social sciences diverged rather than converged. Political scientists no longer engage in discussions about economics, and administrators are often hesitant to delve into political matters. Furthermore, many economists tend to focus solely on their sophisticated theoretical models, often neglecting consideration of other areas.

The recent global trend is interdisciplinary integration. On a smaller scale, this implies the convergence of disparate societal domains. On a broader scale, it expands to the integration of social sciences with humanities and engineering. In the industrial society, the specialization of knowledge was crucial. However, in the information society, the integration of dispersed knowledge is of paramount importance. Only when we comprehend the social sciences within a unified framework can we combine knowledge about societies with arts and technology. With this vision in mind, I have authored this book, taking the first step toward understanding the entirety of social sciences within a unified framework.

7 Institutions of Four Realms

In the four social domains, there exists a corresponding "governance system" that matches its characteristics. If the term "governance system" sounds heavy, it can also be referred to as an "operating system." Depending on the social domain, there can be a focus on a "top-down" governance system where control is exercised from above, or an emphasis on a "bottom-up" voluntary operating system formed from the grassroots. This is an institution that aligns with the unique characteristics of each domain. Interestingly, Western ideas about these systems were established between the 17th and 19th centuries. Subsequently, they rapidly spread to the East and were embraced as global standards in the 20th century.

Economic System: Capitalism and the Market

The economy operates around the central concept of "money." All economic systems are designed to revolve around money. The collective term for such systems is "capitalism." The essence of capital lies in money. Forms of capital encompass cash, stocks, bonds, machinery, buildings, land, skilled employees, patents, trademarks, and more. Their common denominator is their potential to be money. Ultimately, capital represents money. The system in which economic activities revolve around assets that have the potential to be converted into money is called a "capitalist system."

Adam Smith perceived the essence of economy as "exchange." In the early stages, the division of labor led to the exchange of goods produced by individuals. Money emerged to facilitate the exchange of goods, and the accumulation of capital was required for future business endeavors. Adam Smith begins the second book of "*Wealth of Nations*" with the following statement:

> In that rude state of society in which there is no division of labor, in which exchanges are seldom made, and in which every man provides everything for himself, it is not necessary that any stock should be accumulated beforehand in order to carry on the business of the society.
>
> (Smith 1776, p. 276)

Here, "stock" refers to capital, and the market is the place where exchanges take place via capital. The most representative institution in the capitalist system is

DOI: 10.4324/9781003464730-9

Figure 7.1 Governing institutions and systems of four domains of society.

the "market." The market is a place where goods or services are exchanged for money. Consumers visit the market with money in hand to select goods or services. Suppliers offer their goods or services in the market and sell them to willing consumers for a fair price. The market acts as an intermediary for transactions involving money. This form of capitalism is also known as a "market economy." Max Weber points out as follows.

> Want satisfaction will be said to take place through a market economy so far as it results from action oriented to advantages in exchange on the basis of self-interest and where co-operation takes place only through the exchange process.
>
> (Weber 1922, p. 109)

The market highly values consumers' freedom. In order for the market to function properly, consumers must have the freedom to buy desired goods at desired prices. Occasionally, there are markets where this freedom is not ensured. Some merchants deceive or force vulnerable and powerless consumers into buying goods. Such practices are detrimental to the existence of the market. Once news of such coercion spreads, consumers no longer visit that market. "Freedom" is a precious virtue in the market.

If "freedom" is important for consumers, then the virtue for suppliers is "competition." It is the competition to provide cheaper and better products. Suppliers compete with each other, and consumers freely choose in such a market environment. This landscape of competition and consumer freedom represents the virtues of the market.

Then, who ensures these virtues and order in the market? Initially, merchants in the market organize themselves into associations to regulate undesirable behavior. However, there are individuals who cannot be controlled by merchant associations alone. For instance, there are disruptive consumers who cause disturbances, refusing to pay for expensive services. In such cases, the administration intervenes to uphold market order and virtues. The police might step in to apprehend individuals resorting to violence and merchants who use coercion or deception. The market does not exist independently. For the market to function, it requires assistance from another social realm, which is administration.

Community System: Communism and Community

Communities operate around the central concept of "relationship" or networks. Within the community, individuals are collectively protected and supported. This system is commonly referred to as "communism." When people hear the term communism, they often associate it with the political systems in countries like Russia or China. However, the concept of communal living predates these political systems and has been practiced since ancient times. It involves collective production and consumption. For instance, early Christian churches operated based on communal principles. The adaptation of communism into a political system is a relatively recent development, which has evolved over the past century.

Communism emphasizes the importance of the collective unit, known as the community. Max Weber highlights the characteristics of communism as follows.

> Communist arrangements for the communal or associational organization of work which are indifferent to calculation are not based on a consideration of means for obtaining an optimum of provisions, but, rather, on direct feelings of mutual solidarity. They have thus tended historically, up to the present, to develop on the basis of common value attitudes of a primarily non-economic character. There are three main types: (1) The household communism of the family, resting on a traditional and affectual basis; (2) the military communism of comrades in an army; (3) the communism based on love and charity in a religious community.
>
> (Weber 1922, p. 153)

As Weber pointed out, one of the most fundamental communism is the "family." The principle guiding family life is to provide maximum protection and support for its members. Even if certain family members are not able to contribute to productive activities, the family supports them unconditionally. This principle extends to the elderly who may no longer be able to participate in productive activities due to age. However, there is little concern for children or the elderly from other families, as they are not part of the immediate community. This captures the essence of communism that centers on members within the community.

In 1847, Frederick Engels wrote "The Principles of Communism," which served as a draft for the "Communist Manifesto." In this work, he defined communism as follows:

> Communism is the doctrine of the conditions of the liberation of the proletariat.
>
> (Engels 1847)

In this manuscript, Engels expanded the scope of communism to include the entire proletarian class, who earn their livelihood through the sale of labor. He identified the core of the proletarian revolution as lying in the abolition of private property, which he viewed as the root cause of boundless competition and the miserable state of the proletariat.

> Since competition is in reality merely the manner and form in which the control of industry by private property owners expresses itself, it follows that private property cannot be separated from competition ... Private property must, therefore, be abolished and in its place must come ... the communal ownership of goods. In fact, the abolition of private property is, doubtless, the shortest and most significant way to characterize the revolution in the whole social order which has been made necessary by the development of industry - and for this reason it is rightly advanced by communists as their main demand.
>
> (Engels 1847)

Communist states apply the principles of communism to the entire nation. The state assumes responsibility for the survival and welfare of its people, regardless of their ability to contribute to productive activities. Similar to the family where there is no specific ownership of furniture or televisions, there is no differentiation in the ownership of factories and land within the state. As everything is collectively owned by the whole family, the whole state owns everything in communist countries.

The implementation of communist principles at a national level is a relatively recent phenomenon, having evolved over the past century. Initially, communism was practiced at smaller scales, such as in villages. This is often referred to as the "communal community." Within communal communities, however, not all forms of consumption are collectively supported. Members typically cooperate in activities such as farming or attending funerals, which can be difficult for individual families to carry out alone. In this respect, communal life was a hallmark of agrarian society.

At its core, communism places priority on the bonds within the collective unit or community. While capitalism values monetary wealth, communism values human relationships. The key differentiation is whether individuals belong to the same community or not. However, as the size of the community expands beyond the village level, it becomes difficult for members to maintain close relationships. In large-scale communist states, the bonds within the community often exist more as abstract ideals than tangible relationships. The operation of these states is therefore grounded in an ideology that emphasizes belief in the collective. The organization that upholds and propagates this ideology is the "Communist Party." The primary mission of the Communist Party is the dissemination and preservation of communist ideology among the population. Without a collective and common belief in communist ideology, neither the Communist State nor the Communist Party can sustain itself.

Political System: Democracy and Voting

The transition from small communities to larger ones naturally moves people into political surroundings. In small communities, like families or villages, politics is not essential, as conflicts or disagreements among members can be resolved through dialogue or self-restraint. However, as communities grow larger, resolving conflicts becomes more challenging. Small disagreements can escalate into major disputes, potentially leading to divisions within the community.

To manage and resolve conflicts and disagreements, a "representative" who can gather and convey the opinions of the members is needed. Being a representative is often not a sought-after role, as it requires time and effort and can result in being caught in disputes. To incentivize individuals to take on this role, communities often provide financial support and honorific titles to the representative, who is then recognized as the leader of the community. This recognition encourages more people to aspire to leadership positions.

This process of selecting representatives to manage conflicts and gather opinions is what is known as politics. Political systems vary based on how representatives are chosen. In a monarchy, the successor is usually chosen by the reigning monarch. Aristocratic politics involve a small group of elites selecting the leader. Conversely, in a democratic system, leaders are chosen based on the collective opinions of the citizens. The term "democracy" is derived from "demo," meaning the people or citizens, and "cracy," meaning rule or governance.

The Bill of Rights 1689, which set limits on the powers of the monarch and defined the rights of Parliament and free elections in England, is regarded as a cornerstone of modern democracy. John Locke, who influenced this legislation, is renowned as a political philosopher who laid the groundwork for democratic political philosophy. Locke wrote as follows.

> And thus every man, by consenting with others to make one body politic under one government, puts himself under an obligation to every one of that society to submit to the determination of the majority, and to be concluded by it.
>
> (Locke 1689, Chapter VIII)

In this statement, Locke implies the fundamental principles of democracy, establishing a political and governmental body through the social contract and majority rule of election system.

Before Locke, the political philosopher who argued for the formation of governance through the social contract was Thomas Hobbes. Hobbes discussed the fundamental equality of power, asserting that even the weakest individual in this world can kill the strongest. From such equality arises a struggle of every man against every other man. Ultimately, everyone is tormented by the fear of not knowing when they might be killed. The only way to escape this fear, according to Hobbes, is for everyone to relinquish their individual sovereignty and create a single ruler. In *Leviathan*, published in 1651, Hobbes states the following:

> The only way to erect such a Common Power … is to confer all their power and strength upon one Man or upon one Assembly of men … This is more than Consent, or Concord; it is a real Unitie of them all … This done, the Multitude so united in one Person, is called a COMMON-WEALTH, in latine CIVITAS. This is the Generation of that great LEVIATHAN.
>
> (Hobbes 1651, p. 87)

Leviathan, symbolizing a formidable monster with immense power, directly signifies the government. While Locke's contract is renewed through regular elections, Hobbes's contract demands eternal obedience. Locke's social contract is democratic and egalitarian. If the government fails to uphold the contract, citizens can revoke it. However, Hobbes's contract is irreversible. In essence, Locke's contract is a pact of freedom. In the context of modern society, if Locke's contract pertains to the realm of politics, Hobbes's leviathan aligns with administration. The bureaucratic organization within the administrative domain maintains an everlasting contract with citizens. In the political realm, political leaders regularly enter into new contracts through elections.

Democracy employs a voting system to gauge the opinions of the populace. Citizens can either directly participate in elections to choose crucial policies or have representatives who participate in elections on their behalf. The former is known as "direct democracy," and the latter is called "representative democracy." In modern society, most nations operate under a representative democracy. Generally, representatives are elected by geographic regions. These elected representatives work in the Parliament or Assembly to create laws and review government budgets. As it is impractical for a single representative to handle all tasks, representatives with similar political views form "political parties." Parties that advocate for progressive changes are commonly referred to as the "liberal party," while those favoring the preservation of traditional values are known as the "conservative party."

The electoral process extends beyond choosing representatives for communities. Administrative leaders, such as presidents, mayors, and governors, are also elected. Unlike members of Parliament, these administrative leaders focus on the executive functions of governments rather than engaging in party politics.

Even until several decades ago, elections were accompanied by significant expenses. Collecting the opinions of citizens through voting demanded immense work and effort. The logistics of traveling to polling stations and counting ballots were complicated, and illiteracy was widespread. Consequently, participation rate in voting was not high. However, with advancements in information and communication technology in the 21st century, voting has become far more accessible with almost no cost. The challenge now lies in ensuring that elections are conducted both secretly and transparently.

Administrative System: Bureaucracy and Civil Servants

While political leaders are chosen through electoral processes, the administrative apparatus operates independently from politics. Linking the administrative system directly to politics would create immense confusion with every change of political leadership. As such, a system that maintains the order and functioning of the administration regardless of political changes is necessary. This system is known as "bureaucracy.'

There are common misconceptions regarding bureaucracy. Often, the term "bureaucracy" is used pejoratively. Describing an organization as mired in bureaucracy implies inefficiency or rigidity. Many scholars in public administration criticize bureaucracy, contributing to its negative perception. Negative perceptions of bureaucracy tend to reinforce themselves.

However, Max Weber, one of the prominent theorists of bureaucracy, viewed it as a positive embodiment of modern rationality. The term "bureaucracy" combines the French word "bureau," meaning desk or office, with "cracy," denoting rule or governance. Essentially, it signifies governance through desks or in offices. Weber emphasized the positive rationality of bureaucracy.

> The decisive reason for the advance of bureaucratic organization has always been its purely technical superiority over any other form of organization ... Precision, speed, unambiguity, knowledge of the files, continuity, discretion, unity, strict subordination, reduction of friction and of material and personal costs - these are raised to the optimum point in the strictly bureaucratic administration, and especially in its monocratic form.
>
> (Weber, 1922, p. 973)

Bureaucracy possesses not only technical rationality but also rationality grounded in an impersonal principle. In medieval Europe, society was governed by feudalism, where lords wielded arbitrary control over their territories. For activities like getting married, relocating, or starting a business, individuals had to seek permission from their lord. Max Weber observed a dynamic shift with the advent of bureaucracy. Instead of appealing to a lord, individuals began going to an office or a "small room" to submit documents and receive official approval for various endeavors. This shift reduced the lord's arbitrary influence, as approvals were granted based on standardized criteria. This "rule by offices" eliminated the whims and caprices of individual rulers. Bureaucracy aligns with the development of modern democracy in the sense that it follows impersonal rule rather than a personal monarch (Weber 1922, pp. 984–985).

Bureaucracy, with its emphasis on impartiality, provided the framework for the rationality that modern society seeks. Through bureaucracy, individuals could set up businesses, produce goods, and make plans without the fear of a ruler's arbitrary intervention. In this context, bureaucracy can be seen as an institutional mechanism that facilitated the Industrial Revolution.

> The progress toward the bureaucratic state, adjudicating and administering according to rationally established law and regulation, is nowadays very closely related to the modern capitalist development.
>
> (Weber 1922, p. 1394)

In bureaucracy, work is conducted methodically through documents and procedures, minimizing arbitrary decision-making. Those who execute these functions are known as "bureaucrats." To ensure the effective operation of a bureaucratic system, individuals who are proficient in reading and processing documents need to be appointed as bureaucrats. Moreover, to shield them from undue influence from higher offices, their tenure must be secured by institutional protection. These bureaucrats are typically referred to as "civil servants," and the civil service system is a central component of bureaucracy.

In South Korea, civil servants are appointed through a public examination. Once appointed, civil servants are obligated to maintain political neutrality, meaning they must refrain from engaging in any political activities. Concurrently, they have the right to job security, ensuring they cannot be arbitrarily dismissed. This balance of duty and the right of civil servants guarantees the independence of the administration from politics and ensures that civil servants can carry out their jobs impartially for the citizens.

While bureaucracy emerged in Western society a few centuries ago, variants of bureaucratic systems have existed in Eastern societies for almost 2000 years. In Eastern societies, bureaucracy was often rooted in Confucianism, which emphasizes humanism and rituals. This Confucian bureaucracy sought to limit the arbitrary power of rulers through adherence to humanistic principles. However, it also recognized the authority of rulers as a natural aspect of social order, limiting the extent of efficiency and impartiality in Eastern bureaucratic systems.

Anarchism

There are four distinct governance systems for the four realms that make up society: democracy in politics, bureaucracy in administration, capitalism in economy, and communism in communities. Over the years, a vertical image has taken root in people's minds. The top-down governance of politics and administration dominates the realms of economy and community. This vertical image has rapidly transformed in modern society. It has evolved into a rather interdependent image where the bottom-up demand from economy and community generates the top-down supply of politics and administration. It is now more of a horizontal image, where politics and administration provide governance services, while economics and communities contribute some necessary inputs to governance.

There has long been a movement seeking to deliberately dismantle the vertical relationship caused by the governance of politics and administration. It is anarchism. Anarchy, a word derived from Greek, combines "an" (without) and "archy" (ruler) to mean "without a ruler." Proudhon is famous as the first anarchist. He detested the oppressive rule of the state. In his book, Proudhon argued as follows.

> As a state religion is the rape of the conscience, so a state political administration is the castration of liberty.
>
> (Proudhon 1851, p. 265)

And he asserted that a private contract could replace the government:

> The CONTRACT solves all problems - The producer deals with the consumer, the member with his society, the farmer with his township.
>
> (Proudhon 1851, p. 268)

His claim is that if individuals are allowed to freely enter into contracts, all problems would be solved.

In the 21st-century information society, anarchism persists. The primary obstacle for digital citizens on the globally connected internet is the physical barrier imposed by the politics and administration of individual countries. Digital citizens desire privacy, freedom of the press, and freedom of digital content, but governments regulate them strictly. Particularly, transactions involving the exchange of money over the internet are not free. In the late 20th century, the world of information saw the emergence of cyber-anarchism or crypto-anarchism, aiming to exclude state control. Bitcoin, introduced in 2008, allows financial transactions across borders through its network. Moreover, Bitcoin serves as a crucial tool for crypto-anarchism by enabling transactions free from government surveillance. The world envisioned by crypto-anarchists is one where individuals, free from the barriers of national borders, build their own network states.

In 1988, Timothy May, emulating the Communist Manifesto by Marx and Engels, declared "The Crypto Anarchist Manifesto." May declared:

> A specter is haunting the modern world, the specter of crypto anarchy ... Just as the technology of printing altered and reduced the power of medieval guilds and the social power structure, cryptologic methods will also fundamentally alter the nature of corporations and government interference in economic transactions ... Arise, you have nothing to lose but your barbed wire fences!
>
> (May 1988)

After 140 years since the Communist Manifesto in 1848, the anarchist manifesto presented by May has not yet been embraced as a serious revolution. However, May's declaration is far from dead. In the digital world, crypto-anarchism is spreading vigorously. The last sentence of the Communist Manifesto was "Working Men of All Countries, Unite!" Timothy May did not need this last sentence because digital workers worldwide were already united beyond borders.

Metaphors vs. Ideology

While describing institutions unique to the four social realms, we explored classical works by renowned scholars. Throughout the 17th to 19th centuries, European society underwent rapid transformations. Intellectuals endeavored to comprehend the essence of this rapid change and its direction. However, capturing the nature of a dynamic and emerging society that defies human senses is challenging. A cognitive tool that alleviates this difficulty is metaphor.

Metaphor intuitively expresses experiences that are challenging to describe. When we say, "Do not waste your time," we use the metaphor "Time is money." When expressing "Time flies," we metaphorically compare time to a bird. When discussing the invisible and intangible nature of time, we rely on metaphor.

Similarly, when discussing a society that is invisible and intangible, we rely on metaphors. Adam Smith often used terms like productive hand, unproductive hand, and invisible hand, metaphorically comparing the economy to the hand of a human. Thomas Hobbes used war analogies to describe politics and employed the metaphor of the sea monster, Leviathan. John Locke discussed democratic politics by metaphorically using the contract of merchants. Karl Marx metaphorically likened workers to commodities and used the metaphor of battle. Max Weber often compared bureaucracy to an efficient machine.

To understand rapidly changing societies, renowned scholars used metaphors. However, their metaphors soon evolved into ideologies. An ideology that pursues absolute good leads people to antagonize and reject other ideologies. However, metaphor is relative and rejects absoluteness. Comparing a person to a flower, a tree, or the sky – all are possible at the same time. Essentially, all metaphors acknowledge their own limits and strive for coexistence. It is crucial not to forget that the institutions proposed by intellectuals are fundamentally metaphors. When institutions are embraced as metaphors, they effectively describe society. However, when metaphors are accepted as ideologies, they become blind to social reality, losing their insights.

Metaphor is a double-edged sword. On one hand, it simplifies and clarifies complex social phenomena, but on the other hand, it conceals the various meanings embedded in these phenomena. George Lakoff and Mark Johnson discuss metaphors remarkably clearly in "*Metaphors We Live By*." As a conclusion to their book, they cautioned against metaphors in political economy. Their concern becomes more crucial when the metaphor transforms into ideology.

> When we accept the LABOR IS A RESOURCE metaphor and assume that the cost of resources defined in this way should be kept down, then cheap labor becomes a good thing, on a par with cheap oil … The blind acceptance of the metaphor can hide degrading realities.
>
> (Lakoff and Johnson 1980, p. 237)

8 Public vs. Private Area

Society can be divided into the public and private areas. Politics and administration fall under the public area, while the economy and community are part of the private area. So, how do we differentiate between the public and private areas? The concept that distinguishes the public from the private area is "publicness." An area possessing characteristics of publicness is considered public, while an area devoid of publicness is considered private. The concept of publicness has been in use for a long time, but it lacks a clear definition. Scholars who discuss this concept present various perspectives.

"Publicness" encompasses the commonality of society, openness to society, the rights of social members, and considerations for fairness and equality within society. From the scholarly discussions, a common thread can be identified. "Publicness" places prime importance on society as a whole, while the private lives of individuals remain free from public scrutiny. A consensus among most scholars is that politics and administration fall within the public area, while the economy and community belong to the private area.

In the public area, where considering society as a whole is deemed important, the pursuit of personal interests, known as "private interests," is discouraged. Individuals involved in the public area are expected to prioritize the collective interest of society, known as the "public interest." Politicians and civil servants who engage in pursuing private interests in the public area are often criticized for involvement in corruption.

In contrast, in the private area, pursuing personal interests is considered natural. People seek to protect their safety and maximize their benefits. They may even harm the interests of others to enhance their own. However, in the private area, individuals do not solely pursue self-interest. They may advocate for the interests of the organizations they belong to. For example, employees of a company can secure their own interests by contributing to the interests of the company. In this case, the company's interests are referred to as "private interests" rather than "public interest." The same applies to the community area. Even if parents make sacrifices to support their family, it is not referred to as serving the public interest. Similarly, if an individual makes sacrifices for the benefit of a religious group, it is not termed a sacrifice for the public interest. This is because, in modern society, family and religion are categorized as parts of the private area.

DOI: 10.4324/9781003464730-10

Figure 8.1 Public and private areas are among the four domains of society.

In the public area, which prioritizes society as a whole, most activities are transparent and open to scrutiny. Police officers on duty are not allowed to have privacy. Most police stations have CCTV installed to record the actions of police officers. Even in emergency situations, police officers may attach cameras to their bodies. Of course, there are exceptions, such as military operations or police investigations, which may necessitate secrecy. However, in most cases, activities in the public area, including their budgets, are disclosed as a matter of principle. This is to enable monitoring and prevent corruption within the public area.

On the other hand, in the private area, most activities are afforded confidentiality. The private area is a space where individuals' privacy is safeguarded, and within this space, individuals can experience true freedom. The word "privacy" is itself derived from the notion of the private area. The saying "My home is my castle" particularly emphasizes the complete protection of privacy within the home. The private area is entrusted to individuals and communities, allowing them to act without being subjected to scrutiny by others.

The distinction between public and private is more of a relative concept than an absolute one. While most organizations within the administration are considered public, informal gatherings among civil servants for recreational activities fall into the private domain. When a civil servant within the administration completes their duties and leaves the office, they enter the private area. Moreover, the activities of politicians do not solely belong to the public realm. When a prominent politician publishes an autobiography and earns economic profit, it is considered an economic activity and thus falls within the realm of privacy. There are instances where an influential politician provides consulting services to companies and receives substantial compensation; in such cases, there might be public scrutiny for corruption rather than private activity. Sometimes the line between the public and private is unclear and ambiguous.

Public Roles in the Community

There are times when organizations belonging to the private area are required to play a public role. Although newspapers and broadcasting companies fall within the economic area, many people consider their roles as public. News produced and transmitted privately has an impact on society as a whole. During the period when Covid-19 was shaking the world, fake news was rampant. There were reports claiming that the Covid-19 virus was intentionally spread, and widespread misinformation about vaccines, including their side effects and even conspiracy theories. Societies worldwide were thrown into confusion by unverified news surrounding Covid-19. Governments in each country also vacillated between excessive control and excessive laissez-faire.

Sometimes, false news can bring about unexpected fortunes. On November 9, 1989, during an official press conference where East Germany announced its policy of travel freedom, an East German official, without much thought, responded with "immediately, without delay (Sofort, unverzüglich)." An Italian journalist present at the press conference then spread the false news of the "collapse of the Berlin Wall." This misinformation traveled around the globe at lightning speed, and on that night, excited Berlin citizens climbed the wall, causing it to crumble. The scene was broadcast worldwide. The false news played a role in advancing the reunification of Germany.

The cases where misinformation brings good fortune are exceptional. Most misinformation leads to social chaos and disasters. Particularly, in the 21st century, the uncontrolled production of fake news on social media platforms has already emerged as a societal issue. Operators of internet media generate sensational fake news to attract people's attention. Such sensational fake news is adopted by other social networks and spreads to even more people. More concerning is the spread of politically motivated fake news on social network services. Politicians may be falsely portrayed as corrupt or extreme-minded. Due to the recommendation algorithm for showing news with high similarity, most people are susceptible to distortion by fake news. Those who encounter fake news frequently on the internet gradually come to believe it as true. Society becomes polarized and hatred deepens as a result of fake news. As fake news spreads through social media, there is an argument that it should go beyond the private realm of internet media. And there are calls to hold operators of internet media accountable for their fake news.

While belonging to the community area, schools are organizations with a public nature. Schools should not teach students about the personal preferences of teachers. Even if a teacher believes in the health benefits of vegetarianism, they should not instruct students not to eat meat. Teaching students about political ideologies, including liberalism and conservatism, is also discouraged. Despite being in the private realm, schools fulfill a public role in educating the next generation.

Also, a "CSO (civil society organization)" is a private organization that performs a public role. Sometimes CSO is referred to as NGO (non-government organization) or NPO (non-profit organization). NGO has public concern as its mission and works in the public area, emphasizing that it does not belong to the administrative area and is not a government organization. Usually, NPO works in the business area, but its main purpose is not to make a profit but to contribute to social goods.

CSOs perform a public role, engaging in activities for various purposes such as human rights protection, environmental conservation, and the elimination of discrimination. In the process of their activity, they expose social issues and demand citizen participation. CSOs generally do not belong to the realm of politics. Their involvement in politics might be detrimental to their purity. However, CSOs often encourage citizens to actively participate in politics. This is because the political participation of citizens allows the advocacy of CSOs to be reflected in politics.

Sometimes CSOs contribute to global solidarity. Issues like climate change transcend national boundaries, and their resolution cannot be achieved through the efforts of any single nation. It is estimated that there are over 40,000 NGOs operating internationally. Well-known international NGOs include "Greenpeace," which advocates for environmental protection, and "Doctors Without Borders (Médecins Sans Frontières)," which provides medical services in underserved regions.

It is not uncommon for organizations within the economic area and those within the community to perform public roles. However, just because these organizations undertake public roles doesn't necessarily make them public organizations. On the contrary, they possess a distinct identity by operating within the private area while fulfilling public roles. As a light shining through the shadow appears brighter, performing public roles within the private area might be more effective. This contrasting effect works on the premise of distinction between public, consisting of politics and administration, and private, composed of economy and community.

Public Policy as Intervention

Public policy can be defined in a nutshell as the intervention of public organizations in the private area. According to Peters, "Public policy is the set of activities that governments engage in for the purpose of changing their economy and society (Peters 2015, p. 1)." He emphasizes the importance of approaching policy intervention from a design perspective. Careful consideration should be given to which areas of the private area to intervene and what policy tools to use when intervening. Of course, the overarching direction of policies is determined in the realm of politics. When politicians decide on the grand set of values to pursue, the government designs specific routes and means of intervention. The definition of policy as an intervention of the public into the private is the clearest and most visual definition.

The term "intervention" presupposes noninvolvement in the original state. The economy and the community have historically operated independently without administrative interference. This autonomy guarantees the privacy of both the economy and the community, as well as individual freedom. However, with the onset of administrative intervention, individual freedom and privacy become constrained. Consequently, there has been longstanding resistance to public intervention in private matters.

Adam Smith, the author of "*The Wealth of Nations*," opposed public intervention in the economy. He argued as follows:

> (Merchants) generally, indeed, neither intend to promote the public interest, nor know how much they are promoting it... they intend only their own gain, and they are in this, as in many other cases, led by an invisible hand to promote an end which was no part of their intention ... I have never known much good done by those who affected to trade for the public good. It is an affectation, indeed, not very common among merchants, and very few words need be employed in dissuading them from it.
>
> (Smith 1776, p. 456)

Adam Smith did not trust the concept of the public itself. On the contrary, he believed that individual merchants in the private sector, freely pursuing their own interests, contribute to the wealth of society.

However, there has been a growing recognition that government intervention becomes inevitable when market failure occurs. Markets, influenced by individuals with a narrow focus on pursuing their own interests, have experienced confusion through misguided speculation and hoarding. This has resulted in a failure to supply goods that many people need, and unethical products such as drugs have flooded the market. This is commonly referred to as market failure. Such market failures justify government intervention. When the market falls into disarray, the government cannot stand idly by. The government must intervene to rectify the market's confusion and paralysis. This governmental intervention is referred to as public policy.

Government intervention is not limited to the market; it also extends to the community. Government interference may occur when the community fails to care for its members or when the community collapses. For instance, when the community fails to provide support for elderly individuals who cannot be cared for at home, the government establishes nursing homes to look after them. As many young people move to urban areas, leaving behind depopulated village communities, the government establishes nursing homes to maintain a sense of community. This form of government intervention is commonly referred to as "social welfare policy."

There is little opposition to government intervention in the face of community failure. Instead, there is a demand for more proactive government intervention and support. Government intervention in communities typically takes the form of financial assistance. In contrast, government intervention in the economy focuses more on regulation than support. Due to these differences, there has been a strong voice opposing government intervention in the economic area, while in the community area, there is often a demand for more government intervention. Just as the ebb and flow create the appearance of a coastline, modern society has taken shape through alternating support and opposition to public policy intervention.

9 Value vs. Fact

Society's four realms can also be differentiated based on values and means. In the public area, politics determines the values to pursue, while administration provides the means to achieve those values. In the private area, the community sets forth the values to pursue, and the economy furnishes the means to realize those values.

In this context, it is important to clarify conceptual meanings. The terms "values" and "ends" have similar meanings, while "means" and "facts" are closely related. Values often become ends to pursue, and the means of pursuing activities can be found in the world of facts. Therefore, means are conceptually akin to facts.

Now, let's consider values and facts. Values and facts are opposing concepts. Facts denote the current state, while values signify the desired future state. Now, let's think about the relationship between ends and means. These are not opposing concepts but rather interconnected. The means are the tools to implement ends. Now, let's connect these four concepts again. Value and fact are no longer opposing concepts. In the world of values, there are ends to pursue, and in the world of facts, there are means to use.

In the political realm, liberal parties generally emphasize "equality," while conservative parties emphasize "growth." Voters cast their ballots for parties that advocate the values they prefer. The party that receives the most support gains the legal authority to determine the values that govern society. Politics, through elections, decides the values a society pursues. Often, the values chosen through elections reflect the pressing social needs in that society. A society facing repeated economic decline tends to highly value the virtue of economic growth. A society where the gap between the rich and the poor has been widened deeply tends to prioritize the value of equity. In this way, elections play a role in revealing the path for the future of society.

However, the values chosen through elections are not always guaranteed to be good. The values chosen by the majority of voters can lead society astray. In the 1932 German parliamentary elections, Hitler's Nazi Party obtained 37% of the vote, making it the first party. Many Protestants who couldn't vote for the Communist Party turned to the Nazi Party. The choice of the German people to give power to the Nazi Party ultimately brought suffering to the whole world. Although political elections can end with misguided choices, elections remain the only procedure that the majority of people can agree on to select the future values of society.

DOI: 10.4324/9781003464730-11

Figure 9.1 Value and fact among four domains of society.

These values become the ends that administration should pursue. But how can we achieve the value of equality? Administration can achieve these ends by collecting more taxes from the wealthy and providing more financial support to the less fortunate. The act of collecting taxes and allocating support is the means to achieve the value of equality. Means are tangible actions that can be observed in the factual world. In contrast, the ends of equality exist in the world of values and are more of an idea than a concrete fact.

In the community realm, various values exist. Firstly, one of the most crucial values is the survival and continuity of the community. The family itself is considered a value that must be preserved, and nations may endure wars for their survival. Secondly, individual members within the community are inherently important values. Families support grandparents who have lost their productivity until the end of their lives, and governments invest significant manpower and budgets to rescue even one citizen kidnapped by pirates. Thirdly, the mission pursued by the community is a fundamental value. In religious communities, values range from love for humanity to devotion to God. For Christians, the gospel and worship are paramount values, while for Buddhists, the realization of nirvana is crucial. Some individuals, instead of denying their beliefs, choose martyrdom. Fourthly, fellowship and peace provided by the community are important values. Communities often refrain from intense debates to avoid conflict. Fifthly, the external reputation of the community is considered an important value. To prevent tarnishing the community's reputation, it may even expel a powerful member involved in scandals.

In contrast, in the economic realm, all values are ultimately tied to money. The value of goods is evaluated in monetary terms, and the value of services is also assessed based on money. Even an individual's worth is often translated into monetary terms in the economic realm. "Money" becomes the most tangible expression of value in the economy. However, upon reflection, money itself has no intrinsic value. Strictly speaking, money, especially in the form of banknotes, is just a representation of value. Banknotes have no inherent worth but are a social agreement to exchange for goods or services. Therefore, money serves as a means within a socially agreed-upon framework and does not possess value in and of itself. Thus, the economic realm is primarily concerned with means. Money, in the form of banknotes, exists in the factual world, as it is tangible and can be physically handled. It serves as society's agreed-upon means of exchange.

When distinguishing the four realms of society based on values and means, administration and economy are associated with the world of means, while politics and community are associated with the world of values. Administration represents the means grounded in practical authority within the public area, and economy deals with means in terms of money within the private area. In contrast, politics and community establish ends and values. In the community realm, individuals find diverse values within the communities they are a part of. In the political realm, electoral outcomes determine the ends and values.

Now, we can combine the categories of public and private with the categories of value and fact. This combination reveals that each of the four domains of society possesses unique characteristics. The community holds private values, while the economy provides private means. Politics is the arena for generating public values, and administration provides public means.

Dreamers vs. Counters

Those engaged in the world of values are generally warm and passionate. Politicians are kind to voters, and those involved in elections often demonstrate fervent passion for either progressive or conservative values. Passion is crucial in the world of values. Max Weber emphasizes passion as an important virtue for politicians. However, he notes that politicians must also bear responsibility for their passion, requiring the ability to maintain a certain distance. While politicians need passion, they should not be consumed by it. Weber stated as follows.

> To be sure, mere passion, however genuinely felt, is not enough. It does not make a politician unless passion, as devotion to a "cause," also makes responsibility to this cause the guiding star of action. And for this, a sense of proportion is needed. This is the decisive psychological quality of the politician: his ability to let realities work upon him with inner concentration and calmness. Hence his distance to things and men. "Lack of distance" per se is one of the deadly sins of every politician.
>
> (Weber 1919, p. 36)

Here, Weber emphasizes the virtue of calmness in contrast to passion. While passion dreams, calmness calculates. Those engaged in the world of facts are generally cool and objective. Government officials in the administration scrutinize documents submitted by residents from an objective standpoint. Business persons in the economic realm must calculate pragmatically how well their products will sell in the market and decide on the pricing. In the world of facts, objective rationality is emphasized over subjective emotion.

Often, kindness towards customers is emphasized as an important virtue for employees in businesses. It is indeed true that kindness towards customers is crucial. However, kindness towards customers is a conditional kindness, based on the premise of transactions involving products and services. The kindness required in a community is not conditional but unconditional. The Bible teaches not to show favoritism to the rich and not to mistreat the poor in a church. However, it's different in a department store. Customers who make significant purchases are usually classified as VIP customers and are treated with special kindness.

In this way, administration and economy dealing with facts emphasize the rational dimension, while politics and community handling values prioritize the emotional dimension. In practical terms, public administration in the public area and management in the private area are similar as they both are concerned with implementing means. Public policy in the public area and economics in the private area often revolve around budgetary considerations. Politics and sociology share a common focus on values, especially in terms of addressing conflicts in values. However, political science emphasizes resolving conflicts in the public area, while sociology focuses on values in the private area.

Values and facts can be discussed in the dimension of time. Facts are expressed in data, representing records of the past, while values are aspirations for the future that one desires to achieve. Those who confront facts are counters, while those embracing values are dreamers. The future direction of society lies in the realms of community and politics. Values are precious because they have not yet been realized, providing coordinates and hope for the future. Dreamers exist in the realms of community and politics.

In the community, education cherished for children is an investment in the future. Religion in a community shares dreams about the more distant future. Acts 2:17 in the New Testament states, "I will pour out my Spirit upon all flesh, and your sons and your daughters shall prophesy, and your young men shall see visions, and your old men shall dream dreams." People gathering in Christian churches do not inquire about each other's past; they unite as one with the same faith and hope for the future.

Separation of Powers

In the world of politics, politicians and citizens engage in fierce competition through elections to determine what values their society will pursue in the future. While the past actions of politicians may emerge as important election issues, their significance lies in assessing the trustworthiness of the promises politicians make for the future. Politics is about future choices, not the past.

In contrast, the society's past is recorded in administrative documents and economic capital. Economic capital indicates how much profit was generated in the past within that society. The data on population and housing managed by the administration also constitute historical records about the social foundations. Counters, who confront current facts, exist in the realms of administration and economy.

The separation of powers into legislative, executive, and judicial branches is often discussed as a cornerstone of democratic governance. The legislature creates laws, the executive implements them, and the judiciary adjudicates violations. The legislative branch constitutes the "political realm," whereas the executive and judiciary form the "administrative realm." The legislative branch creates laws with new values as social ends. These laws represent aspirational values, and the legislative branch is future-oriented. The executive branch brings these laws into effect in the present, which is referred to as "implementation." The judiciary assesses violations of the law, which are accidents that have occurred in the past. The judiciary thus reviews past accidents and determines legal consequences.

Charles de Secondat, known as Montesquieu, advocated the separation of the three powers in his book "The Spirit of Laws." These powers encompass the legislative, executive, and judicial branches, aligning with the future, present, and past perspectives of society. Montesquieu believed that separating powers based on these time perspectives was crucial for maintaining a peaceful balance. He expressed the idea that if the same individual or body were to wield two out of three powers – enacting laws, executing public resolutions, and trying the causes of individuals – it would lead to the downfall of everything (Montesquieu 1748, pp. 173–174).

A person possessing two out of the three powers can execute the remaining one. When these powers are separated, they can exercise their authority legitimately without fearing others. According to Tocqueville, there is one more condition to accomplish full democratic governance: all three powers must originate from the citizens. Three powers must be separated and endorsed by citizens. Tocqueville said that the United States is the first country to realize these conditions.

> In America the people appoints the legislative and the executive power, and furnishes the jurors who punish all offences against the laws. The American institutions are democratic, not only in their principle but in all their consequences; and the people elects its representatives directly, and for the most part annually, in order to ensure their dependence.
>
> (Tocqueville 1840, p. 196)

These three powers operate with different time perspectives. I once suggested a catchphrase: "The judiciary deals with the past, the administration focuses on the present, and the legislature is responsible for the future." With this catchphrase emphasizing time perspectives, I advocated for the establishment of a future research institute within the National Assembly of Korea. At the time, many politicians in the National Assembly were skeptical of my proposition, questioning why the political assembly should be involved in the future planning of society.

In the past, the government in South Korea planned a blueprint for the nation's future. People with such experiences were convinced that "planning for the future is the task of administration." However, administration is primarily concerned with tangible actions and the present. While it is essential for public officials to be concerned with and propose policies for the nation's future, the authority and responsibility to determine the direction society should take lie with the legislature.

Unfortunately, many politicians did not understand that the future belongs to the realm of politics. Many politicians who value traditional authority consider the essence of politics to be rooted in the legitimacy of the past. They prioritize factors such as royal lineage or patriotic activities in the past. This is often referred to as the politics of privilege. They believe that only deserving individuals should hold political power. They regard political power as a favorable benefit to enjoy. However, in democratic societies, political power is not a seat for enjoying privileges but rather a position for shaping the future direction of society.

Many individuals do not clearly understand their roles within the political, administrative, economic, and community realms. It is only when individuals have a clear understanding of their positions within these realms that they can effectively fulfill their respective roles and missions. When record-keepers look to the future, they cannot find data to record, and when decision-makers look at the past, there is no future to choose.

Optimism and Pessimism

The current facts and future values often form a cyclical relationship. Those who recognize the abundant resources in present society may think optimistically about the future of society, leading them to invest in savings and pensions. These investments, in turn, have a positive impact on the future of that society. Ultimately, as more people anticipate the future of society optimistically, the society develops and flourishes even more.

However, young people witnessing the decline of the city they belong to tend to have a pessimistic outlook on the future of that region and seek to escape. As young people exit the society, the region undergoes even more rapid desolation. This phenomenon is observed in Japan and Korea and is referred to as "local town extinction (地方消滅)." In 2014, Japan was shocked by Hiroya Masuda's report, which predicted that 896 towns and villages across Japan would no longer be viable by 2040, describing it as "local town extinction." Similarly alarming, in South Korea, it is reported that more than 50% of regions are at risk of extinction.

In this way, the current facts influencing the values of the future, and vice versa, creating a cyclical relationship, are known as a self-fulfilling prophecy (Schelling 1978, p. 115). Robert Merton used this concept to explain the process through which collective behavior unfolds. For instance, there is a rumor circulating that a small-town bank is at risk of bankruptcy. Upon hearing this rumor, depositors rush to withdraw cash from the bank. As the bank that does not hoard all deposits in cash reaches a point where it cannot provide cash to depositors, the rumored bankruptcy becomes a reality. Even if the bank is financially sound, the mere rumor of bankruptcy can lead to its downfall. This illustrates the frightening power of a self-fulfilling prophecy.

> The self-fulfilling prophecy is, in the beginning, a false definition of the situation evoking new behavior, which makes the originally false conception come true.
>
> (Merton 1968, p. 477)

People with a pessimistic outlook on the future of society cannot work for the society anymore. Some even seek to acquire small valuables before the complete collapse of society. In the event of riots in a city, residents may loot department stores and convenience stores to seize goods. When a rumor circulates that a company is on the verge of collapse, employees cannot focus on their work. Eventually, as the factory comes to a halt, the pessimistic rumor proves to be true. Thus, a pessimistic prophecy about the future leads to the current tragedy.

Conversely, people who are optimistic about the future of society willingly show loyalty to that society. Even in times of crisis for a company, an employee who is confident that the company will not perish remains committed, even if they do not receive their wages. When South Korea faced a national bankruptcy crisis in 1997, many Koreans remained optimistic about the future. In January 1998, a gold collection campaign took place, with 3.49 million people participating over four months, gathering 225 tons of gold and supplementing $2.1 billion in foreign exchange.

In schools, the term "self-fulfilling prophecy" is often used in a positive context, known as the "power of positive thinking" or the "Pygmalion effect." In Greek mythology, Pygmalion was a sculptor who fell in love with a statue of a woman he had created. With his deep love, the statue eventually became a real person. In the field of education, this concept is referred to as the "power of positive thinking" or the "power of praise." When a teacher positively affirms and praises a student, saying that they will become an outstanding individual in the future, the student diligently studies and eventually achieves great success. The reverse is also true. If a teacher scolds and curses a student, the student may become trapped in a vicious cycle.

On Value/Fact Dichotomy

In this way, facts and values, means and ends, and the present and the future become social concepts that mutually influence and dynamically shape society. However, most philosophers deny the interaction between facts and values. The dichotomy that values cannot be inferred from facts is common sense among philosophers. The philosopher who first clearly articulated this was David Hume. Hume cautioned against the erroneous confusion of the two. He wrote as follows.

> I am surprised to find that, instead of the usual copulations of propositions, is, and is not, I meet with no proposition that is not connected with an ought or an ought not. This change is imperceptible but is, however, of the last consequence.
>
> (Hume 1739, p. 302)

Hume points out that intellectuals often conflate facts with imperatives, asserting imperative statements without thorough consideration. For example, when reporting the extravagant spending of the wealthy, they suddenly argue that one should not waste too much. Hume's caution has been interpreted as Hume's law, positing that values cannot be derived from facts.

Subsequently, most philosophers and thinkers have accepted the distinction between facts and values (Putnam 2004). Unlike the beliefs of philosophers, in the world of society, facts and values are closely intertwined. When reports about child abuse frequently appear in the media, public opinion forms around the importance of preventing child abuse. If it is reported that drug addiction is on the rise, an imperative to crack down on drugs emerges. In the social realm, it is evident that facts influence values. And the emerging values result in new policy interventions that alter previous facts. Thus, a cycle exists where facts influence values, and, in turn, values influence facts. The social world differs from the world of philosophy. Facts in the administrative and economic areas interact with values in communities and politics and even form cycles. While it is possible to distinguish facts and values in the social world, they cannot be separated.

10 Competition vs. Cooperation

Four realms of society exhibit distinct modes of action. In the economic and political realms, "competition" is the primary mode of action. In contrast, in the administrative and community realms, "cooperation" is the normal mode of behavior. Politicians compete in elections to gain more votes. Businessmen compete in the market to earn more money. In the bureaucratic system of administration, public officials perform their duties through cooperation between superiors and subordinates, as well as collaboration between other public institutions. In community groups, members are encouraged to cooperate rather than compete with each other.

In the public world of politics, competition centers around the pursuit of values, with the means entrusted to administration. Conversely, in the private world, competition revolves around money, serving as the private means. The pursuit of values in the private area is entrusted to communities that operate on cooperation among members. While public competition in politics is associated with values, private competition in the economy focuses on means. Similarly, public cooperation of administration involves means, while private cooperation in communities deals with values.

In the private world, individuals can choose the values they wish to pursue. If one wants to follow Buddhism, one may go to a temple; if one prefers Christianity, one can attend a church. Individuals embrace the values presented in Buddhist scriptures as part of the temple community and those in the Bible as part of the church community. It is a matter of personal choice. However, money, being a limited resource, becomes a subject of competition. Individuals seeking to obtain limited financial resources have no choice but to compete.

In the public area, a nation cannot officially embrace contradictory values simultaneously in the same space. Political choices, such as whether to prioritize the natural environment or economic development, often become sources of conflict. Elections serve as the means to resolve such conflicts, determining which values to pursue through competition among politicians and political parties.

Once the public values to be pursued are determined through political competition, administration is responsible for their execution. However, public officials in administration do not need to compete over which means to employ. If a public official can use the desired means, they do so; if not, they refrain from using it. Why is that? If a public official cannot access a particular resource, it means that the resource was not allocated for use in the political realm. For example, when a

DOI: 10.4324/9781003464730-12

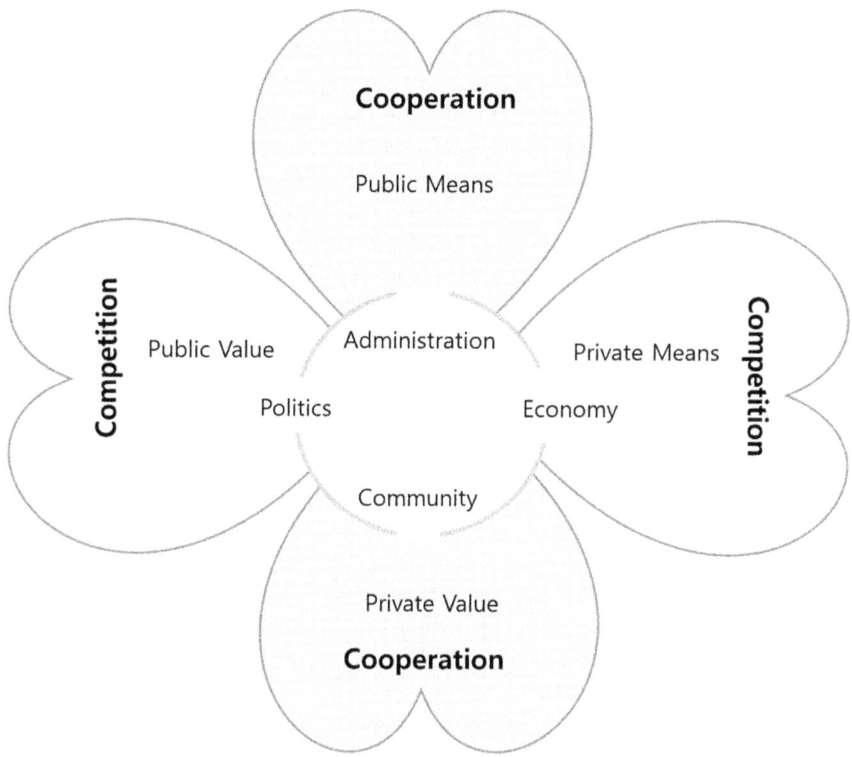

Figure 10.1 Competition and cooperation among four domains of society.

public official responsible for supporting impoverished elderly citizens needs 100 million dollars but is allocated only 10 million dollars, they have no choice but to work within the budget of 10 million dollars. There is no need to compete with other departments to secure the remaining 90 million dollars. The task of a public official is to select and provide support to eligible elderly citizens within the given budget range without delay. Seeking cooperation is the responsibility of a public official. Later on, the public official can persuade politicians about the necessity of a larger budget. However, the persuasion by a public official is intended for cooperation. Competitive persuasion, aimed at taking the budget away from other departments, goes beyond the role of a public official.

Number of Cooperation and Competition

Cooperation and competition are inherently social concepts. People cannot cooperate alone, and they cannot compete alone. Society is a combination of cooperation and competition. While competition is emphasized in politics and economy, cooperation also takes place simultaneously. To compete against a powerful opponent, the cooperation of the weaker ones is necessary. Moreover, competition within a dominant group can result in its fragmentation. In other words, cooperation for the sake of competition can occur, and such cooperation collapses due to internal competition. This form is often referred to as "merging and splitting."

As competition and cooperation lead to repeated mergers and divisions within groups, representative patterns emerge in terms of cooperation and competition. Most converge into dyadic or triadic structures. Triadic structures, in particular, are mysterious. In Christianity, the Trinity represents a triadic structure with God the Father, Jesus Christ the Son, and the Holy Spirit. In the history of Asian kingdoms, various kinds of three-kingdom structures can be observed. One of the most widely read books in Asia for an extended period is "*Romance of the Three Kingdoms*." Authored by Luo Guanzhong in 14th century, this historical novel covers the Three Kingdoms period of the 3rd-century China. One of the most famous scenes depicts three heroes – Liu Bei, Guan Yu, and Zhang Fei – taking an oath of fraternity in the Peach Garden. They swore as follows:

> We three - Liu Bei, Guan Yu, and Zhang Fei - though of different families, swear brotherhood, and promise mutual help to one end. We will rescue each other in difficulty; we will aid each other in danger. We swear to serve the state and save the people. We ask not the same day of birth, but we seek to die together. May Heaven, the all-ruling, and Earth, the all-producing, read our hearts. If we turn aside from righteousness or forget kindliness, may Heaven and Human smite us!
>
> (Chinese Text Project, https://ctext.org/sanguo-yanyi/ch1)

The entire scene of this oath follows a triadic structure. Three heroes become one, and these heroes serve both the state above and the people below. With the heavens above and the earth below, their commitment to be one stands. Again, a triadic landscape. The "Oath of the Peach Garden" is not just a scene in the novel; its influence has endured among Asians who dream of revolution. Aspiring politicians and soldiers dreaming of revolution, as well as even those involved in organized crime and local troublemakers, desired to emulate their oath. To achieve this, three individuals had to come together. So many faithful triadic groups emerged among ambitious individuals in Asia.

In Western politics, the union of three leaders is referred to as a "triumvirate" or "triarchy." The most famous triumvirate is the political alliance among Caesar, Pompey, and Crassus in 60 BC, a period when the Roman Republic faced instability and struggled to effectively manage crises. To overcome the veto power of the Senate, the three leaders agreed to join forces and dominate the Roman government for nearly a decade. The Second Triumvirate occurred among Octavian (Augustus), Lepidus, and Mark Antony in 43 BC, lasting another decade. In 30 BC, after their defeat at the Battle of Actium against Octavian, Mark Antony committed suicide with Cleopatra, the queen of Egypt. In 27 BC, Octavian became the first emperor of Rome and held the title of Augustus.

Many contemporary competitions unfold in triangular structures. In the mid-20th century, the global political economy was characterized by the competition among Europe, the Soviet Union, and the United States. In the 21st century, this dynamic has shifted to a triangular structure involving the United States, Europe, and China. Even in market competition, the top three companies typically dominate most markets.

The separation of powers is also applied to the governance of a nation. The US Constitution establishes a "trias politica" system that strictly separates the powers of the legislature, executive, and judiciary, maintaining a system of checks and balances to ensure stable governance. Even in this context, the triangular structure serves as the framework for competition.

In the late 20th century, the South Korean government deliberated on how many mobile communication companies to license. Due to the limitations of frequency bands, the number of companies was restricted. Allocating a frequency to only one operator would result in a complete market monopoly for that operator. Allocating frequencies to two operators posed the risk of creating an oligopoly. So, the question arose: how many operators should be allocated frequencies?

It is fortunate for me to participate in this policy discussion. Surprisingly, there were no economic theories to consult for such policy decisions. Ultimately, it was decided to allocate frequencies to three operators. With three operators, if the market share of one operator increases, the other two can join forces to restrain it. Additionally, even if three operators manage to form a collusion, there is a big incentive for one operator to break out. In the end, it was determined that allocating frequencies to three operators is advantageous for maintaining market competition. The wisdom that influenced this policy decision is an ancient Asian proverb called "three legs balancing (三足鼎立)," which suggests that a pot with three legs will not tip over. Traditionally, pots used for containing hot embers were crafted with three legs to prevent them from tipping over. The knowledge applied in making crucial economic policy decisions was not from sophisticated academic disciplines but from traditional wisdom.

A pattern of competition and cooperation that commonly appears, no less than the triangular structure, is the dual structure, known as the dyadic structure. Through numerous processes of mergers, a competitive structure is formed between the two strongest forces. The world's religions unfold in a dyadic structure as Christianity with 2.6 billion followers competes against Islam with two billion followers. Additionally, global economic warfare unfolds in a dyadic confrontation between the United States and China. The domestic politics of many countries converge into a dual-party system of conservative and progressive parties. This is often depicted in extreme terms as a struggle between good and evil or a war between light and darkness. Dyadic structures often unfold in extreme confrontations, leading to social conflicts and dilemmas.

Dilemmas Imposed on Society

Administration is expected to execute what politics determines. However, there are many instances when politics cannot decide clearly what values to pursue. Frequently, public administrators are tasked with pursuing economic growth and social equality simultaneously. However, choosing economic growth may jeopardize social equality, and vice versa. In such circumstances, administrators face a dilemma. Making policy choices in this dilemma is never easy.

Arthur M. Okun discusses the most fundamental dilemma of economic policy. Economic policies aim to satisfy both equity and efficiency simultaneously. However, equity and efficiency have a significant trade-off relationship (Okun 1975). Policies that seek to improve economic efficiency tend to reduce the fairness of distribution. Conversely, policies aiming to enhance equity often result in decreased economic efficiency. Okun emphasizes that policymakers need to understand the dilemma posed by these conflicting objectives.

The policy dilemma has been studied by Professor Lee Chong-Bum and his colleagues for over 30 years in South Korea, and it remains an important research topic (Yoon et al. 2000). Unresolved political conflicts may transform into administrative dilemmas. In a modern society where more diverse values are cherished and considered important, administrative dilemmas increase rapidly. Administrators face a hard time dealing with these dilemmas, as it is difficult to choose between conflicting values. However, they cannot ignore the dilemma. Ignored dilemmas in administration might lead to economic crises and subsequently to deeper conflicts in society and politics once again.

Faced with conflicting values or alternatives, an administrator finds themselves in a dilemma. To protect the city's environment, emissions from factories need to be prohibited. However, if emissions from factories are banned, the factories would have to close, leading to job losses for residents. Studies on dilemmas have identified three types of reactions to such situations. First, administrators facing a dilemma may choose to delay their decision. Recognizing that any choice between environmental protection and factory operation will result in negative consequences, administrators often postpone making a final decision. Second, administrators facing a dilemma may exhibit inconsistent behavior. For instance, an administrator who advocated for prohibiting factory emissions might later argue that such a prohibition is excessive regulation. The administrator's decision tends to change depending on the economic situation of the city. Third, administrators respond to the dilemma through symbolic actions. If an administrator finds it hard to resist pressure from environmental groups, they might opt for a policy prohibiting factory emissions. However, since shutting down the factories is not desirable, the administrator may not actively enforce the emission control policy. In this way, administrators navigate through dilemmas using strategies such as time delay, inconsistent choices, and symbolic actions.

Baruch Spinoza, a prominent figure in 17th-century Enlightenment philosophy, discussed abnormal behavior in dilemmas. Spinoza explores Buridan's ass, questioning the existence of free will. Buridan imagined a hungry and thirsty ass placed equidistantly between a pile of hay and a water puddle, unable to decide which to approach first. Eventually, the ass dies from hunger and thirst. Spinoza argues that humans face similar difficulties in similar circumstances.

> I say that I grant entirely that a man placed in such an equilibrium (viz. who perceives nothing but thirst and hunger, and such food and drink as are equally distant from him) will perish of hunger and thirst.
>
> (Spinoza 1677, p. 151)

Two thousand years ago, Pontius Pilate found himself in a dilemma between the cries of the Jews urging for the crucifixion of Jesus and his conscience, recognizing the innocence of Jesus. Pilate, while accepting the voices of the Jews, symbolically washes his hands to shift the moral responsibility onto the Jews. In a similar vein, Hamlet becomes entangled in a dilemma upon discovering that the murderer of his father is now his mother's husband. He faces the dilemma of seeking revenge for his father, knowing that doing so would result in the loss of his mother's love. The famous soliloquy emerges from the extreme of this dilemma: "To be or not to be, that is the question." This soliloquy articulates the confused mind experiencing a dilemma.

Modern society is full of dilemmas. In the United States, where approximately 50,000 people lose their lives to firearms each year, gun regulation has been a long-standing dilemma. There is a growing argument that individual gun ownership should be prohibited to reduce the escalating casualties from mass shootings. However, the Second Amendment to the US Constitution recognizes the right of citizens to own guns for self-defense against crime, and the powerful National Rifle Association (NRA) opposes gun regulation. Within the dilemma of gun regulation, policy decisions regarding gun regulation continue to be delayed.

The global dilemma of the 21st century revolves around refugees. As of 2023, the UN has identified over 35 million refugees. Particularly, there has been a sharp increase in refugees since the Syrian civil war in 2015. Their destination is often European countries. EU nations are faced with the dilemma of whether to accept or reject them. Arguments in favor of accepting refugees on humanitarian grounds clash with concerns about social instability. While some countries make symbolic gestures of actively welcoming refugees, in reality, there are nations that aim to suppress the influx of refugees. Governments of countries facing this serious dilemma find themselves unable to make a rational choice, as no option appears truly reasonable.

Dilemmas in private areas are frequently observed within communities. One common example is the dilemma faced by a father attempting to escape from North Korea, who must choose which of his children to save. While crossing the river, both children are swept away by the strong current. He is forced to decide between rescuing his daughter or his son. His choice to save one means losing the other. In such dilemmas, human rationality often falters.

Contrary to this, observing dilemmas in the economic domain is not as straightforward. While consumers often ponder over which product to purchase, their choices may not necessarily constitute a dilemma. Similarly, companies deliberating whether to invest in employee training or facility improvement are not necessarily ensnared in a dilemma.

Dilemmas are often observed in the domains of administration and community, where cooperation is emphasized over competition. It appears that cooperative individuals are more susceptible to dilemmas. If this holds true, could competition serve as a strategy for resolving dilemmas?

This is a story from the Middle East. A father had two sons, and he owned a farm. Faced with the dilemma of deciding which son would inherit the farm, the father proposed a competition to his sons. The proposition was that the son who first crossed the desert would inherit the farm. The father aimed to resolve his dilemma through the competition between his two sons. However, a problem arose. While competing in the desert, the two sons, intending to concede their inheritance to each other, rode their horses slowly. If the older son went slowly, the younger son went even slower, and vice versa. Unable to escape the scorching desert, the two sons found themselves in danger. The father's dilemma turned into a more serious dilemma for the two sons. At that moment, a wise solution occurred to them. They decided to exchange horses. Riding each other's horses, the older son shouted at his horse to run faster, and the younger son shouted at his horse to run faster. Eventually, the horses they rode picked up speed and crossed the desert. In this way, the dilemma within cooperation was resolved through competition. The virtues of competition and cooperation pursued by the four social realms can provide each other with an escape route from dilemmas.

Another way to overcome a dilemma is to limit the options available in the dilemma situation. Jon Elster discussed the dilemma of Ulysses (Elster 1979). In the Greek myth, Ulysses embarked on his journey homeward, navigating perilous waters that brought him near the Sirens. The Sirens, enchanting sea nymphs, sang captivating songs. Sailors who heard these songs were lured to their deaths by crashing into rocks. Ulysses wanted to hear the Sirens' songs, but he knew that listening to them would lead to his death. Ulysses faced a dilemma. To overcome this dilemma, Ulysses tied himself to the mast of the ship and blocked the ears of his crew. He commanded them to row towards the planned route, no matter what happened. In this way, Ulysses could hear the Sirens' songs while ensuring that the ship stayed on course. Ulysses overcame the dilemma by restraining his own choices.

Elster discusses that many people use self-binding methods, similar to Ulysses, to overcome dilemmas. Many individuals find themselves in a dilemma between spending and saving. To navigate this dilemma, people often enter into contracts that automatically allocate a portion of their income to savings. These contracts help them overcome dilemmas by limiting their choices. One of the most notable examples of such a contract is marriage, where couples make vows in front of witnesses, committing to each other and foregoing the possibility of future happiness with other partners.

There is a more serious form of self-binding. Politicians have incentives to stimulate the economy to win elections. One of the most effective and direct methods is for the central bank to print money and inject it into the market. However, this method leads to long-term inflation and damages the economy. A dilemma arises over whether to expand money for short-term popularity or to maintain economic stability. To prevent falling into such a dilemma, in most countries, politicians are excluded from decisions regarding the money supply, despite being responsible for overall economic policies. This is analogous to the dilemma faced by Ulysses when listening to the Sirens' song. To avoid succumbing to fatal temptations, politicians are bound to the mast as Ulysses was.

> To remove monetary policy from the political sphere would itself be political act; the abdication of politicians and not their dethronement.
>
> (Elster 1979, p. 61)

Part III
Mechanism of Social Science

If the focus of Part II was on what constitutes the realms of society, Part III is about how these realms operate. Only by understanding what society is composed of and how it functions can we truly comprehend the social structure.

The essential functions expected from the realms of administration and economy are "resource allocation," while the core functions of the realms of community and politics revolve around "conflict resolution." In a national society, resource allocation and conflict resolution are the most crucial functions. When these two functions operate effectively, the country can sustain itself and develop continuously.

In markets, the allocation of private resources occurs through the mediation of "price adjustment," while in administration, public resources are allocated using queues as indicators. The market operates through a bottom-up mechanism, while administration proceeds through a top-down mechanism. Traditionally, communities resolve conflicts through spatial separation. Territorial boundaries between conflicting communities create private spaces where conflicts can be circumvented. Achieving spatial separation in politics is inherently difficult. In politics, the coexistence of conflicts over values is facilitated through temporal separation.

DOI: 10.4324/9781003464730-13

11 Resource Allocation vs. Conflict Resolution

What functions do the four realms of society perform? This is an exceptionally difficult question. As formidable as the question is, the answer is equally challenging. However, surprisingly, the answer emerged in my mind. Over the past 40 years, through reading books, papers, engaging in conversations with numerous scholars, and attending conferences, answers to this question have accumulated in my mind. One day, while lecturing my students on the functions of social institutions, an answer spontaneously emerged from my mind. The answer that flowed out of my mind is as follows: the functions expected from the realms of administration and economy are "resource allocation," while the functions of the realms of community and politics revolve around "conflict resolution."

Resource Allocation

Administration focuses on public means, while the economy focuses on private means. Both administration and economy perform tasks related to acquiring, providing, and utilizing means. Means needed to achieve any purpose or value are collectively referred to as "resources." Economic activities can be understood as the circulation of the resource known as "money" within the processes of producing, distributing, and investing in commodities and services. Similarly, activities in the realm of administration can be interpreted as the provision of public resources such as budgets, facilities, and public personnel. In this way, economic and administrative activities perform the function of "resource allocation."

I remember being impressed when I read an economic paper emphasizing the importance of resource allocation. At that time, I thought that resource allocation was not only important in the economic realm but also crucial in the realm of administration. What is the most important thing for a company to survive and grow continuously? What is the most important thing for a country to continue to exist and develop? It is the task of allocating more resources to those contributing to the survival and growth of companies and countries. This is the essence of the function called "resource allocation."

A family had two children. The younger child was a diligent and well-behaved student, while the older one was a troublemaker, always getting into mischief. One day, the older child got involved in assault and battery. Consequently, the older child ended up in prison. It was possible to release him if a substantial

DOI: 10.4324/9781003464730-14

Figure 11.1 Functions of the four domains of society: Resource allocation and Conflict resolution.

compensation was paid to the victim. The parents faced a difficult dilemma: if they paid the compensation, they couldn't afford to send the younger child to college. The choice for the parents was difficult – whether to focus resources on the troublemaking older child or allocate them to the diligent younger child. While it might seem sympathetic to allocate resources to the older child, it raised questions about the family's future. If resources were directed towards the older child, the younger one would have to discontinue his studies. Moreover, once released from prison, the older child might engage in further misconduct. The family would increasingly find itself in crisis. Supporting the younger child to continue his education is a choice that ensures the future of the family. Such resource allocation demands the parents' rational judgment.

The core idea asserted by Adam Smith in "*The Wealth of Nations*" is resource allocation. The wealth of nations depends on how resources are allocated – whether to diligent and productive hands or to idle and unproductive ones. Smith believed that capital could be employed by diligent and productive individuals to generate wealth, whereas revenue was often consumed by idle and unproductive parties. Regarding their allocation, Smith declares the following:

> The proportion between capital and revenue, therefore, seems everywhere to regulate the proportion between industry and idleness. Wherever capital predominates, industry prevails: wherever revenue, idleness. Every increase or diminution of capital, therefore, naturally tends to increase or diminish the number of productive hands, and consequently … the real wealth and revenue of all its inhabitants.
>
> (Smith 1776, p. 337)

The government faces dilemmas as well, particularly when deciding whether to provide financial support to a major company facing a bankruptcy crisis. If a large corporation fails, numerous jobs disappear. Politicians representing the region where the factory of this large corporation is located, along with those who have received lobbying from the corporation, engage in lobbying campaigns. The lobby advocates for providing financial support to save the troubled corporation. However, such a choice comes with significant repercussions. Rescuing a financially troubled major corporation not only deprives its competitors of the opportunity to expand their market shares but also reinforces the notion known as "too big to fail (TBTF)." This expectation arises from the belief that the collapse of a large corporation would have a profound impact on society, leading to the anticipation that politics and administration will provide support.

When such expectations take root, leaders of major corporations may focus more on cultivating relationships with politicians rather than striving to produce high-quality products. This approach is not only a safer option but, if done well, can even lead corporate leaders to venture into politics. This situation, where politics and the economy become closely intertwined, is commonly referred to as "crony capitalism." The economic development in Korea occurred under the protection of military dictatorships, giving rise to the phenomenon of crony capitalism. In 1997, Korea experienced a financial crisis, leading to a change in political power and the dismantling of the belief in the "too big to fail" aspect of crony capitalism. Historically, significant crises often come with rare opportunities to eliminate past vices.

In 2012, Acemoglu and Robinson published the book *Why Nations Fail: The Origins of Power, Prosperity, and Poverty*. The book delves into the reasons some nations succeed while others fail, even when they share similar populations and resources. Examples include neighboring countries such as the United States and Mexico, Europe and Russia, and North and South Korea. What distinguishes these nations, leading to their categorization into success or failure? Acemoglu and Robinson pinpoint these distinctions in terms of inclusiveness and exclusiveness. Exclusiveness denotes the concentration of power among a few, while inclusiveness signifies the open participation of people. The authors focus on both economic and political arenas, asserting that a nation exclusive in both domains is destined to fail, while one inclusive in both tends to prosper.

However, they do not provide a clear answer to the question of what happens in nations where politics is exclusive but the economy is inclusive. I have discussed this with students and concluded that the key lies in how resource allocation takes place. Inclusiveness is only a condition for effective resource allocation. Moreover, inclusiveness in one domain promotes inclusiveness in another, while exclusiveness in one reinforces exclusiveness in another.

For a long time, Koreans were indoctrinated to believe that exclusive politics could bring about economic development. However, witnessing the harms of crony capitalism, Koreans have learned the importance of inclusive politics. In an inclusive political environment, crony capitalism disappears, and corporations focus on securing their economic competitiveness. A circular relationship is established.

Observing corrupt and flawed resource allocation, citizens chose inclusive politics, ultimately leading to an inclusive economy. An inclusive economy no longer advocates for exclusive politics. Citizens, having witnessed how the exclusiveness in politics and the economy distorts resource allocation and leads to economic decline, opted for inclusive politics and economy.

Conflict Resolution

Resource allocation takes place in administration and economy. However, the direction of resource allocation is determined by politics and the community. If many people consider economic development a crucial value, resources are allocated to entrepreneurs contributing to economic development. If there are many who prioritize the value of protecting the vulnerable, resources are allocated to the vulnerable through administration. The values chosen by society in the domains of the community and politics determine the direction of resource allocation.

Community generates private values, while politics determine public values. Emphasizing one value as crucial often means that other values are pushed aside as less important. Those who support the discarded values express dissatisfaction. As dissatisfaction grows, society descends into turmoil. Implementing values selected at higher ranks transitions to administration and economy. However, values relegated to lower ranks still linger in the domains of community and politics.

The values of high rank and low rank inevitably come into conflict with each other. Uncontrolled value conflicts can escalate into extreme fights, ultimately tearing apart societies. It is necessary to manage or resolve these conflicts to avoid catastrophe. Conflict management focuses on the outcomes resulting from conflicts, while conflict resolution concentrates on the conflicting values that serve as the root cause. However, conflict management and conflict resolution are not clearly distinct, and both do not fundamentally solve conflicts. Social conflicts are inherently challenging to address. All conflict resolutions are merely temporary solutions. Therefore, once a conflict is resolved, it needs to be addressed again.

There are conflicts that persist for thousands of years without resolution. Many conflicts between nations and ethnic groups, dating back to ancient times, still remain unresolved. In particular, ethnic conflicts can escalate into collective massacres advocating ethnic cleansing. Religious conflicts are also difficult to resolve. When the values of Christianity and Buddhism clash, resulting in value conflicts, achieving a complete resolution is nearly impossible. Judaism, Islam, and Christianity have endured conflicts for thousands of years, and resolution can only be achieved through compromise and partial sacrifices.

For a long period, the values of the ruling class overwhelmed those of the subordinate class. Privileges were bestowed upon the children of the ruling class, and the religion of the ruling class was officially recognized. Throughout society, the values of the ruling class took precedence. However, human civilization has gradually evolved in a direction that considers the values of the weaker. The distinction between the subordinate and ruling classes is disappearing, and all adults can now cast an equal vote in elections. Women's rights have improved in households and businesses. With the advancement of civilization, more diverse values emerge in society, leading to an increase in conflicts of values. The resolution of such conflicts has become crucial for modern communities and politics.

Even if temporarily reconciled, value conflicts resurface eventually, necessitating further adjustments. This is why the term "resolution" is used for conflicts instead of "solution." We learn about "problem-solving" at school; however, social conflicts cannot be solved at once. Conflicts repeat and can only be "resolved." In a world of abundant values, conflicts over values occur on a daily basis. Ultimately, the core function that politics and communities should be responsible for is "conflict resolution." Without addressing and resolving ongoing conflicts over values, the peace and order of a society cannot be maintained.

Grand Circle

In a national society, resource allocation and conflict resolution are the most crucial functions. When these two functions operate effectively, the country can develop continuously and positively. However, resource allocation and conflict resolution do not occur independently. They are closely interconnected and move in tandem with each other.

There are two relationships between resources and values. Firstly, there is a reinforcing relationship where higher values receive more resources. This is often referred to as the cycle of the rich getting richer and the poor getting poorer. In the shadow of prosperity, there is poverty. The values of groups that do not receive resources are gradually considered less significant. This is also evident in everyday life. Those who wear expensive clothes and drive luxurious cars are treated better, while those who wear shabby clothes and take the bus are not highly regarded.

Secondly, there is a balancing relationship, where higher priorities are given to lower values. This relationship arises because as the gap in values widens, conflicts over values intensify. Resources are allocated to resolve the value conflicts. Parents often show more significant concern for weaker and deprived children than for healthy ones. Healthy children may not necessarily require the same level of attention from parents. The government's budget follows a similar pattern. It is natural to demand an increase in the government budget for impoverished areas.

Values and resources form a vast cycle. Resources flow towards high values or towards low values with high conflicts. This creates the fundamental dynamics of society. In a positive cycle between values and resources, resources tend to accumulate in highly valued locations. Conversely, in a negative cycle between values and resources, resources are dispersed to areas with low value. If the former represents the centripetal force of society, the latter corresponds to the centrifugal force of society. A society where the centripetal force is greater tends to shrink, while a society where the centrifugal force is greater tends to expand over time. In this way, the centripetal and centrifugal forces emerging from the processes of value conflicts and resource allocation in society drive social cyclical movements.

12 Resource Allocation in Economy

Market Price Adjustment

Resource allocation in the economy is achieved through the market. The market is where consumers and suppliers meet to exchange goods, existing in physical spaces or cyberspace through the internet. Consumers pay money for goods, while suppliers receive money for providing them. What functions does the market as a whole perform? What functions do societies expect from markets?

Through market transactions, money flows from consumers to suppliers. Suppliers compete with each other, aiming to attract consumer choices by supplying better products at lower prices. Through the competitive mechanism of the market, consumers can purchase better products at lower prices. Ultimately, consumers' money concentrates on the most competitive suppliers. Resource allocation is achieved through the market.

Thomas Sowell's *Basic Economics*, a renowned textbook in economics without graphs and equations, declares "resource allocation" as the core of economics. This is because the essence of economics is on the use of scarce resources having alternative uses. Demand and supply for millions of goods, and the resulting prices through market transactions, allocate resources. Sowell explains this in plain language:

> The over-all coordination of these innumerable isolated decisions takes place through the effect of supply and demand on prices and the effect of prices on the behavior of consumers and producers. Money talks—and people listen … From the standpoint of the economy as a whole, this means that resources tend to flow to their most valued uses when there is price competition in the marketplace.
>
> (Sowell 2015, chapter 2)

This mechanism can be explained using causal loop diagrams, which are powerful visual tools of system dynamics. Causal loop diagrams depict arrows that start from causes and point to effects. Arrows with a "+" indicate positive causality, while arrows with a "-" indicate negative causality. The right side represents the feedback loops in the demand sector, while the left side represents the feedback loops in the supply sector. The center is occupied by the "price" of goods, forming the central axis. When the price of a product increases, the demand for that product decreases. This negative causality is represented by the upper arrows in the demand

DOI: 10.4324/9781003464730-15

section. Conversely, when the demand for the product increases, the price of that product rises. This positive causality is represented by the lower arrows in the demand section. Price influences demand, and in turn, demand affects price. Thus, the two arrows form a loop and circulate.

The left side represents the feedback loops in the supply sector. When the price of a product increases, suppliers supply more goods to the market. This positive causality is represented by the upper arrows in the supply sector. However, when the supply of a product increases, the price of that product decreases. This negative causality is represented by the lower arrows in the supply sector. Both supply and price form feedback loops that circulate.

The price adjustment mechanism in the market consists of two feedback loops. Feedback loops also have polarities of + and -. Negative (-) feedback loops possess the property of maintaining equilibrium, while positive (+) feedback loops possess the property of deviating from equilibrium. A positive feedback loop reinforces any changes in the loop, while a negative feedback loop suppresses any changes. The two feedback loops that form a normal market are both negative feedback loops. The feedback loop in the demand sector exerts a force to maintain equilibrium through adjusting demands. Similarly, the feedback loop in the supply sector seeks to maintain equilibrium with the reaction of the suppliers.

Now, let's imagine a fire occurring in a warehouse where goods are stored, causing a decrease in the supply of goods. In that case, the price of goods will temporarily increase. However, consumers will reduce their demand for goods with increased prices. As demand decreases, the price of the product will decline. In this way, the demand sector temporarily lowers the price of goods that have suddenly increased to restore equilibrium. The feedback loop in the supply sector operates in the same way. When the price of goods rises, suppliers increase their supply, and as the supply increases, the price of goods decreases. The feedback loop in the supply sector also exerts a force to return the price to its original equilibrium state. Now, let's consider what would happen if the price of goods suddenly drops. In this case, the feedback loops in both the demand and supply sectors act in reverse to increase the price of the decreased goods. I encourage you to review the causal loop diagram.

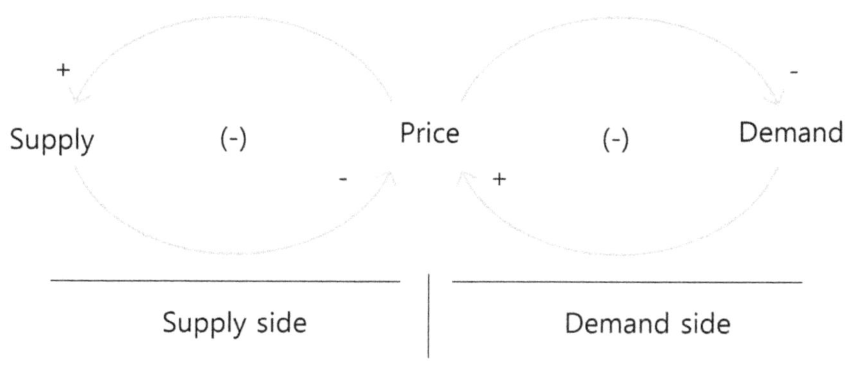

Figure 12.1 Causal loop diagram for price adjustment mechanism of the market.

Price as Knowledge in Society

The economist who clearly elucidated the functioning of the market's price-adjustment mechanism is Friedrich Hayek. In 1945, he published an insightful paper titled "The Use of Knowledge in Society." At that time, debates among intellectuals were focused on comparing the market economy of the United States with the planned economy of the Soviet Union. The planned economy, which involved the central collection and calculation of all information, was often considered superior to the decentralized market economy in terms of resource allocation. Centralized and controlled planned economies were believed to be more capable of resource allocation than dispersed market economies.

Hayek emphasizes that all information in the economy cannot be collected by the center. In the process of utilizing resources to produce and distribute goods, diverse knowledge and information of countless individuals are involved. However, the central government is unaware of the secretive know-how and capricious changes in preferences used daily by workers, capitalists, engineers, merchants, and consumers. Here, Hayek states that the difficulty of resource allocation exists.

> The economic problem of society is thus not merely a problem of how to allocate "given" resources ... it is a problem of the utilization of knowledge not given to anyone in its totality.
>
> (Hayek 1945, pp. 519–520)

Intellectuals are bewildered in such situations. How can one act without sufficient knowledge? Here lies the longstanding arrogance and misconception of intellectuals. People often act without knowing more than they act with knowledge, especially concerning society. Hayek explains this as follows:

> As Alfred Whitehead has said in another connection, It is a profoundly erroneous truism, repeated by all copy-books and by eminent people when they are making speeches, that we should cultivate the habit of thinking what we are doing. The precise opposite is the case. Civilization advances by extending the number of important operations which we can perform without thinking about them. This is of profound significance in the social field.
>
> (Hayek 1945, p. 528)

In a society where members and their knowledge are dispersed, the prices in a market economy serve as a lighthouse. The almost singular information that society's members possess is the market price. When the price of a good rises, consumers reduce their consumption. Observing the rise in the price of goods, retailers release stored products from warehouses. As the price of goods rises, suppliers employ more workers to increase production. Society's members may not know why market prices change, but they act agilely in response to market prices. Regarding this, Hayek explains with the following metaphor:

> It is more than a metaphor to describe the price system as a kind of machinery for registering change, or a system of telecommunications which enables

individual producers to watch merely the movement of a few pointers, as an engineer might watch the hands of a few dials, in order to adjust their activities to changes of which they may never know more than is reflected in the price movement.

(Hayek 1945, p. 527)

Hayek's argument is that, compared to a centrally planned economy, a decentralized market economy effectively utilizes the knowledge of society's members. Serving as a lighthouse that informs the entire market situation, prices allow individuals, who are most familiar with their own circumstances, to make the most appropriate decisions. There is no central authority that can instruct every ship at sea on which direction to move and at what speed. Hayek's paper provides insight into the difference between individual knowledge and societal knowledge.

Speculation, Bubble, and Fashion

Market mechanisms do not always function flawlessly. Distortions in market mechanisms often occur. Market distortions arise from speculation in the consumption sector and fluctuations in the supply sector. Causal loop diagrams can also easily explain situations where market distortions occur. When the price of a product increases, speculative demand in the consumption sector does not decrease but actually increases. This is because individuals anticipate making substantial profits by reselling the product later. When price and demand change in a positive causal relationship, the polarity of the feedback loop in the demand sector shifts to positive (+). Positive feedback loops exert a force that deviates from equilibrium. In the presence of speculative demand, product prices become unstable.

Speculation often leads to economic bubbles. A bubble refers to a situation where the price of a commodity is significantly higher than its "intrinsic value." For example, if the price of an ordinary small car exceeds one million dollars,

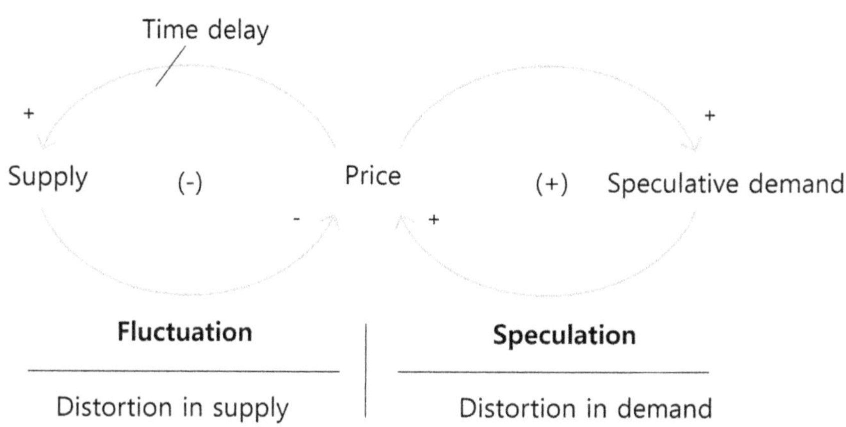

Figure 12.2 Causal loop diagram for market distortion: fluctuation and speculation.

it can be considered a bubble. This is because one should be able to purchase a similar car at a much lower price. Bubbles distort the resource allocation in the economy.

The most serious speculation in history was the bubble of Tulip Mania in Denmark. In the 17th century, the price of tulips, especially those of rare colors, rapidly increased. The price of rare tulips reached a bubble, exceeding 20,000 US dollars in today's currency. The bubble led to more speculation, as investors expected to make even greater profits. They poured substantial funds into buying rare tulips. However, the tulip craze soon faded away, leaving speculators to lose their entire fortunes overnight.

The background of speculation often involves a reinforcing circle between trends and bubbles. As the trend of favoring tulips spreads in society, speculation on tulips begins, causing prices to skyrocket and generating a bubble. The abnormal bubble in tulip prices creates an illusion about tulips, sustaining the trend. However, every trend is a temporary social phenomenon. Once a trend fades, the illusion disappears, and the price falls to the ground.

In modern society, fashion trends related to clothing are constantly evolving. Once, short skirts were in fashion, shortly followed by the trend of long skirts. Clothing that has gone out of fashion often sees a significant drop in price, while bubbles form in the prices of clothing that have peaked in popularity. This phenomenon of fashion extends to academic disciplines as well. When statistics is in vogue, salaries for statisticians are high, but when psychology becomes trendy, salaries for psychology majors rise. Recently, salaries for artificial intelligence majors have been overwhelmingly high. Does this specialized knowledge genuinely generate substantial profits for companies? Alternatively, it could be that companies with a high number of employees in trending disciplines experience a surge in their stock prices. These are structural mechanisms that amplify bubbles, trends, and fashions throughout society.

Since 2007, for over a decade, there has been a Big Data craze among intellectuals in Korean society. It was an unfounded belief that Big Data technology would lead Korea's future. I argued that their belief in Big Data's ability to accurately predict the future is not true. However, it took a long time to realize the bubble. It is a rule that one fashion does not fade away until there comes a new one. With the emergence of the artificial intelligence trend, the old trend faded out.

The recent major bubble debate revolves around Bitcoin. When it entered the market as digital cash in 2009, Bitcoin's price was only $0.05. However, by 2013, it surpassed $100, reached over $10,000 in 2017, and crossed $50,000 in 2023. Bitcoin is a form of encrypted digital currency with no intrinsic value. It solely possesses the exchange value as highlighted by Marx. If no one desires Bitcoin, its price would approach zero. Over the decade from 2013 to 2023, the price of Bitcoin increased by more than 500 times, leading some scholars to argue that it is a speculative bubble. Others contend that Bitcoin is necessary for borderless, free transactions and that it holds not only "exchange value" but also "use value." This debate is ongoing. If a network state, transcending borders, emerges as dreamt by crypto-anarchists, Bitcoin's price is likely to rise further. However, if nation-states with territorial boundaries manage to suppress the emergence of a network state, the bubble embedded in Bitcoin's price may deflate.

Fluctuation and Economic Cycle

The distortions in the supply sector, referred to as fluctuations, are attributed to "time delay." These occur when a rise in product prices doesn't promptly translate into an increased supply. For instance, in the housing market, an upturn in housing prices doesn't immediately lead to an augmented housing supply due to the time needed for constructing new houses. When time delay is present in negative feedback loops, the corrective forces acting to restore equilibrium operate with a slight delay, causing misalignments in their effects. The accumulation of these misalignments gives rise to fluctuations.

Fluctuations are often referred to as waves. Products that experience a time delay in supply are exposed to waves. Agricultural products and livestock, which require time for cultivation and breeding, are prime examples of products susceptible to waves. The housing market is also vulnerable to waves. When the housing market is booming, there is a shortage of houses for sale. In response, construction companies start building additional houses. However, by the time they can supply new houses, the boom in the housing market is over. Many construction companies struggle to find consumers and face bankruptcy. The "boom and bust cycle" is, in fact, a result of suppliers not fully understanding the effect of time delay.

The economic domain is filled with the dynamics of fluctuations, waves, and cycles. One of the most famous economic cycles is the Kondratiev wave. This is a long-term economic cycle occurring every 40–60 years, discovered by the Soviet economist Nikolai Kondratiev about a century ago. Many economists have attempted to explain the causes of economic cycles, and among them, Joseph Schumpeter's theory of technological innovation has been widely accepted.

Schumpeter is a remarkable economist. He explains complex economic mechanisms with easy and clear sentences without using any formulas. Reading his sentences is like watching a movie; pictures are painted. Firstly, Schumpeter describes external factors that bring about changes in the economy, including natural disasters, changes in crop yields, the discovery of new continents, and revolutions in social institutions. He then presents technological innovation as internal factors that bring about massive changes. Schumpeter points out that there is a time lag for economic agents to adapt to these changes, particularly emphasizing the importance of "lag effects" for suppliers.

> Major innovations entail construction of New Plant (and equipment)—or the rebuilding of old plant—requiring non-negligible time and outlay.
>
> (Schumpeter 1939, p. 90)

Thus, the fundamental factors bringing about business cycles are the significant technological innovations, the time delay involved in implementing them, and the secondary time delay in the adaptation process of the rest of society.

System dynamics scholars emphasize that business cycles can arise from everyday delays in corporate activities, even without massive technological innovations. The daily decisions of numerous firms, each aiming to return to their usual equilibrium state, generate fluctuations.

> The cycle arises from the negative feedbacks through which firms seek to maintain inventories at appropriate levels. Delays in these feedbacks caused by the hiring process mean production cannot be adjusted instantly to desired levels. The delays in these negative loops cause the oscillation.
>
> (Sterman 2000, p. 789)

However, these small waves can either offset or mutually amplify each other. The phenomenon of mutually amplifying waves is called entrainment. Predicting the business cycle arising from the amplified waves of everyday economic activities is difficult.

> It means the business cycle originates in the private sector from the ordinary, everyday decision-making processes of millions of firms and individuals. It also means stabilization of the business cycle through government monetary and fiscal policy is difficult.
>
> (Sterman 2000, p. 784)

The possibility of a business cycle occurring without a massive technological innovation is akin to a tsunami engulfing the coast without a massive earthquake. The whole is different from the sum of the parts. The whole society is completely different from the sum of the decisions by individuals.

Opportunity in Waves

Fluctuations can present tremendous opportunities as well as great loss. In the Genesis of the Old Testament, Joseph interpreted Pharaoh's dream, predicting seven years of good harvest followed by seven bad years. As the appointed Prime Minister of Egypt, Joseph stored grain during the years of abundance, successfully overcoming the subsequent years of scarcity. He sold the stored grain to residents of Egypt and beyond. This led to Pharaoh gaining ownership of all the land, possessions, livestock, and even people, establishing Pharaoh as a powerful ruler. Joseph's success allowed him to reside in Egypt with his 11 brothers, contributing to the formation of the Israelite people. Waves present opportunities. Those who take the chance in the wave make a big fortune, while others in the same wave lose their all.

A theory has been developed to leverage economic cycles for profit. In his 1938 book, Ralph Nelson Elliott discovered useful patterns in the waves of the stock market. Studying price changes on the New York Stock Exchange, he discovered the typical pattern of waves. Changes in stock prices consist of three impulse waves followed by two corrective waves (Elliott 1938). When stock prices are increasing, three consecutive upward impulse waves occur, followed by two corrective waves in the decreasing direction. In the scenario of decreasing stock prices, three consecutive downward impulse waves occur, followed by two corrective waves that restore stock prices. This provides a simple pattern to interpret the complex changing prices in stock markets.

Elliott did not explain why three consecutive impulse waves are followed by two consecutive corrective waves. All human behavior follows a rhythm. There is a rhythm of day and night, as well as a weekly rhythm of weekdays and weekends. Even if we cannot explain the cause of the rhythm, knowing the pattern of the rhythm allows us to predict the future. Ancient people who did not understand why the sun rises were still able to accurately predict the time of sunrise.

Although Elliott did not provide any theoretical grounds, his wave principle has been widely used. Consider a situation where the price of a stock you own begins to increase. When is the appropriate time to sell? If the stock is entering an upward trend, it is expected that three upward waves will follow. It is advisable to wait until at least two waves have occurred before selling the stock. The appropriate timing is determined when it is perceived that the third wave has arrived. Elliott's wave theory, though simple, provides strategic timing guidance, while economic theories that are extremely complex fail to provide insight into when to sell. Due to this allure, Elliott's wave theory continues to be widely used among stock investors. However, it has its limitations, as it does not explain the underlying reasons for the occurrence of three impulse waves and two corrective waves.

I have shared my understanding of the structure of Elliott Waves with students. The formation of the five waves is influenced by information barriers among investors. In the context of stock markets, there are three types of investors: insiders from the company, institutional investors, and the general public. Those most familiar with confidential situations within a company are the insiders, followed by institutional investors. The general public primarily observes changes in stock prices. Let's consider a scenario where research at a pharmaceutical company is successful. Insiders, being the first to know about this information, begin buying shares of the pharmaceutical company. Subsequently, institutional investors, noticing signs of successful research, also start acquiring shares. Observing the stock price of the company rise, the general public enters the buying parade. This sequence gives rise to the occurrence of three impulse waves. The correction phase begins with information about stock prices when investors believe the stock prices have risen sufficiently. During the correction phase, there is no information barrier between insiders and institutional investors. As insiders and institutional investors sell their shares, the general public, surprised by the price drop, follows the second corrective wave. In this way, information barriers among investors bring about three impulse waves and two corrective waves.

Distortions in Resource Allocation

Speculation and fluctuations distort resource allocation in the market. Speculation in the consumption sector artificially raises product prices, with the housing market being a typical example. Consumers end up paying more money to purchase houses, leading to an increase in the number of people who cannot afford them. Excessive profits concentrate on consumers who purchas houses for speculation. As a result, serious distortions occur in resource allocation.

Fluctuations in prices mean significant losses for producers, as exemplified by the pig farming industry. Hardworking farmers, dedicated to raising pigs and supplying them to the market, experience losses when pig prices drop. Some farmers, having suffered significant losses due to price declines, decide to discontinue pig farming. However, shortly after, pig prices surge again. In the end, only the distributors who have stored pork in warehouses benefit, while the farmers directly involved in pig raising incur losses in various ways. As a consequence of these distortions in resource allocation, the livestock industries of farmers further decline.

In the presence of speculation and fluctuations, the price adjustment mechanism distorts resource allocation. In a normal market, resources concentrate on diligent suppliers. However, in a distorted market, large-scale distributors, rather than diligent producers, reap the benefits. Furthermore, in cases where speculative demand arises, huge resources are concentrated on speculative consumers, endangering the entire society in a bubble.

13 Resource Allocation in Administration

Queueing Mechanism

If the market operates on competition, administration embodies "distribution." The government provides resources to those in need rather than favoring those leading in competition. While there are times when the winner of a competition takes resources, there are also situations when resources should be allocated regardless of competition. There are even times when support is needed for those who have lost in competition. The market caters to the former, while administration addresses the latter.

While the market concerns individuals and businesses, administration deals with society as a whole. Resources allocated through the market are owned by individuals or companies, but there are resources that should be communal. These include roads, railways, the internet, schools, hospitals, parks, air, and natural landscapes, among others. These resources, termed "social infrastructure," should be accessible to all members of society and not privately owned. The allocation of resources to develop social infrastructure is the domain of administration, not the market. Resource allocation in administration seeks the welfare of society at large and the protection of the vulnerable.

While resource allocation in administration occurs through "distribution," it must rigorously limit the discretion of civil servants, embodying the essence of "bureaucracy." Typically, administration establishes transparent eligibility criteria for recipients, thereby eliminating the discretion of civil servants. For example, criteria such as annual income level and number of family members to support can be set.

Nevertheless, resources are always limited, and the needs of some individuals may be more pressing than others. Since it is difficult to establish precedence rules beforehand, the principle of "queueing" or waiting in line is adopted. Civil servants distribute resources to those who arrive first. Queueing is an age-old and objective principle of distribution, prevalent wherever administrative distribution takes place. For instance, in areas where market functions are paralyzed due to natural disasters, administration provides relief supplies, and people queue for these resources. Queueing has also been widespread in communist countries where markets were not as functional.

"Queueing" is often viewed negatively by scholars, particularly those critical of bureaucracy. They associate long queues in government offices with inefficiency. This critique reflects a lack of understanding of administrative essence. Critics,

DOI: 10.4324/9781003464730-16

entrenched in capitalist culture, fail to recognize that queueing is fundamental to administration. Queueing may not appear elegant or theoretically profound, but it is an essential mode of public resource allocation. Similar to economics, which developed from everyday market transactions, a robust theory of public administration should acknowledge and build upon the simple act of queueing.

"Queueing" possesses the power to transform abstract concepts into tangible reality. The taste of restaurant food is subjective, with some trusting evaluations from renowned food critics and others relying on reviews from popular YouTubers. In such instances, there is a fair criterion: the number of people waiting in-line in front of the restaurant. The concept of lines can be applied to notions of beauty and popularity.

The model for government resource allocation is "planning by central government." In this model, the central government collects information related to the current state of society to assess where resources are lacking and makes decisions on resource allocation. A huge number of government officials responsible for different sectors of society provide information about their respective situations to the central planning department. In this process, officials in charge of each sector report how much resources they need. How does the central planning department prioritize resource requests coming from different sectors? The key criterion used in prioritizing is the "line length." How long and how urgently are officials making resource requests waiting in line? This is the heuristics employed by bureaucrats in the central planning department.

During my younger years, I served as a consultant in the budget department of the central government. As an expert in information technology, my role was to provide advice on whether the information technology budgets of various administrative departments were justified and to what extent they could be reduced. Extensive documents, laden with detailed information, were submitted along with budget requests. These extensive documents signaled the urgency and necessity of the budget requests. Additionally, a key indicator of their priorities was the length of time administrative personnel waited in line and the enthusiasm with which they

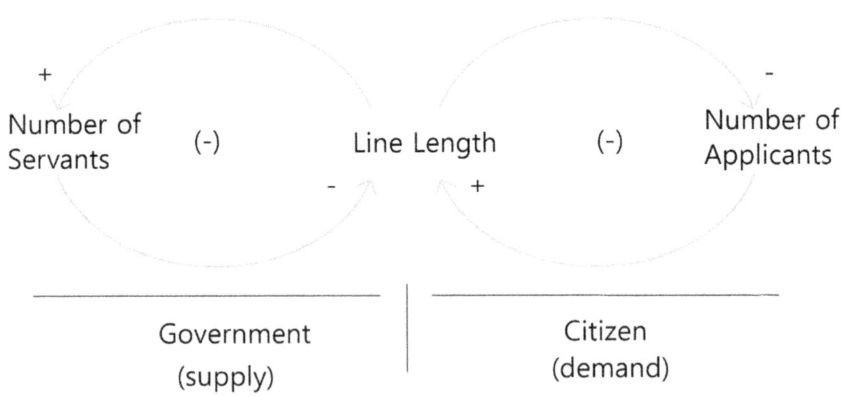

Figure 13.1 Causal loop diagram for queuing mechanism in administration.

presented their needs for resources. Ultimately, the priority of resource demands was determined by the length of the queue and the passion exhibited by those making the requests.

A causal loop diagram can explain the "queueing" mechanism. The crucial element here is the "line length." As the number of applicants increases, the length of the queue grows. However, as the queue lengthens, the number of new applicants decreases as people are deterred by the waiting time. This forms a negative feedback loop between the "line length" and the "number of applicants." This is analogous to the demand sector in the market.

Administration, which provides distribution, corresponds to the supply sector of the market. If the line length increases, administration allocates more civil servants to handle distribution, consequently shortening the queue. Like the supply sector in the market, administration also operates through a negative feedback loop.

Structurally, the "queueing" mechanism in administration is parallel to the "price" mechanism in the market. Just as "money" serves as the linchpin in the market, "queues" are pivotal in administration. Administration can be said to have a "line adjustment" mechanism analogous to the market's "price adjustment" mechanism.

Distortions in administration can be analyzed through causal loop diagrams, similar to market distortions. Distortions in the "queueing" mechanism arise from the supply side due to time delays in personnel allocation. What happens when there is a time delay in adjusting administration personnel? If the queue has been lengthy for an extended period, it naturally tends to shrink as applicants become weary and abandon their waiting efforts. By the time new civil servants are allocated, the line has already shortened, and they have little work to do. However, they cannot stay idle wasting their time. In order to justify their employment, unnecessary tasks are created.

This phenomenon of work expansion in the bureaucracy was known as "Parkinson's Law." Northcote Parkinson stated as follows:

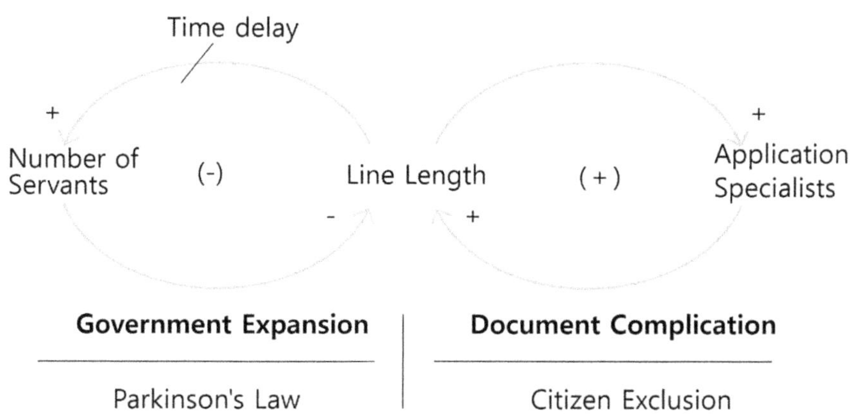

Figure 13.2 Causal loop diagram for distortions in queuing mechanism in administration.

> Work EXPANDS so as to fill the time available for its completion … The fact is that the number of officials and the quantity of work are not related to each other at all. The rise in the total of those employed is governed by Parkinson's Law and would be much the same whether the volumes of the work were to increase, diminish, or even disappear.
>
> (Parkinson 1957, pp. 2–4)

In modern society, Parkinson's Law has become widespread. Anthropologist David Graeber argues that roughly half of societal work is meaningless and serves no purpose (Graeber 2018, p. 285). He refers to this phenomenon as "bullshit jobs."

> A bullshit job is a form of employment that is so completely pointless, unnecessary, or pernicious that even the employee cannot justify its existence. Some jobs are so pointless that no one even notices if the person who has the job vanishes. This usually happens in the public sector.
>
> (Graeber 2018, p. 3)

In the resident sector of administration, what distortions are evident? As the queue lengthens for receiving administrative services, specialists in queueing emerge. Some act as proxies, standing in line on behalf of others, while others are experts adept at navigating the labyrinthine paperwork. As the line extends, actual individuals in need are increasingly supplanted by these specialists. A distortion arises when the administration starts to favor these specialists over the intended recipients – the residents.

With the influx of specialists, the complexity of paperwork escalates. The administration deliberately complicates the documentation process to lessen its own burden, knowing that specialists can manage the intricacies. Ordinary residents, who find it onerous to handle the convoluted paperwork, are marginalized. The original residents, for whom the administrative services were designed, rapidly vanish from the queue, leaving only specialists.

I have personally encountered such a distortion. During my service as the president of an academic society, we needed to register the society as a corporation and routinely update documents. The process was so complex that laypersons could not manage it. We were compelled to expend substantial funds to engage lawyers and tax accountants. Such stringent requirements were unnecessary for an academic society whose sole focus was scholarly activities. When our staff members prepared the documents and attempted to submit them, they were rebuffed. Only by employing lawyers and tax accountants to process the paperwork was the submission successful. In the end, citizens are excluded in favor of allocating resources to specialists.

14 The Academic Study of Queueing

Ever since I was young, I have believed that "queueing" lies at the very essence of administration. The concept of queueing invariably surfaces in my thoughts whenever I contemplate administration. This is particularly true when considering the distribution aspect of administration, as it naturally involves the "queueing" of recipients. However, many people harbor negative sentiments towards the concept of "queueing" in administration. As such, when I posit that the essence of administration is queueing, many administrative scholars respond with skepticism. Certainly, it is unjust for residents to endure unnecessarily lengthy queues at government offices. However, viewing queues themselves as inherently negative phenomena is an ingrained bias. It is equally mistaken for administrative scholars to have such a negative predisposition towards queues as it is for economists to hold a negative view of money.

While administrative scholars have reservations about queueing, there are scholars who regard queueing as critically important. Scholars in industrial engineering and operations research developed "queueing theory," which studies the dynamics of waiting lines. In a factory setting, multiple machines and employees are engaged in processing and assembling various parts into finished products. A central question in industrial engineering and operations research is how to configure these machines and employees to optimize factory efficiency. They need a simple and lucid concept of factory efficiency, and this is where the concept of "queue" becomes instrumental.

Queueing theory analyzes the factory through the lens of queues. It interprets the manufacturing process as parts queueing in front of machines. In other words, parts enter the factory and join queues ahead of the machines. After being processed by one machine, they proceed to the next and queue once more. The entire processes in the factory are seen as a series of queueing. Now, the efficiency of the factory can be measured by the total line length of queues. The shorter the line length of the queue, the more efficient the factory is evaluated. System researchers found that the concept of queue as efficiency works well beyond factories, including traffic signal systems, military operations, and even computer design. Queueing theory is indispensable in the realm of industrial engineering and operation research.

Queuing theory is typically applied with the assistance of computer simulation, as mathematical models of queues in the real world are often too complex to calculate. This application is known as "system simulations," sharing the same

DOI: 10.4324/9781003464730-17

perspective of queues. System simulation models machines and employees as "servers" and the parts as "entities" that queue before the servers (Kim and Kim 1993). The servers represent permanent entities, whereas the parts are temporary entities. In the simulation, the parts are portrayed as living their lives within the factory – entering the factory (generate), waiting for servers (queue), and exiting the factory (terminate).

I was surprised to learn that system simulations focus on temporary entities rather than permanent entities. Through extensive trial and error, researchers in system simulation found that modeling systems from the perspective of temporary entities simplifies the process. This marked a revolutionary shift in the perspective of understanding the world. A similar question arises in deciding whether a school should be modeled based on teachers (who are constant in the school) or on students (who enter, attend classes, and graduate). While it might seem natural to model the school based on teachers, system simulation researchers concluded that focusing on students is simpler and more convenient.

Can a similar insight be applied to public administration? Should the focus be on permanent entities like civil servants, or on temporary entities like residents who visit government offices temporarily? According to the wisdom of system simulation researchers, the focus should be on the temporary entities – the residents. However, most public administration scholars fail to view administration from the perspective of residents.

Fortunately, there have been efforts to understand policies from the perspective of residents. James Q. Wilson categorized public policies based on how they impact people (cost vs. benefit) and how people react to them (distributed vs. concentrated). From these two dimensions, he identified four domains of regulatory politics: majoritarian, client, interest group, and entrepreneurial (Wilson and Dilulio 2008, pp. 467–481). I believe that his classification provides the most elegant and powerful framework for understanding the politics of public policies. Similarly, Schneider and Ingram classified public policies in terms of the target population, according to their degree of power (strong vs. weak) and reputation (positive vs. negative). With their classification, we can understand why some policy tools are adopted and rejected (Schneider and Ingram 1993).

A Poem for Temporary entities

In my youth, I delved into the study of queuing simulation, and I found the perspective on temporary entities fascinating. In my first book on system simulation, I highlighted the beauty of temporary entities by drawing parallels with "Prelude," a poem by Yoon Dong-Joo, one of Korea's most beloved poets. In "Prelude," special attention and beauty are given to temporary entities. The opening line, "Till I die," portrays the poet as a temporary entity. The "winds among leaves," transient as they are, represent temporary entities. "I'll love all things of dying" embodies the empathy and adoration for temporary entities. The line "Now I must walk the way given to me" represents the poet's destiny to perish as a temporary entity, reminiscent of his own demise in a Japanese prison during the occupation of Korea.

"Prelude" also captures the majesty of permanent entities, such as the sky and stars. While the poet reveres and admires the permanent entities, he feels a deep connection to the temporary ones. As he gazes at the sky and is stirred by the winds among the leaves, he proclaims, "I'll love all things of dying." The poet does not aspire to become the sky or a star. The poem culminates with "On this night, winds sweep over the stars." This line seems to reflect the fate of the poet, who, like all temporary entities, is destined to pass away as a poet of resistance. The beauty of system simulation, which models the factory by focusing on temporary entities, resonates through this poem.

PRELUDE

By Yoon Dong-Joo
November 1941

Till I die
Under the heaven
I prayed no shame on my soul.
Even winds among leaves
Ached my heart.
As all sings of the stars,
I'll love all things of dying.
Now I must walk the way given to me.

On this night
Winds sweep over the stars.

15 Spectrum of Resource Allocation

In markets, the allocation of private resources occurs through the mediation of "price," while in administration, public resources are allocated using "queues" as indicators. The market operates through a "bottom-up" mechanism, whereby individuals voluntarily engage in exchanges. Through price adjustments, the freedom of choice for consumers and producers reaches a state of equilibrium, inherently bottom-up. Conversely, administration operates through a "top-down" mechanism, wherein resources are allocated in a hierarchical manner. Viewing the entire country from an elevated perspective, akin to a bird's eye view, reveals which residents need support. Resources are allocated according to predetermined rules and regulations, where allocation aligns with queues in societies.

In real-world situations, the institutions we encounter often fall somewhere between markets and administration. Take the example of a restaurant. Typically, a restaurant is categorized as part of the market. However, it does not operate solely on market mechanisms. There are instances when the number of customers exceeds the seating capacity. Can the restaurant arbitrarily increase the prices of dishes due to high demand? This proves to be almost impossible. Customers unable to find a seat wait in line at the entrance. This demonstrates how an administrative queuing mechanism operates within a restaurant, which is primarily market-based. Resource allocation in the real world exists on a spectrum between the market and administration. In this spectrum, a restaurant is positioned closer to the market.

Comparatively, a school aligns more with administration. Students wait in lines for classes, meals, and borrowing books from the library. Even in private schools, students are accustomed to queuing. At the same time, monetary payments are required to avail the school's services. Tuition fees vary depending on the school, with private schools generally charging higher fees compared to public schools. Thus, schools also exhibit a blend of market and administrative mechanisms, though they lean more towards administration.

Banks occupy a middle position on the spectrum between market and administration. Essentially, banks are part of a capitalist society and are considered part of the market. However, when customers visit a bank, they usually wait in lines. Customers accept a waiting line as a natural part of receiving services at a bank.

DOI: 10.4324/9781003464730-18

There are exceptions, such as VIP customers who do not wait in lines but are guided to VIP rooms for personalized services. Regular customers do not usually protest the preferential treatment afforded to VIP customers, acknowledging that individuals with significant deposits are entitled to certain privileges and recognizing that banks are market-based institutions.

There is a book titled *What Money Can't Buy* by Michael Sandel, discussing ethical collisions between markets and administration (Sandel 2013). Upon my first encounter with this book, I was struck by the title of the first chapter, "Jumping the Queue." This phrase signifies bypassing a queue to receive services. In the first chapter, Professor Sandel discusses how monetary influence can undermine the fundamental nature of administration, epitomized by queuing. Take, for example, the process of acquiring a designated airplane seat at the airport. Economy class passengers often wait in lengthy queues, whereas first-class passengers receive immediate service without waiting. To a certain extent, this differentiation is accepted by passengers. However, one airline proposed that by paying an additional $50, economy-class passengers could receive the expedited services akin to first-class passengers. Professor Sandel critiques this as using money to "jump the queue."

He also highlights that this phenomenon extends to the public domain. For instance, in a public hearing for issues of local development, there is a limit to the number of participants. To secure a seat, individuals must queue for tickets. Among those wishing to attend are companies pursuing local development and environmentalists who oppose it. Wealthy companies employ individuals to queue on their behalf, while the less affluent environmentalists have no choice but to stand in line themselves. Consequently, the environmentalists arrive at the hearing fatigued, whereas the company representatives are refreshed and alert. Clearly, the latter have an advantage in the ensuing debate. Professor Sandel criticizes this advantage as "jump the queue."

In everyday life, we sometimes pay with money, and at other times, we wait in queues. The domains of the market and administration are intertwined. In some instances, the combination of money and queues is perceived as natural, while in others, as Professor Sandel points out, it may feel unjust. It is crucial to understand that resource allocation permeates society, often occurring without the perception and knowledge of its participants. Resources are distributed sometimes through a bottom-up approach with money, and at other times through a top-down mode via a waiting line. This combination of resource allocation collectively shapes society.

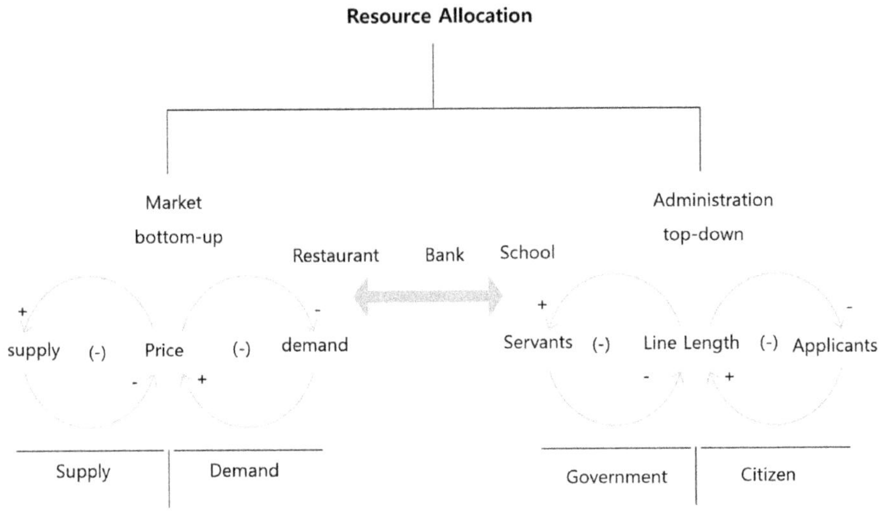

Figure 15.1 Spectrum of resource allocation between market and administration.

16 Conflict Resolution in Community

Spatial Separation

Conflicts within communities can be broadly classified into two categories: internal conflicts, which occur within a single community, and external conflicts, which arise between different communities. Internal conflicts pertain to disputes between individuals who belong to the same community. Despite sharing common values, such as within families or religious groups, communities may experience conflicts over the relative importance of their members. These internal conflicts within a community can often be suppressed or kept discreetly.

In contrast, conflicts between different communities typically stem from the incompatibility of colliding values. For example, conflicts between Christian and Buddhist communities are rooted in differing religious beliefs. Likewise, clashes between animal rights advocates and hunting organizations reflect conflicting values. In such cases, compromises are seldom reached, as yielding on values that a community holds dear is often perceived as a renunciation of those values. Buddhists, for example, cannot be expected to compromise their faith for the sake of Christianity, and vice versa.

The general approach to resolving community conflicts involves "spatial separation" as a means of facilitating "coexistence." Territorial boundaries between conflicting communities create private spaces where conflicts can be circumvented. For instance, Christian values are cultivated within the confines of churches, whereas Buddhist values are fostered within temples. Even internal conflicts within a community are often addressed through separation as a form of coexistence. In the context of family conflicts, tensions may be alleviated by family members occupying separate rooms.

There are instances where individuals, who typically coexist through spatial separation, may unite when confronted with external threats, such as a wildfire that necessitates collaborative efforts from Christians and Buddhists alike. In such scenarios, individuals may perceive themselves as part of a larger community, leading to a sense of unity and a diminishing of prior conflicts.

However, spatial separation can also have the adverse effect of aggravating conflicts between communities. As communities become more isolated from one another, the absence of interaction breeds misunderstandings, prejudices, and stereotypes due to a lack of mutual understanding. This isolation can culminate in animosity between groups, and in extreme cases, result in "genocide." Instances of

DOI: 10.4324/9781003464730-19

Table 16.1 Conflict resolution by spatial separation in communities

Coexistence by spatial separation
More prejudice more conflicts

communal violence and retaliatory massacres based on religious or ethnic differences have been observed globally.

What precipitates such appalling atrocities? Media narratives often attribute these acts to the inherent malevolence of individuals orchestrating the massacres. For example, criticism is leveled against soldiers involved in civilian killings. However, Hannah Arendt, who documented the trial of Adolf Eichmann, one of the culprits of the Holocaust, posited that such massacres must be analyzed through the lens of societal structures. Arendt found that Eichmann was not inherently evil, but merely a shallow and clueless man. She suggested that the lack of empathy and thoughtfulness of individuals, the banality of evil, constitutes the social evil leading to the Holocaust (Arendt 1963). The root cause that escalates this ordinary evil into the monumental tragedy of mass killings lies within the societal structure.

Arendt identified the bureaucratic system of the Nazi regime as a structural catalyst for the unethical massacres. I contend that "spatial separation" is another critical contributing factor. Though spatial separation may appear to offer a temporary resolution to conflicts, it can, over time, deepen the fissures that underlie these conflicts. The cruelty towards Jews can be attributed to spatial separation. Initially, Jews were separated and herded into ghettos, with the goal of expelling them from German territories. The societal structure of spatial separation fosters an individual-level "thoughtlessness," which, in turn, can lead to the catastrophic outcomes of mass violence and genocide.

Inequality among Communities

Groups are diverse. Their members differ in religion, political beliefs, and even skin color. Because of these differences, groups gather and spatially separate into distinct entities. However, this spatial separation is not limited to horizontal separation. It often extends into vertical separation. Vertical spatial separation is a form of segregation accompanied by inequality. Some groups occupy high positions while others are relegated to lower spaces. Wealthy groups, possessing abundance, situate themselves in elevated positions, while impoverished groups find themselves in lower positions. Knowledgeable and educated groups ascend to higher societal spaces, whereas uneducated and ignorant groups find themselves in lower spaces.

In the context of war, the victorious tribe may enslave the defeated tribe. The former becomes the noble class, while the latter is relegated to the status of a slave. Moreover, these class statuses are inherited by their descendants, perpetuating the noble class and passing down the slave class through generations. In this manner, societal inequality becomes institutionalized.

Jean Jacques Rousseau distinguished human inequality into two types: natural inequality and social inequality.

> I conceive that there are two kinds of inequality among the human species; one, which I call natural or physical because it is established by nature, and consists of a difference in age, health, bodily strength, and the qualities of the mind or of the soul; and another, which may be called moral or political inequality because it depends on a kind of convention, and is established, or at least authorized by the consent of men.
>
> (Rousseau 1754, p. 11)

Rousseau argued that the latter, social inequality, emanated from disparities in property through the institution of private property. Through the private property system, a group that accumulated wealth became the aristocratic class.

Examining the history of humanity, victorious nations in wars often plundered the property of defeated nations, enslaving their children and women. This history of inequality has perpetuated racial disparities between savages and civilized people, with discrimination between them considered natural. However, Rousseau attributes such differences to the aggravating cycle of inequality.

> The savage and the civilized man differ so much in the bottom of their hearts and in their inclinations, that what constitutes the supreme happiness of one would reduce the other to despair ... this is not by any means the original state of man, but that it is merely the spirit of society, and the inequality which society produces, that thus transform and alter all our natural inclinations.
>
> (Rousseau 1754, pp. 46–47)

Inequality among social classes is manifested through vertical spatial separation. Those dwelling in lower places gaze up at those in higher positions, while those in elevated positions look down upon those beneath with contempt. Over a long period of time, such inequalities within groups became accepted as natural. Individuals belonging to the common class show respectful attitudes toward those in the aristocratic class. Even if lacking notable talents or virtues, simply being part of the high class makes individuals deserving of some respect. It is taken for granted that the offspring of a king would become the next ruler. Even in the contemporary era of capitalism, corporate leaders pass down their wealth to their children.

Such inheritance practices are often observed in the political area as well. Politicians who have secured influence in a local region pass on their political leadership to their children, convincing residents that their offspring are the most faithful and capable heirs. Surprisingly, this political inheritance is readily accepted by residents. Modern societies like North Korea and the Philippines serve as typical examples. In North Korea, the leadership has successfully continued through three generations. Similarly, in the Philippines, the Marcos family has held power over two generations.

Vertical spatial separation leads to collective discrimination and oppression. Throughout human history, ruling classes have oppressed and exploited the subordinate classes. Individuals belonging to groups in lower social strata often find it challenging to ascend to higher positions, regardless of their exceptional talents. Invisible discrimination abounds in society. Many women face barriers to climbing the corporate ladder simply because of their gender. Likewise, individuals not graduated from prestigious universities may encounter obstacles in career advancement. Discrimination based on skin color can hinder job opportunities, and being from a specific region might result in exclusion.

One famous example of persistent group stratification up to the modern era is the caste system in India. The Indian caste system is highly complex, being determined by various factors such as race, religion, and family occupation. It generally consists of four classes: Brahmans, Kshatriyas, Vaishyas, and Shudras, with Dalits (untouchables) being a group outside these categories. Brahmans play roles as religious priests or teachers, Kshatriyas perform the roles of warriors and rulers, and Vaishyas take on the responsibilities of farmers and traders. These three classes dominate from the position of conquerors, while Shudras constitute a group providing labor for the dominant classes as non-conquerors. Dalits do not belong to any of these four classes. Over 90 million people classified as Dalits traditionally lived in isolation from residents of other classes. They couldn't attend the same schools and were even prohibited from touching the cups used by higher classes. They faced discrimination in education, religion, and economy, leading to a life of poverty. Many individuals belonging to Dalits convert to Buddhism or Christianity to escape this discrimination, but it remains difficult for them to overcome the stigma associated with their family names, language, and skin color.

For a long period, apartheid in South Africa imposed oppression on the black population. Apartheid was a set of laws that enforced the separation and discrimination of whites and blacks. It regulated black people entering cities where whites lived and established residential areas for black people on the outskirts of cities. Apartheid was so thorough in its racial segregation that in 1949, laws were enacted to prohibit marriages between whites and blacks. Opposition to apartheid persisted until the early 1990s, during which over 20,000 people lost their lives. Nelson Mandela, who led the anti-apartheid struggle, spent 27 years in prison. Eventually, due to the struggle of the South African people and international criticism, apartheid was abolished in 1991, and Mandela was elected president in 1994.

The "Indian reservation" in the United States is another example of vertical spatial separation in contemporary civilized society. The 18th-century expansion of Europeans into North America inevitably led to conflicts with Native Americans. Those Native Americans defeated in these conflicts were often compelled to reside on allocated but largely barren lands, known as "Indian reservations." According to Wikipedia, there are 326 Indian Reservations covering 2.3% of the US territory, with approximately one million Native Americans residing there. The defeated Native Americans have been forced to reside in this separated space for more than 200 years. In 1971, the American rock band "The Raiders" released a song titled

"Indian Reservation," conveying their pain to a global audience. The song became widely known as "the lament of the Cherokee Reservation Indian."

Trap of Inequality

Vertical spatial separation, discrimination, and oppression that occur at the community level are challenging to address at the individual level. There is often a hopeful message that if individuals work hard on a personal level, they can overcome such discrimination. The message conveys that with a humble attitude and diligent effort, individuals, regardless of being women, immigrants, or having lower education, can climb to high social positions. However, this hopeful message typically applies to only exceptionally lucky individuals. For most people, hope turns into despair, and they believe they failed because of their insufficient abilities and efforts. The existence of individuals who have overcome group disadvantages makes them attribute their failure to personal shortcomings. The societal-level message of hope ends up perpetuating despair and self-blame for the majority. This is a trap of social inequality.

In 1971, Pastor Kim Jin-Hong, who initiated his ministry in the slums, documented in his diary the desperate nature of life in poverty.

> After falling into the slum, why can they not escape from it? Their mindset may be partly responsible. I have heard that they have a mindset that leads them to a life of poverty, but that cannot be. Even I find myself incapable of thinking about the future, now that I am hungry. Incompetence and lethargy are the result of poverty, not the cause.
>
> (Kim Jin-Hong 2002, p. 187)

Pastor Kim's confession reflects his exhaustion due to hunger and the resulting inability while living in the slum. Determined to overcome extreme poverty, he resolved to work together with impoverished neighbors. Subsequently, he became one of the most authentic and spiritually impactful testimonies in the Korean society.

In the 20th century, many scholars began advocating for a critical approach to the unequal social structure. Theodor Adorno, Max Horkheimer, and Jürgen Habermas are exemplary scholars of Critical Theory. Critical Theory aims to clarify that numerous discriminations and oppressions in society are not individual faults but result from the societal spatial structure that vertically separates communities of people. Taking a step further, it emphasizes the need to dismantle the societal vertical separation to liberate individuals trapped in such unequal oppression. The essence of Critical Theory lies in the idea that this change can be initiated not by individual elites but by the awareness and collective movements of individuals in lower strata. Pastor Kim embodied Critical Theory not only in words but also through living with and among the poor.

In 1861, the American Civil War aimed to abolish the societal institution that enslaved black people and sought to emancipate them. This war led to the liberation of black people from the status of slavery. However, societal discrimination against black individuals did not disappear. In 1944, Gunnar Myrdal published a book exposing the reality of racial discrimination in the United States. His book was titled *An American Dilemma: The Negro Problem and Modern Democracy*. As the title suggests, the United States society is caught in a dilemma between the tragic state of African Americans being denied their civil rights and the lofty belief that all human beings are born equal. Myrdal argues that the "Negro problem" in American society should be acknowledged as a "white man's problem."

Myrdal argues that black individuals are trapped in a vicious cycle. White discrimination forces black people into a lower level of education and health, and the resulting lower education and health status justifies white prejudice and discrimination.

> The Negro is judged to be fundamentally incorrigible, and he is, therefore, kept in a slum existence which, in its turn, leaves the imprint upon his body and soul, making it natural for the white man to believe in this inferiority. This is a vicious circle; it is, indeed, one of the chief examples of cumulative causation.
>
> (Myrdal 1944, p. 101)

Discrimination creates inferiority, and inferiority justifies discrimination. Myrdal's vicious circle is reminiscent of the cycle observed by Rousseau in the inequality between savages and civilized people.

Robert Merton interprets the vicious cycle emphasized by Myrdal as a self-fulfilling prophecy. Prejudice against black individuals becomes a reality through social interactions, and the dire reality of black people reinforces white prejudice. The way to break free from this vicious cycle is to reduce white prejudice or improve the situation of black individuals beyond critical points. Myrdal referred to this as the "principle of cumulation." He was aware of the mechanism by which a vicious cycle turns into a virtuous one. As well-known to modern system dynamics scholars, when the value of a variable exceeds a critical mass, the vicious cycle transforms into a virtuous one (Schelling 1978, pp. 91–102).

In the 1960s, the social movement to overcome discrimination against black individuals gained momentum. The speech "I Have a Dream" by Reverend Martin Luther King continues to inspire many people to this day. For a while, I listened to Reverend King's speeches almost to the point of memorization. The most impressive speech for me was his final one, "I've Been to the Mountaintop." Moses, who led the Israelites for 40 years in the desert, could not enter the promised land but went up to a mountain, looked at the promised land, and died. Reverend King's speech foreshadowed his own impending death, similar to Moses. He looked upon the land, promised for all black people, from the mountaintop as Moses did. Expressing his happiness, he concluded his last speech. The next day, he was fatally shot by a white assailant. His final speech poignantly illustrates that an individual's life is not confined to the personal realm but is connected to a higher dimension of societal life.

Spatial Integration

At first, spatial separation is accepted as a natural occurrence. The wealthy gather and live together, while the poor reside among themselves. White individuals tend to live in communities with other whites, and black individuals gather in neighborhoods predominantly occupied by other blacks. Refugees who sought asylum in Europe often settle on the outskirts of cities. Natural spatial separation gradually solidifies into closed-off spaces. Isolated spaces intensify misunderstandings and biases towards each other. Ironically, spaces initially separated naturally tend to escalate conflicts.

Initially, spaces separated horizontally out of necessity may evolve into vertical separation over time. The separation between the rich and the poor began voluntarily for economic convenience. However, in affluent neighborhoods, police are stationed, while impoverished neighborhoods become havens for drug dealers. Simply residing in a low-income neighborhood raises suspicion of drug addiction, leading to police checks. What initially started as economic separation based on necessity transformed into moral and social status-based segregation. Consequently, societal discrimination against those positioned in the lower realms of vertical spatial separation is deemed acceptable as time goes by.

Spatial separation as a natural method of conflict resolution tends to lean more towards conflict avoidance. It minimizes the chances of conflict by reducing the frequency of face-to-face encounters. Instead of facilitating conflict resolution, spatial separation tends to exacerbate bias and disliking. However, spatial separation for conflict resolution is a cost-effective method that does not demand extensive resources. Living in spatially separated areas, especially for the poor, can offer the benefit of reducing living expenses. For the wealthy, it contributes to the appreciation of property values in affluent neighborhoods. From an economic perspective, spatial separation appears attractive. However, in the long run, it amplifies conflicts, leading to significant societal costs.

As society enters these stages, critical reflections on spatial separation emerge. Social movements against spatial separation come into play. The segregation of restaurants between black and white has been abolished. The educational approach of separating children with disabilities from those without is gradually shifting towards inclusive education. In France, refugee villages formed on the outskirts of Paris led to the deterioration of the local economy and security. Spatial separation only exacerbated the situation. Paris, recognizing the desirability of spatial integration over separation, has implemented policies to purchase housing in central areas and offer it to refugees at affordable rents, aiming for a more mixed spatial arrangement.

However, spatial integration cannot solve all the problems. Policies advocating spatial integration face criticism from citizens. The first criticism is that the issue is not significant enough to warrant a substantial investment of taxes. The second criticism is the concern that spatial integration might actually increase social conflicts more than separation. The third criticism is the resistance from citizens residing in the areas targeted for spatial integration, fearing insecurity, and decline in housing prices. The fourth criticism is the concern that the cohesion of minority communities is being disrupted. As the Māori people of New Zealand migrate to urban areas, many critics focused on concerns that Māori communities and cultures are disappearing. Fifth, spatial integration tends to produce more failures than successes for minorities. The harsh reality is that minorities with invisible discrimination and handicaps find it difficult to survive in the intense competition in large cities. Thus, spatial integration, emerging to address the problem of spatial separation, presents another dilemma – not just a dilemma for majorities but a dilemma for minorities as well.

17 Conflict Resolution in Politics

Temporal Separation

Achieving spatial separation in politics is inherently difficult. Unlike other areas of society, politics operates predominantly in the public domain, where the notion of private space is virtually nonexistent. In the political arena, spaces are intended to be open and accessible to all. Consequently, spatial separation is not a viable means of conflict resolution within politics. Instead, politics employs temporal separation as a method for managing conflicts.

In the public domain, conflicts over values are often attenuated through the electoral process. In the world of elections, the principle of "winner takes all" applies. A politician elected as president acquires the authority to appoint the entire cabinet. However, the winner is constrained by time. In South Korea, the president is elected for a single five-year term, while members of the National Assembly serve four-year terms. As these terms near their conclusion, the underlying conflicts in values re-emerge. Fresh elections are held, and the contest of values resumes. Values that had previously been victorious may be reaffirmed, or alternatively, values that had been defeated may gain ascendancy. This cyclical nature of elections, with the potential for a change in prevailing values, serves as a mechanism for resolving intense conflicts in the political area. Despite any deep-seated political disagreements, there is an understanding that opportunities for competition and change recur every four to five years.

In politics, the coexistence of conflicting values is facilitated through temporal separation. Values that have been defeated in the current election cannot be dismissed outright, as they may emerge victorious in subsequent elections. Conversely, there is no imperative to unconditionally adhere to the values that have prevailed in the current election, as they can be supplanted in the next cycle. The prospect of temporal shifts in dominance fosters an environment in which individuals can endure present setbacks with an eye toward future opportunities.

The coexistence through temporal separation echoes a concept prevalent in Eastern philosophy. Eastern thought often expounds on the cyclical nature of dominance, where the strong become weak, and the weak become strong. Confucius, for instance, spoke of this alternating shift in dominance through the concept of "One yin and one yang (一陰一陽), this is the truth (道)." This represents the cyclical transition wherein yin dominates at one point in time, and yang takes precedence at another. In politics, there's a saying that, just as flowers cannot maintain their vivid color for ten days, power cannot be sustained for ten years.

DOI: 10.4324/9781003464730-20

Table 17.1 Conflict resolution by temporal separation in politics

Coexistence by temporal separation
Value alignment less conflict

This notion serves as a mechanism for resolving conflicts over values within the political area.

Through temporal separation, conflicting values gradually intermingle and find shared commonalities. For example, when a liberal party assumes power, it might implement policies with an emphasis on equality. When a conservative party wins the subsequent election, it does not abruptly dismantle all the equality-focused policies instituted by the previous political power. This is because a sudden rollback of such policies could provoke a substantial backlash.

Psychologists and Nobel laureates in economics, Amos Tversky and Daniel Kahneman, discovered that people tend to be more sensitive to losses than gains (Tversky and Kahneman 1981). The distress experienced from losing ten dollars is greater than the elation derived from gaining the same amount. Consequently, if a liberal party raises the minimum wage by one dollar, and then a conservative party comes into power and reduces it by one dollar, the conservative party could face vehement opposition. As a result, the winning party often retains a significant portion of the values and policies introduced by the preceding party. Through this process, different values among political parties become increasingly integrated, and conflicts over values gradually abate. Temporal alternation of political powers serves to mitigate value conflicts.

Prolonged Power

Temporal separation in politics might be ineffective in the face of "prolonged power," where ruling powers remain unchanged for several terms. Prolonged power manifests in various ways, from "strong dictators" who reject political competition, to "popular leaders" who enjoy widespread support from the people. The former is often classified as illegal prolonged power, while the latter is deemed legal. However, all forms of prolonged power undermine temporal separation and ultimately lead to undesirable outcomes in politics.

In his essay "*On Liberty*," John Stuart Mill seriously discusses the pitfalls of the democratic electoral system (Mill 1859). The trap he highlights is "the tyranny of the majority," which becomes a social evil, more formidable than other forms of political oppression. The tyranny of the majority manifests itself in real politics as prolonged power, which imposes a hopeless consciousness of inferiority on others. Mill emphatically stated as follows:

> There needs protection against the tyranny of the prevailing opinion and feeling; against the tendency of society to impose, by other means than civil penalties, its own ideas and practices as rules of conduct on those who dissent from them.
>
> (Mill 1859, p. 9)

One of the longest-ruling political leaders in modern states is Fidel Castro, known as both a founding father and revolutionary leader of Cuba, who held power for 52 years. Despite being closely located to the world's superpower, the United States, he has led the forefront of anti-American sentiments. Since the establishment of North Korea in 1948, Kim Il-sung ruled for over 45 years until his death, after which his son and grandson continued the prolonged rule. Surprisingly, their prolonged rule has surpassed 76 years. Japan's Liberal Democratic Party (自由民主党), except for a brief interruption of five years, has maintained its majority position since 1955.

Prolonged power has a positive meaning of political stability. However, more precisely, it denotes the stability of the ruling power. While long-term rule signifies the success of the ruling power, it also points to the failure of the political system. Prolonged power, in itself, indicates the paralysis of political functionality. If the ruling power remains unchanged, the temporal separation of political values comes to a halt. All values, except those endorsed by the ruling power, lose the opportunity for political representation. Many citizens cannot project their values into politics and become second-class citizens. This is the direct harm of prolonged power.

Indirect harms of prolonged power are more serious. Prolonged power leads to the corruption of the ruling class. In the 19th century, British historian John Dalberg-Acton wrote, "Power corrupts. Absolute power corrupts absolutely." The power that succeeds in prolonged rule is absolute power. Most politicians and bureaucrats try to prove their loyalty to absolute power. They often go unpunished even if they engage in bribery. Over time, corruption spreads throughout the entire ruling class.

The next stage of prolonged power is the corruption of the entire society. Corruption initiated within the ruling class accelerates corruption in the economic domain. For businessmen, survival through bribery becomes a faster and safer method than survival through competition. This leads to the formation of collusion between businesses and politics, eroding competition in the economic sector. Ironically, entrepreneurs who assert their competitiveness based on high performance are considered traitors seeking independence from political leaders. Cynicism that mocks those who work hard spreads throughout society. The entire society falls into a swamp of incompetence.

A direct method to prevent prolonged power is through a constitution limiting the political leader's term. The President of South Korea serves a single five-year term, preventing prolonged power. In the United States, the president can only serve two terms. Regardless of the high support from the citizens, challenging a third term is not permissible. There is even a warning against the risk of the re-election of the president. While Tocqueville praised democracy in America, he cautioned against the danger of the president's re-election.

> Intrigue and corruption are the natural defects of elective government, but when the head of the State can be re-elected, these evils rise to a great height and compromise the very existence of the country.
>
> (Tocqueville 1840, p. 156)

Unlike the presidential system, parliamentary cabinet systems rarely concern themselves with prolonged power and thus lack specific rules to prevent it. However, parliamentary cabinet systems are not immune to prolonged power. For example, Germany's Chancellor Angela Merkel served four terms over 16 years. While a parliamentary system inherently operates with decentralized powers, any form of prolonged power restricts the resolution of political conflicts. Although those in power might celebrate prolonged rule as a political success, it often signifies hopelessness for others.

18 Spectrum of Conflict Resolution

Conflict resolution methods can be classified as spatial separation and temporal separation. These two approaches are rather extreme ideal types. In reality, many situations do not neatly fit into the extremes and instead involve a combination of spatial and temporal separation to resolve conflicts.

Take, for example, the planning of group trips, where conflicts might arise due to differing preferences regarding the destination, such as domestic trips vs. international travel. One way to resolve this conflict is through spatial separation: dividing into two groups based on their preferences. However, in groups where there is a strong emphasis on concerted action among members, employing spatial separation may not be viable. In such instances, a temporal separation approach can be adopted. This might entail casting votes between domestic trips and international travel, with the understanding that the next trip will be to the destination not chosen this time.

In response to societal changes, conflict resolution methods can also undergo transformations. The escalating conflict between smokers and nonsmokers has changed due to the rise of the anti-smoking culture. In the past, conflicts were often addressed through spatial separation by designating areas for smokers and nonsmokers. However, this approach encountered issues as smoke could still permeate nonsmoking areas, compelling nonsmokers to close windows to avoid exposure. With the rising prominence of the anti-smoking culture, the voices of nonsmokers have gained support. This has led to introducing voting processes to designate specific areas as smoke-free zones. The conflict resolution approach for smoking has shifted from spatial separation to temporal separation, where nonsmokers hold the majority.

There are many instances when methods of conflict resolution shift from political voting to spatial separation. This is particularly evident in the aspirations for independence among minority communities. These communities often find it difficult to protect their rights through political voting due to their minority status, as they frequently end up on the losing side. Voting does not afford them future opportunities and only perpetuates their sense of defeat and exclusion. Consequently, minorities often seek separation and independence from the dominant majority communities. Local autonomy systems, which afford minorities the opportunity to succeed in local elections, exemplify instances where spatial separation is applied to politics. In such systems, minorities unable to win the election for

DOI: 10.4324/9781003464730-21

Table 18.1 Spectrum of conflict resolution between community and politics

Community			*Politics*
Spatial separation	Group touring	Neighbor smoking	*Temporal separation*
More prejudice/more conflicts	←------------------------------→		Value alignment less conflict
Private value	Rotation and Toleration		Public value

national president can wield influence in local politics, thereby safeguarding their local autonomy.

Rotation and Toleration

In reality, various methods are used to mitigate the drawbacks of spatial and temporal separation. Representative methods include rotation and toleration. In the corporate world, job rotation alleviates conflicts arising from spatial separation, while in the political realm, tolerance is a virtue to lessen the disaster of temporal separation.

One method of managing employees in large organizations is "job rotation." This approach simultaneously addresses temporal and spatial separation to resolve conflicts. In large organizations, the development of work specialization and compartmentalization often leads to conflicts between different departments. For instance, production and marketing departments have distinct job skills, cultures, and grievances. They may refuse to understand each other's goals and problems, leading to conflicts. To address these issues, job rotations are introduced, exchanging the chief officer of the production department with that of the marketing department. This involves both the temporal separation, as the leader of each department changes, and the spatial separation, as most employees in each department remain together.

When working in the same department for an extended period, the relationship between leaders and employees often evolves into personal and human connections. If their personal relationship is intimate, covering up each other's mistakes can undermine the organization's efficiency. On the other hand, if their personal relationship is discordant, communication and collaboration for work may be hindered, affecting the organization's effectiveness. To mitigate these risks, job rotation is introduced, moving leaders from one department to another after a certain period. Job rotation implements temporal separation by ensuring that leaders change relatively frequently. Employees with uncomfortable relationships with their leaders can endure, knowing that a new leader will come in shortly, bringing hope for a change.

Furthermore, job rotation alleviates communication barriers caused by spatial separation between departments. When the sales of a product decline, leaders of the production and marketing departments often blame each other. The production department accuses the marketing department of passive marketing, while the marketing department blames the production department for quality problems. Spatially separated, these departments fail to understand each other's situations, leading to escalating conflicts. To overcome this situation, job rotation is employed. By experiencing new tasks and cultures in a different department, the leader gains a comprehensive understanding of the separated spaces. Through job rotation, leaders can facilitate smoother communication and alleviate conflicts between departments.

However, the job rotation approach cannot be implemented in the world of politics. One prominent form of spatial separation in the political realm is regional division. Conflicts may arise between the eastern and western regions of a country or between the northern and southern regions. In such divided spaces, a politician representing one area cannot become a representative for another region. The same holds true in terms of ideological separation. A progressive politician cannot effectively represent conservative ideology.

In the realm of politics, tolerance proves to be effective. The essence of tolerance lies in accepting the differences between oneself and others. Typically, tolerance is considered a virtuous attitude exhibited by political winners toward the losers. Tolerance presupposes temporal separation and requires that winners refrain from retaliating against the losers.

In the 17th century, Europe witnessed severe persecution of Protestants by Catholics, and the struggles between Catholics and Protestants expanded into the realm of politics. In the midst of this turmoil, in 1689, John Locke wrote "*A Letter Concerning Toleration*." Locke argued that state intervention in religion is meaningless and emphasized that individuals should not be oppressed based on their different religions or denominations. Toleration involves recognizing that citizens in a society can have different religions and political beliefs (Locke 1689b). Tolerance acts as a virtue in politics, mitigating the harms of temporal separation.

While rotation is used to mitigate the drawbacks of spatial separation, toleration is emphasized to overcome the limitations of temporal separation. However, these methods cannot resolve all conflicts. Conflict still persists. It's important to recognize that diverse resolution methods cannot guarantee the permanent elimination of conflicts. Even conflicts that appear to be resolved can resurface or erupt unexpectedly. Conflict resolution is an ongoing process that necessitates continuous attention, care, and empathy to sustain peace.

Part IV

Dynamics of Failure

If the mechanisms discussed in Part III were to function efficiently, society as a whole would operate smoothly. However, mechanisms created by humans are never perfect. As times flow and environments change, mechanisms that once functioned effectively may begin to falter. It is inherent in human-created social systems to experience failures – this should not come as a surprise but rather as an expectation. Moreover, there is no reason for despair or discouragement. Recognizing failure paves the way for learning. Through learning from failure, evolutionary rationality is secured.

However, a society that refuses to acknowledge failure and rejects change cannot achieve evolutionary learning. When failures persist without changing through learning, they can eventually lead to revolution. A revolution promising all good things often means hell to many people. This part examines how the four realms of society have experienced failures and learned from them.

DOI: 10.4324/9781003464730-22

19 Market Failure

Public Goods

The market has long been regarded as the most efficient among human-made institutions. Adam Smith, referring to the market as the "invisible hand," emphasized its superiority over the visible hand of administration. However, it has been discovered by later scholars that there are instances when the market fails to function properly. One of the most notable examples is regarding goods known as "public goods." These goods are essential for society to function, yet the market cannot adequately supply them. This has been recognized as fundamental "market failure."

Public goods are goods or services that can be jointly consumed by everyone. Examples include parks, roads, streetlights, fire departments, police services, and the military. Such public goods are difficult to supply through market mechanisms because it is almost impossible for businesses to invest and generate profits from them. Economists have found the reason for this in the non-excludability and the non-rivalry of public goods.

In contrast, "private goods" exhibit excludability and rivalry. Consider a private car – since I possess the car key, others cannot access it, demonstrating excludability. However, if someone steals the key and drives my car, I cannot use it, illustrating rivalry. Excludability relates to the prevention of others' access, and rivalry pertains to the competition for consumption. Similarly, a home is a private good. By closing the front door, I can prevent others from entering. But if someone trespasses and occupies my home, I cannot use it. Thus, it satisfies both excludability and rivalry. Private goods with excludability and rivalry can be supplied and exchanged in the market.

On the other hand, public goods exhibit non-excludability and non-rivalry. Consider a grand park with a forest and a river. Non-excludability means it is impossible to exclude people from accessing the good. For instance, one cannot install fences around the park to prevent nonpaying individuals from entering. Non-rivalry means that one person's consumption does not limit others' use. Even if one person rests in the park, others can freely use it. Goods with non-rivalry don't require consumer fees because, even with many people using them, the goods do not deplete or become limited. Moreover, fees cannot be imposed on goods with non-excludability since it is impossible to block access for non-paying consumers.

Consequently, the market cannot provide public goods, representing a market failure. So, how can public goods be provided? Quite literally, they can be provided through the intervention of the public agencies. The government provides

DOI: 10.4324/9781003464730-23

Figure 19.1 Market failure of public goods.

public goods by constructing parks, building roads, and installing streetlights. The government maintains the military to defend citizens from external threats and organizes the police to protect citizens from internal crimes. Ultimately, public administration might enter into areas where the market fails. As administration intervenes more, the public area expands.

Grand Infrastructures

In a national society, one of the most fundamental public goods is "infrastructure," also known as "social overhead capital (SOC)." The term "social" implies that it is accessible to everyone, and "overhead" means that it is not directly associated with any specific production but is utilized for overall societal development. Infrastructure with these characteristics includes various public facilities such as ports, roads, railways, electricity, and gas that serve as the foundation for social activity. Due to the substantial costs involved in constructing such infrastructure, it is typically funded and built by the government's budget. Historically famous infrastructures include China's Grand Canal, Great Wall, and Silk Roads. To comprehend their overall structures, satellite photos would be necessary.

The Grand Canal of China, primarily constructed during the 7th century Sui Dynasty, is a canal stretching 1,776 km, connecting the southern city of Hangzhou to the northern city of Beijing. It is considered the world's longest canal and is of such magnitude that it could be described as an artificial river. The Sui Dynasty undertook the construction of this colossal canal to supply the bountiful harvests from the fertile lands of southern China to the armies in the north. However, the Sui Dynasty, having expended excessive resources in building the canal, eventually collapsed.

Over the subsequent 1,000 years, the Grand Canal remained the principal conduit linking northern and southern China. It played a crucial role in transporting grain to Beijing and facilitated cultural exchanges and political integration between the two regions. Although the dynasty that constructed the Grand Canal met its demise, the canal itself became a symbol of the unification between the southern and northern regions of China.

Just as roads and canals connecting regions within a country are crucial, infrastructure blocking invasion routes from outside the nation is also essential. In the northern region of China, the world's longest wall, known as the Great Wall of China, was constructed. Stretching over 5,000 km, it is recognized as one of the longest human-made structures. Built by numerous Chinese dynasties over a span of more than 2,000 years from the 7th century BC, the Great Wall served the purpose of preventing invasions from nomadic tribes in the northern regions. While it is often exaggeratedly claimed to be visible from the Moon, it remains a mountain-like wall constructed to artificially obstruct invasion and plunder from outside.

The most remarkable road of the ancient period is the Silk Road. Originating in China and extending to India, Syria, and even Rome, the Silk Road was a network of trade routes. It served as a trade route from the 2nd century BC to around the 16th century, covering a distance of nearly 9,000 km. The Silk Road, named after the silk textiles produced in China, encompassed various commodities such as tea, perfumes, and horses. Moreover, the exchange along the Silk Road facilitated the transmission of paper and gunpowder, influencing the development of ancient civilizations. The Silk Road was not just a conduit for the exchange of goods; it also facilitated the interchange of ideas and religions. Shortly after the opening of the Silk Road, Buddhism, originating in India, spread to China through this route. Subsequently, Buddhism became one of China's major religions and extended its influence to Korea and Japan. Thus, while the Grand Canal served as an infrastructure connecting the north and south of China, the Great Wall thwarted invasions from northern tribes, and the Silk Road became a passage for the exchange of culture between China and Europe. A notable point here is that the Grand Canal and the Great Wall were constructed by the public realm, whereas the Silk Road was forged by merchants privately.

In modern society, there exists infrastructure that connects the entire globe. It is the road that reaches from one end of the Earth to the other within a second – the information highway known as the internet. The internet is also a global public good constructed by governments, requiring massive investments. During the Cold War era in the 1960s, the US Department of Defense researched a communication network that could survive extreme situations like nuclear warfare. They implemented Advanced Research Projects Agency Network (ARPANET), adopting a novel "packet switching" approach instead of the traditional "circuit switching." Circuit switching involves sending information over fixed connections between the sender and receiver. In contrast, packet switching attaches the recipient's address to the information, eliminating the need for permanently connected circuits. Packet switching provides flexibility, bypassing broken connections, among other advantages. In 1989, ARPANET was expanded for commercial purposes, marking the beginning of internet services. The internet rapidly expanded globally, connecting nearly every corner of the Earth, and individuals now access it through smartphones. In the 21st-century information and communication era, the most crucial infrastructure is the internet, which might be recorded as the first global public good for all of humanity.

Invisible Public Goods

There are invisible public goods essential for the survival of society, including languages, cultures, religions, and sciences accumulated by previous generations. These forms of knowledge serve as the intellectual infrastructures of a society. Systematically organizing and transmitting this knowledge through education to future generations is a public good necessary for the entire society. As a public good, it is not provided within the realm of the economy.

Modern society's education is predominantly provided by the government. The government constructs schools, selects teachers, and allocates them to schools. Schools are operated with government budgets. There are also private schools established by individuals or companies. While public schools focus on fundamental and universal education, private schools emphasize specialized knowledge or religious interests. These private schools fall within the realm of the community rather than the economic domain. Interestingly, public schools are perceived to belong to the community domain as well, rather than the administrative domain. In the process of blocking partisan influences in universal education, schools have come closer to the community, regardless of whether they are public or private.

Historically, schools originated within communities. There were small schools where local residents gathered to teach children basic literacy. Teachers in these small community schools were often retired elders. Additionally, religious communities also established schools. Before the advent of modern civilization, religious knowledge was regarded as philosophy and science. Even in contemporary society, schools are established to spread religious beliefs. Many prestigious universities in Korea have evolved from Christian institutions founded by Western Christians in the early 20th century.

The sharing of knowledge continues even in the information society. However, surprisingly, education in the information society is actively taking place in the realms of the economy and community. Learning through searching the internet, sharing knowledge and discussions on social media, and receiving intellectual assistance through artificial intelligence are predominantly carried out by private IT companies. What is even more astonishing is that these services are mostly provided for free. Education, once offered by ancient local communities, medieval religious institutions, and modern public administrations, is now being supplanted by internet companies in digital communities. Instead of the previous model of universal education provided by public schools, internet companies are increasingly offering personalized education at almost no cost. This represents a silent educational revolution, a change that 21st-century social scientists should pay attention to.

20 Market Failure

Unethical Market

Unlike market failures stemming from public goods, there are instances where the market operates efficiently but is still deemed a failure, as seen in unethical markets. For instance, sexual exchange for money is a prominent example of an unethical market. Another unethical market involves the trade of human organs. A significant market arises between individuals awaiting organ transplantation and those looking to sell their organs. Violent organizations, such as loan sharks, often become involved in this market. Perhaps the most unethical and sizable market is the "drug market." Consumers, ensnared by addiction, become enslaved to drugs, while suppliers reap substantial profits from their dependency. In the drug market, both suppliers and consumers are vulnerable to addiction.

Even if a market operates efficiently, society cannot tolerate unethical markets. Markets involving the trade of unethical goods and services are inherently harmful and unacceptable. In response, the government directly intervenes in such markets, prohibiting their formation. When suppliers and consumers engaged in the drug trade are identified, they are promptly apprehended.

In some cases, unethical markets can escalate into international conflicts. The most prominent example is the Opium Wars between China and Britain. In the mid-19th century, there were two wars between Britain and China. British merchants illegally exported opium to China, reaping enormous profits. The widespread opium addiction among the Chinese population emerged as a serious social problem. The Chinese government banned the opium trade and confiscated opium from British merchants. In order to protect British opium merchants, the British government waged war against China. After suffering defeats in these unethical wars, China was forced to sign unequal treaties with Britain.

After signing the unequal treaties, the Chinese government paid substantial reparations to Britain for the destroyed opium. Additionally, Hong Kong was under British rule from 1842 until 1997. Following the Opium Wars, China experienced a rapid decline, subjected to widespread exploitation by Western empires. The Opium Wars were known as one of the most unethical wars waged to protect unethical markets. Moreover, China's defeat in this war led to significant political upheaval throughout Asia. As a result of this painful experience, the Chinese government has maintained a strong stance against drug-related crimes to this day.

Not all unethical transactions are prohibited. For instance, narcotics should be allowed for patients suffering from extreme pain. Some countries permit euthanasia

DOI: 10.4324/9781003464730-24

Figure 20.1 Market failure of unethical markets.

involving the use of large quantities of narcotics. There are also arguments for the legalization of sex work, viewing it as a matter of personal choice. Additionally, proposals for legalizing organ trade with strict conditions have emerged. Globally, over a million people are waiting for organ transplants, and many die due to a shortage of organs. Moreover, there is a phenomenon known as "transplantation tourism," where individuals from wealthy countries travel to poorer nations for illegal organ transplants. However, most countries still prohibit the trading of human organs.

There are also markets where the degree of unethical behavior is relatively mild. Gambling falls into this category. While gambling is prohibited by law in most countries, small-stakes gambling is generally permitted. Moreover, a considerable number of governments actively promote lotteries. In such cases, lotteries are considered public gambling. Gambling is even encouraged for public entertainment. Many people participate in gambling games where they predict the outcomes of sports matches such as football and baseball. Recently, online gambling conducted over the internet has been growing in scale and emerging as a social issue.

Ethics of Land

Trading human bodies is unethical. Since the human body is valued as the essence of human beings, any direct trading or activities that harm it (such as drug trade) are deemed unethical. A similar concept is found in "land trading." Land is perceived as a unique resource due to its finite supply. It is considered too valuable to be owned by individuals alone. Landlords, who own large tracts of land, disproportionately accumulate wealth from society. This is why land trading is regarded as unethical. One of the most notable scholars advocating this view is Henry George.

Henry George, a political economist in 19th-century America, wielded significant intellectual influence over his contemporaries. In 1879, George published a book with the lengthy title *Progress and Poverty: An Inquiry into the Cause of Industrial Depressions and of Increase of Want with Increase of Wealth – The Remedy*. His book gained fame for selling millions of copies, ranking second only to the Bible. His ideology, promoting the "public concept of land," is known as Georgism, which continues to influence many intellectuals to this day.

His book begins with a compelling question: "Despite the tremendous progress brought about by the Industrial Revolution, why does poverty still persist?" Hence, George titled his book "Progress and Poverty." The Industrial Revolution brought about vast technological advancements, leading to exponential increases in productivity. However, wages for laborers still barely allow them to make ends meet. Is this due to exploitation by capitalists? Not necessarily. George points out that the situation of capitalists is not significantly different from that of laborers.

George argues that the sole fundamental cause of poverty lies in the cost of land, namely, rent. He contends that as rent increases, wages for labor and interest on capital decrease. The rent of land increases at a faster rate than productivity, leading to an exacerbation of societal inequality. Ultimately, all profits of laborers and capitalists flow to landowners.

> The reason why, in spite of the increase of productive power, wages constantly tend to a minimum which will give but a bare living, is that, with an increase in productive power, rent tends to even greater increase, thus producing a constant tendency to the forcing down of wages.
>
> (George 1879, p. 282)

Furthermore, the land is susceptible to speculation, making it an attractive target for those seeking substantial future profits. Speculation on land increases its value and drives up rent beyond the level that the labor and capital of society can afford.

> Given a progressive community, in which the population is increasing and one improvement succeeds another, land must constantly increase in value.
>
> (George 1879, p. 264)

George argues that this speculation on land is the fundamental cause of recurrent industrial depressions. And the cause of poverty persisting amidst social progress and prosperity, as well as the occurrence of recurrent economic depressions, can be attributed to the rent of land. Ultimately, the private ownership of land is the source of all social inequality and the fundamental evil. George's solution is clear:

> There is but one way to remove an evil … To extirpate poverty, to make wages what justice commands they should be, the full earnings of the laborer,

> we must therefore substitute for the individual ownership of land a common ownership … We must make land common property.
>
> (George 1879, p. 328)

Georgists consider profits from land rent to be unethical, similar to the unethical nature of trading human beings for profit. This isn't due to the perception of land as sacred, as suggested by the Old Testament passage, "The land must not be sold permanently, because it is Mine" (Leviticus 25:24). Rather, it's because all the wealth of society becomes concentrated in the hands of landlords. Additionally, Georgists regard landlords who accumulate society's wealth through land rent without engaging in productive activities as lazy, immoral, and therefore unethical.

Administrative Intervention

As markets fail, the scope of administrative intervention expands. The provision of public goods, which markets cannot supply, becomes the responsibility of the administration. Additionally, the administration prohibits and monitors unethical markets. Public goods and unethical markets represent extreme concepts of market failure. The reality of market failure and administrative intervention lies somewhere in between these extremes.

In the age of information and communication, the internet is considered the most crucial social infrastructure. However, if left solely to the market, there is a high likelihood that the internet will not be adequately provided. It demands substantial initial investment and presents challenging issues regarding profit-sharing. Governments actively encourage and support private sector investments in the internet, sometimes even taking direct initiative in its construction.

Moreover, the administration consistently monitors and regulates the financial industry. While the financial industry itself is not inherently unethical, there is a risk of setting interest rates for loans at levels deemed unacceptable by society. Additionally, there is a possibility of luring unsuspecting consumers into high-risk investments. To address these unethical practices, the government constantly monitors and supervises financial institutions.

In society, blood supply occurs through two methods: voluntary blood donation and paid blood sales. In the United States, both methods coexist. Although paid blood sales themselves are not considered unethical, they result in unethical social outcomes. As more individuals donate blood voluntarily, the price of selling blood decreases. Eventually, donors may realize that their actions harm those engaged in

Table 20.1 Spectrum of government intervention for market failure between public goods and unethical markets

Government interventions in response to market failures		
Public goods	←-----------------------------------→	*Unethical markets*
Defense – infrastructure – internet – blood-supply – loan-shark – euthanasia – drug		

paid blood sales, leading to a decline in voluntary donations. Over time, this reliance on blood sales may result in a significant transfer of blood from the poor to the wealthy, representing an unethical social phenomenon. To prevent such unethical outcomes, the administration intervenes. The administration discourages blood sales while actively promoting voluntary blood donation. Fortunately, voluntary organizations such as the Red Cross and Red Crescent play a leading role in blood donation. The administration supports these organizations, ensuring the maintenance of an ethical blood supply.

Unanticipated Consequences

There are cases where certain unethical markets are partially allowed. Depending on the country, the sex trade may be permitted but regulated and monitored by the administration. That is because a strong regulation against unethical markets can lead to unintended consequences. Senge describes the side effects of drug crackdown as follows:

> Even more insidiously, they learn that a new citywide outbreak of drug-related crime is the result of federal officials intercepting a large shipment of narcotics – which reduced the drug supply, drove up the price, and caused more crime by addicts desperate to maintain their habit.
>
> (Senge 1990, p. 58)

Ignoring the complexity of societies, the cure can be worse than the disease (Senge 1990). In the United States, there was a period when alcohol prohibition was strictly enforced. However, the desire for alcohol did not disappear; instead, it led to clandestine production and trade. Those caught engaging in this trade faced heavy fines, resulting in a skyrocketing price for alcohol to reflect these costs. Consequently, individuals involved in the secret production and sale of alcohol were able to make significant profits. Where illegal funds accumulate, violent organizations tend to emerge. In American society, alcohol prohibition laws gave rise to organized crime by gangs. Eventually, the main issue became the proliferation of violent organized crime rather than alcohol consumption itself. Thus, outright bans on unethical markets often lead to unexpected side effects.

Governmental intervention in abortions presents similar dilemmas. Many argue that abortion procedures, seen as unethical acts of ending fetal life, should be regulated as crimes. However, there may be serious repercussions when punishing abortion as a crime. Pregnant women in need of abortion may turn to illegal operations, endangering their lives. In 2016, a report from Brazil revealed that an average of four pregnant women died each day due to illegal abortions. In light of these alarming statistics, there is a growing argument for legalizing abortion to ensure access to safe medical services.

Since 2004, the South Korean government has classified the sex trade as a criminal activity and intensified punishments against it. Strong government intervention has led to a significant reduction in the sex trade, resulting in fewer women being victimized by forced prostitution. However, media reports on the sex trade scene present a different narrative. They suggest that the sex trade has not disappeared but has instead gone underground into an invisible world. According to these reports, the sex trade continues in a more clandestine and perverse manner, causing even greater harm than before. Based on such reporting, there are arguments proposing the legalization of the sex trade as long as it does not directly violate human rights. Critics suggest that strong government intervention in unethical markets may actually lead to unintended consequences, which could be more disastrous.

The progressive party in South Korea has twice failed in presidential elections, largely due to the unforeseen consequences of its housing policies. Believing that apartment prices in Seoul were too high, they criticized the high prices as a social evil and introduced various taxes aimed at lowering them. They even threatened a "tax bomb" to target wealthy areas in Seoul. However, excessive taxes led to unforeseen consequences. High taxes resulted in a sharp decrease in the number of apartments for sale. As supply disappeared from the market, apartment prices rose at a faster pace than before. Even more serious consequences occurred. As apartment prices in Seoul soared, property taxes on apartments increased steeply. Dissatisfied with the high taxes, many citizens in Seoul did not vote for the progressive party, leading to its defeat in the elections.

Government policy interventions are fraught with unforeseen consequences, especially when addressing unethical issues. Such interventions are often perceived as "policies with good intentions." Politicians, eager to portray themselves as "champions of justice" to voters, often push for these policies aggressively, sometimes showing hostility toward unethical citizens. In the pursuit of "good policies," politicians frequently overlook the "unforeseen consequences" and disregard lessons learned from past failures. This pursuit blinds them, leading to worse catastrophic failures.

21 Community Failure

Welfare State

Massive market failures can result in community failures. During the economic crisis of the Great Depression in the 1930s, countless people lost their jobs, leaving families unable to support their members. Traditionally, families served as fundamental welfare units, securing the livelihoods of all members through earnings from economic activities. They provided for children and the elderly without income. However, the significant market failure caused by the economic depression pushed families into crisis. When a community fails to adequately protect and provide for its members, the government steps in to offer support. A state that guarantees a minimum support for all people is called a welfare state.

To address the economic depression and community failures, President Roosevelt of the United States launched the New Deal policy. This initiative involved massive construction of social infrastructure such as dams, hydroelectric power plants, and roads under government leadership. The New Deal policy aimed to revive the stagnant market by creating jobs through the construction of public goods and introduced social security systems like old-age pensions and unemployment insurance. It not only generated numerous jobs, helping to restore the family as a basic welfare unit, but also provided social security for family members who would otherwise be burdensome for the family to support.

However, following the Second World War, conservative politicians in the United States began to roll back some of the social stability policies introduced by the New Deal, leading the United States to gradually retreat from the welfare state model. Nevertheless, the New Deal policy in the United States presented the possibility of a welfare state to the world.

European countries devastated by the Second World War began transitioning into welfare states. Amidst the war, the United Kingdom established a committee to prepare for social stability after the war, and the report produced by this committee, known as the Beveridge Report, gained fame. The Beveridge Report, titled "*Social Insurance and Allied Services*," advocated for a society without poverty and demanded fundamental changes in the concept of social security.

> The moral is that new measures to spread prosperity are needed. The Plan for Social Security is designed to meet this need; to establish a national minimum above which prosperity can grow, with want abolished ... Abolition of want cannot be brought about merely by increasing production, without

DOI: 10.4324/9781003464730-25

Figure 21.1 Community failure and the emergence of welfare states.

> seeing to correct distribution of the product; but correct distribution does not mean what it has often been taken to mean in the past … Better distribution of purchasing power is required among wage earners themselves, as between times of earning and not earning, and between times of heavy family responsibilities and of light or no family responsibilities.
>
> (Beveridge 1942, pp. 165–166)

As the concept of a welfare state, where the government guarantees the livelihood of family members, spreads widely, the scope of administration expands into the realm of communities. The emergence of the welfare state results in a rapid expansion of the scale of administration, shifting its role from merely compensating and regulating market failures to encompassing the private world of communities. This expansion of the administrative role also leads to an increase in the size of government, leading to what is often referred to as "big government."

Controversy on Populism

There is an argument that excessive social welfare policies can lead to the decline of a nation. This argument is exemplified in the concept of the "British disease," a term used to criticize the United Kingdom for its perceived overreliance on welfare policies, which were believed to have caused economic downturns during the 1970s. Following the Second World War, as welfare policies expanded, labor productivity in the United Kingdom sharply declined. Social security systems not only significantly increased the government's financial burden but also weakened the labor motivation of workers. Furthermore, as tax burdens for welfare policies increased, incentives for investment in industries decreased. Through this process, it is argued that excessive welfare policies led to adverse effects, decreasing national competitiveness. Senge presents these problems in terms of systems thinking.

> The long-term, most insidious consequence of applying nonsystemic solutions is increased need for more and more of the solution. This is why ill-conceived government interventions are not just ineffective, they are "addictive" in the sense of fostering increased dependency and lessened abilities of local people to solve their own problems.
>
> (Senge 1990, p. 61)

Political emphasis on social welfare is sometimes labeled as populism. Criticisms arise against populism for excessively increasing social welfare benefits to gain short-term popular support, as it is believed to lead to long-term fiscal deficits and high inflation, ultimately hindering the national economy. While aiming for popular support, populism aligns with democratic political systems. However, politicians who overwhelmingly gain popular support through populist politics often veer toward authoritarianism, attacking critical intellectuals as social enemies.

Since the 20th century, populism has dominated Latin American politics. Political scientists cite two main reasons for this. First, severe socioeconomic inequalities spread during the colonial rule by European countries. Second, the democratic institutions introduced by these European nations guaranteed relatively free elections. The resentment of the masses due to inequality found expression in support for populism within the framework of free election systems. Consequently, politicians relying on populism came to power, leading to repeated political and economic turmoil caused by populism. Similar phenomena have been witnessed in some Asian countries. In societies marked by significant inequality, externally implanted electoral systems serve to nurture the roots of populism.

Of course, there are positive aspects of populism. The policies of Luiz Inácio Lula da Silva, who was elected president of Brazil three times, have been criticized as populist, but his policies are generally considered successful. One of Lula's flagship populist policies is the Bolsa Família program, where the government provides cash to families whose income falls below the poverty line. Although strongly pursued with the goal of ending hunger among residents in Brazil, the Bolsa Família program, which provides cash assistance, has been criticized as a populist policy that disregards national finances. However, Lula's popular reform policies succeeded in revitalizing Brazil's economy. During his presidency from 2002 to 2010, Brazil recorded an average annual growth rate of around 5%, and the total GDP more than tripled. Lula's poverty alleviation policies are evaluated to have yielded successful results, leading to his reelection and making him Brazil's first three-term president in the 2022 presidential election.

Populism has been spreading worldwide, even in the 21st century. We observe that more nations are being led by populist politicians. Will this trend of populism persist in the future? How can political populists survive in the age of personalized information technologies surpassing traditional mass media? Will social network services contribute to or constrain future populism? What direction will populism take in the future? Is it optimistic or pessimistic? These questions pose a significant challenge for future social scientists.

22 Causes of Community Failures

Community failures that occurred throughout Western societies in the early 20th century were the result of two world wars and economic depression. From small-scale families to larger social communities, they failed to ensure the livelihoods of their members. Are these community failures temporary phenomena or structural ones? If they are temporary failures caused by war and depression, it may be sufficient to wait for communities to recover. However, there have been thoughts that persistent causes are behind community failures. The most representative views are those of the Malthusian catastrophe, Hardin's tragedy of the commons, Olson's free-rider problem, and limits to growth by systems dynamics researchers.

Malthusian Catastrophe

Thomas Malthus, an economist and demographer of the 18th century, sparked much controversy among intellectuals with his pessimistic theory. In his 1798 work "*An Essay on the Principle of Population,*" Malthus argued that the rate of population growth exceeds the rate of increase in food production.

> Population, when unchecked, increases in a geometrical ratio. Subsistence increases only in an arithmetical ratio. A slight acquaintance with numbers will shew the immensity of the first power in comparison of the second.
>
> (Malthus 1798, p. 4)

While the increase in food production occurs at best in proportion or arithmetically, population grows exponentially. He claimed that as society becomes more affluent due to increased food production, it generates more population, ultimately erasing the prosperity of society. This is referred to as the "Malthusian trap" or "Malthusian catastrophe."

Malthus's pessimistic population theory denied the necessity of relief for the poor. He argued that explosive population growth could only be curbed by the starvation of the poor and the consequent restraint of childbirth. In such a scenario, relief for the poor would lead to population growth and ultimately greater unhappiness in the long run. Malthus's theory at the time reduced poor relief in Britain and sparked significant moral controversy. Particularly, Malthus failed to comprehend the industrial and technological innovations occurring during his era. Human technological innovation progressed much faster and brought about far-reaching

DOI: 10.4324/9781003464730-26

changes than Malthus had envisioned. Additionally, the development of various contraceptive technologies eliminated the explosive population growth Malthus had feared. Some sociologists argue that the modern development of contraceptive technology has led to changes in human sexuality, family relationships, and the overall fabric of society.

The advancement of information and communication technology has outpaced the development of the industrial revolution. Gordon Moore, the co-founder of Intel Corporation, proposed Moore's Law, stating that the number of transistors in an integrated circuit (IC) doubles about every two years. Moore's Law was widely accepted to represent the exponential growth of technology in the IT industry. Additionally, the birth rate in the information society is sharply declining. In an information society where everything, including food, shopping, and entertainment, can be handled through the internet and mobile phones, young people tend to postpone marriage or choose not to have children even after marriage. Already, birth rates in Asian countries are approaching one child per woman. A significant decrease in population is occurring. In an information society witnessing the exponential development of technology and natural population decline, Malthus's theory could not be sustained.

Tragedy of Commons

Following Malthus, one of the scholars who discussed the tragedies of communities and became a subject of debate was Garrett Hardin. Like Malthus, Hardin also held a pessimistic view of communities. The theoretical groundwork for the inevitability of community failures was laid out in his paper titled "Tragedy of the Commons," published in "Science" in 1968. Hardin shows the following problematic landscape.

> The tragedy of the commons unfolds as follows: Consider a pasture that is open to all. Farmers in this commons will each try to raise as many cattle as possible.
>
> (Hardin 1968, p. 1244)

Hardin's argument is encapsulated in these two sentences. First, the open pasture accessible to all is referred to as the "commons," where farmers in the surrounding area have equal access. Therefore, the pasture possesses the characteristic of non-excludability. However, if one farmer brings in their livestock and allows them to consume all the grass, other farmers' livestock will be unable to feed, creating a situation of rivalry. While traditional public goods possess the characteristics of non-excludability and non-rivalry, "commons" has only the characteristic of non-excludability, lacking non-rivalry.

In the second sentence, Hardin explains that in this common pasture, each farmer strives to raise as many cattle as possible. While adding one more head of cattle becomes beneficial for the individual farmer, the damage caused by the diminishing grass is collectively shared. Consequently, everyone starts raising

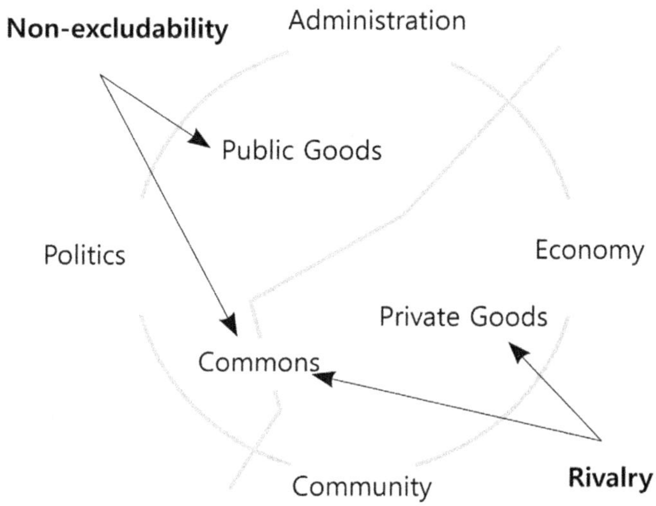

Figure 22.1 Community failures in commons with non-excludability and rivalry.

more livestock. Eventually, the shared pasture becomes depleted, and not a single head of cattle can be sustained. The commons succumb to destruction.

When common resources are entrusted to the collective management of farmers, they are destined to be depleted. The same principle applies to jointly used resources like reservoirs. As the water in the reservoir is accessible to the residents of a village, it possesses the characteristic of non-excludability. However, its consumption involves the characteristic of rivalry as the available water decreases. The residents of the village attempt to supply as much water as possible to their individual farmlands. Consequently, the water in the reservoir is excessively used and quickly depleted. Hardin's conclusion is that commons should not be left solely to the management of communities.

Hardin argues that commons should not be managed by the community of farmers. As each farmer tries to feed more livestock or consume more water, the commons are destined for destruction. Management by the community, without regulation, leads to the tragedy of resource depletion and failure. To prevent this, ultimately, administration must intervene. Administration needs to suppress the freedom of the farmers and control the livestock they raise. The administration, which has been responsible for supplying public goods with the characteristics of non-excludability and non-rivalry, must now take on the task of managing the commons with the characteristic of non-excludability alone.

Like Malthus, Hardin was concerned about overpopulation throughout his life. As measures to curb overpopulation, Hardin argued for the legalization of abortion rights and advocated for strict limitations on immigration. He was even critical of welfare policies, akin to Malthus. Hardin's neo-Malthusian approach faced criticism from many intellectuals.

Free-rider Problem

Mancur Olson offers an alternative explanation for the failure of communities: the free-rider problem. As Olson points out, many social scholars assume that communities or groups will act for the common interest. One of the most prominent scholars in this regard is Karl Marx. Most Marxists believed that the proletarian community would act for the benefit of their collective interest. Olson argues that this line of thinking is mistaken.

> Indeed, unless the number of individuals in a group is quite small, or unless there is coercion or some other special device to make individuals act in their common interest, rational, self-interested individuals will not act to achieve their common or group interests.
>
> (Olson 1965, p. 2)

The free-rider problem is manifest in labor union movements. If wages are increased through labor union activity, all workers benefit. However, memberships in the labor union entails costs such as paying union fees and bearing the burden of participating in strikes. From the perspective of an individual worker, it is advantageous not to join the union. This behavior of enjoying the benefits of the collective while avoiding the associated burdens is termed "free riding." Olson argues that as the size of the community increases, the number of free riders also increases. This is because free riders are more easily identifiable in smaller communities. As the number of free riders grows, it becomes increasingly difficult for the community to obtain collective goods.

We experience the "free-rider" problem in our everyday lives. For instance, when students participate in team projects. Typically, a team consists of five members, and all team members receive the same grade. Most teams have one or two free riders who do not participate in project meetings or contribute actively to gathering materials. In the worst-case scenario, only one person works diligently on the project while the other four act as implicit free-riders. However, a bigger issue is that such unfairness not only occurs in schools but also in companies and governments.

The Pareto Principle, also known as the 80:20 rule, can be applied to the phenomenon of free riders. In the early 20th century, Pareto discovered that 20% of the wealthy population owned 80% of the wealth in society. This 80:20 ratio was also found in various other social domains. For instance, in factories, 80% of quality issues stem from 20% of the causes. Similarly, in ant societies, the 80:20 rule was observed. It was found that only 20% of ants diligently carry leaf fragments while the remaining ants do not engage in any work. This implies that 80% of the ants in the society are free riders.

As the proportion of free riders increases, it becomes increasingly difficult for the community to pursue common interests. To mitigate this problem, financial rewards and recognition are proposed to encourage active workers. Unfortunately, there are occasions where the worst-case scenario unfolds. This occurs when additional rewards and recognition are given not to diligent workers but to free riders. This situation arises when internal politics of the organization are dominated by free riders. Free riders who do not work diligently invest their time in gaining popularity with superiors and colleagues. Eventually, they receive recognition and promotion over hardworking employees. This leads to feelings of betrayal and contemplation of resignation among diligent workers.

Limits to Growth

"*Limits to Growth*," reported to the Club of Rome in 1972 by system dynamics researchers led by Donella Meadows, shed new light on the subject of overpopulation (Meadows, Meadows, Randers, and Behrens III,1972). This book simulated through computers the consequences of economic and population growth under the assumption of limited resources on Earth. They utilized a computer model presented in Jay Forrester's book *World Dynamics* (Forrester 1971). Their computer simulations showed that the world's population and economy would abruptly decline by the mid-21st century. The simulation result of "population decline" depicts a tragic scenario where hundreds of millions of people perish. This book gained unprecedented popularity, being translated into 30 languages and printing over 30 million copies since its publication.

"Limits to Growth" avoided the moral criticisms raised against Malthus and Hardin. This is because, unlike Malthus and Hardin, the report did not advocate for any controversial assumptions or policies. Their only assumption is that the earth has limited resources. Criticism mainly focused on the computer simulation method. However, reality unfolded in a manner similar to their computer simulations. In the late 20th century, famines did occur worldwide, and economic growth rates began to halt. Many scholars compared actual data from the past 30 years with their computer simulations and found remarkably matching results.

The computer model of "Limits to Growth" did not introduce complex assumptions. Unlike traditional economists who assumed infinite resources, it simply acknowledged the undeniable assumption that there are limits to the earth's resources and agricultural land. Computer simulations of their model showed that if one insists on traditional growth, humanity's growth will abruptly stop, leading to an uncontrollable catastrophe of rapid decline. Additionally, their simulation presented a positive scenario: if there is an agreement to significantly reduce the pace of growth, the economy and population can reach a stable equilibrium.

"Limits to Growth" reaffirmed the tragedies of population growth through computer simulations. Furthermore, it demonstrated that a slowdown in economic growth could lead to reaching a stable equilibrium and avoiding catastrophe. Their research shocked Western societies, which had previously taken growth for granted. Subsequently, Schumacher emphasized in his book *Small is Beautiful* the importance of a survival economy rather than a growth economy. Schumacher quotes Gandhi: "Earth provides enough to satisfy every man's need, but not for every man's greed" (Schumacher 1973, p. 29). The key to survival in a finite world lies in abandoning the greed of a few and respecting the needs of the majority. So, how can we implement Gandhi's wisdom? The vision of communities that can share finite resources without reaching catastrophe is revealed through Elinor Ostrom's work.

23 Self-governance by Communities

Overpopulation is interconnected with commons and finite resources. It is a problem within communities where the population uses shared finite resources as commons. Malthus and Hardin argued that avoiding catastrophe cannot be left to the individual's free choice, and therefore, external intervention is necessary. However, they overlooked the choices made by the communities to which individuals belong. The possibility exists for communities to regulate their members. This is called community self-governance.

Self-governance by Elinor Ostrom

The concept of community self-governance over common-pool resources (CPR) emerged relatively recently in Western societies. Elinor Ostrom conducted several research studies to investigate whether communities could effectively manage common-pool resources by themselves. Through her observations and studies of several communities managing the commons, Ostrom demonstrated that communities are indeed capable of governing common-pool resources by themselves without external regulations. She referred to this as "self-governance" in its true sense. Her research was published in 1990 under the title "*Governing the Commons*." Twenty years later, Ostrom was awarded the Nobel Prize in Economics for her groundbreaking work as a political scientist.

The fact discovered in Ostrom's research is that the issue of using and managing commons is intertwined with various different ways of life for residents. The problem of commons is not presented as a one-off game. Moreover, within residents' lives and the environment surrounding common resources, there are numerous uncertainties.

> In contrast to the uncertainty caused by these environments, the populations in these locations have remained stable over long periods of time. Individuals have shared a past and expect to share a future. It is important for individuals to maintain their reputations as reliable members of the community.
>
> (Ostrom 1990, p. 88)

And residents are not passive actors with quick minds, as economists assume. They are not passive actors trapped in the trap that Hardin and Olson claim. Residents

DOI: 10.4324/9781003464730-27

are aware of the selfish trap they can fall into and strive to overcome the dilemmas of commons.

> But self-organizing and self-governing individuals trying to cope with problems in field settings go back and forth across (operational, collective, and constitutional) levels as a key strategy for solving problems.
>
> (Ostrom 1990, p. 54)

Villagers recognized that excessive water consumption from the reservoir would lead to its depletion. They gathered and held meetings to establish limits on the amount of water each household could extract from the reservoir. The villagers actively monitored and enforced compliance with these agreements. Consequently, the reservoir was preserved, and the villagers never experienced water shortages.

Following Ostrom's work, community self-governance over common-pool resources has been observed worldwide. Marine fish, for instance, can be considered a common-pool resource. The sea is accessible to anyone, which presents non-excludability. However, overfishing leads to a rapid decline in fish populations. Fishermen, who have witnessed the tragedy of overfishing over centuries, hold meetings to set limits on the number of fish that can be caught per boat and often prohibit the capture of breeding fish and juveniles. This management of common-pool resources has evolved into cultural and traditional practices passed down through generations. The phrase "living in harmony with nature" epitomizes this responsible management of shared resources.

Subak in Bali Island

One of the most beautiful self-governance systems for managing common-pool resources is Subak in Bali, Indonesia. Subak is a water management (irrigation) system for the terraced rice fields on Bali Island. Developed in the 9th century, Subak has been functioning well to this day. The first sentence introducing Subak on the Indonesian tourism website reads as follows:

> Bali's complex irrigation system has its roots not by order of kings, but its management is very much in the hands of the villagers through village cooperatives, called Subak.
>
> (Website of Indonesian tourism)

This clearly emphasizes Subak as a self-governance system within the community without administrative intervention. Subak is a system that connects temples supplying water and rice fields receiving water. Farmers cultivating rice fields with water from Subak are members of the Subak. While water management is under the authority of the priests in water temples, every decision is discussed at members' meetings.

The Subak system is a vast community that connects farmers and temples. Its common-pool resource is water shared by farmers and priests. The Subak reflects a unique worldview of "Tri Hita Karana," which can be translated as "three ways to happiness." Here, the three ways refer to the relationships between humans, the earth, and the gods. Subak members believe that when these three relationships are harmonious through the Subak system, they can maintain a happy life. Such religious beliefs do not require a monitoring system to ensure conformity. The Subak, which is close to near-perfect self-governance, has evolved Bali's agricultural society into a beautiful culture over thousands of years.

The emphasis on the three relationships in "Tri Hita Karana" closely aligns with the concept of "天地人 (heaven-earth-human)" passed down in Korean society. Moreover, the philosophy of "Tri Hita Karana" suggests that the essence of happiness lies in social relationships. These relationships include one's connection with the divine, with fellow humans, and with nature. With such a worldview that emphasizes social relationships, it is believed that community self-governance has been possible for thousands of years.

New Governance

While Hardin's tragedy of the commons and Ostrom's self-governance represent two extremes in resource management by communities, the reality often lies somewhere in between. In modern times, a notable example of a common-pool resource is "clean air," especially in residential complexes where complaints about smoking are widespread. The air in these complexes can be considered a common-pool resource since it is non-excludable. However, smoking pollutes the clean air, creating discomfort for others. In response, residents voice their complaints and hold meetings to establish smoking regulations. They agree on anti-smoking rules and set fines for those who violate them. This example reflects Ostrom's concept of managing common-pool resources through self-governance.

In practice, there may be individuals who secretly smoke and refuse to pay fines, leading to conflicts among residents. In such cases, administrative intervention can be effective. Instead of dispatching administrative officials or police to enforce anti-smoking regulations, which can be costly and create unnecessary tension, indirect administrative support may suffice. The administration can accept complaints from residents about smokers, issue public warnings against smoking in residential areas, and provide other forms of support. This cooperative approach between the community of residents and the administration is referred to as "new governance (NG)," which empowers the community and encourages compliance (Table 23.1).

Table 23.1 Spectrum of the role of communities in managing commons

	Community on commons	
Tragedy of Commons G. Hardin	←------------------------------------→	Self Governance E. Ostrom
	New Governance (NG)	

Global Challenge

Nature is commonly regarded as a common-pool resource. The pastures described by Hardin, the reservoirs studied by Ostrom, and the water managed by Subak are all crucial components of nature. Likewise, the air we breathe, the forests, and the birds are integral parts of the natural world. Due to the impossibility of restricting access to them, they exhibit the characteristic of non-excludability. Recently, the climate environment affected by the emission of greenhouse gases (GHG) is considered a global common-pool resource.

Late 20th-century scientists warned of a rapid increase in Earth's temperature due to the greenhouse effect, signaling disaster for humanity. Many countries acknowledged the need to reduce emissions of carbon dioxide (CO_2) and other greenhouse gases (GHG) to mitigate such climate change. However, there is a serious problem here. Despite widespread concerns about the global climate environment, few are willing to take action. All governments are, in essence, members of the global community, regarding the climate environment as a common-pool resource. No government wants to impose burdens on its own businesses, fearing that GHG emission regulations could reduce the competitiveness of domestic companies and lead to economic downturns. While all governments agree on the necessity of regulations on GHG emissions, none wants to be the first to act.

A new idea was introduced to address this dilemma: the GHG Emissions Trading System. This system introduces a market mechanism to complement the failures of governments within the global community. In 1997, the Kyoto Protocol adopted an international emissions trading system. Companies intending to produce goods by emitting more GHGs than their allocated allowances must purchase additional allowances from other companies. As the price of GHG allowances increases, factories choose production methods that minimize GHG emissions. They may cease using fossil fuels and instead expand their use of renewable energy sources such as solar or wind power. This approach is anticipated to effectively mitigate GHG emissions in the long term.

The GHG emissions trading market operates internationally as well. Companies from wealthy nations can purchase emissions allowances from companies in underdeveloped countries. If companies from wealthy nations use efficient technology to emit fewer GHGs and produce more goods, then, from a global perspective, GHG emissions can be effectively reduced. In this way, market mechanisms are expected to operate beyond national borders, something that individual governments cannot achieve.

Can the market economy effectively address global environmental issues? Or should we devise a completely different global approach? In the 21st century, we are witnessing an increasing number of global problems, including climate change, refugees fleeing wars and oppression, international drug trafficking, and new pandemics sweeping across the globe. These issues revolve around the global community and manifest as global commons. In the face of global commons, self-interested politicians often turn to nationalism. It is a big irony that as global problems spread, nationalism tends to rise worldwide. This irony leads to the global tragedy of the commons.

When it comes to addressing global problems, governments around the world often resemble the farmers in Hardin's pasture, seeking to maximize their own interests. Politicians fixated on winning domestic elections often advocate for strong nationalism while shunning global solutions. In such circumstances, can traditional market mechanisms effectively address global issues?

A community-based approach could be considered an alternative strategy. In 2016, Facebook CEO Mark Zuckerberg criticized nationalist movements, stating that they were "calling for building walls and distancing people they label as others." The following year, he posted a manifesto titled "Building Global Community," advocating for the global community as a solution to address global challenges.

> Our greatest challenges also need global responses - like ending terrorism, fighting climate change, and preventing pandemics. Progress now requires humanity coming together not just as cities or nations, but also as a global community.
>
> (Zuckerberg 2017)

After the end of World War II, on April 25, 1945, 51 countries signed the charter to establish the UN. Since then, the UN has made collective efforts to maintain peace and order in the world. When considering the entire globe as one society, the UN has taken charge of the public domain. However, the domain of global public has not expanded further. In contrast, with the growth of industrial society, the domain of the global economy has expanded rapidly. Furthermore, as we enter the information age, online global communities are also expanding worldwide. While global private areas are expanding, the global public domain remains relatively small.

As we enter the 21st century, numerous global issues are emerging that transcend the boundaries of individual nations. However, the UN has been ineffective in addressing these global challenges. The UN has been criticized for its inability to effectively address not only physical conflicts between nations but also trade disputes, refugee crises, environmental pollution, and climate issues. Instead of resolving global issues, the UN has often been accused of prolonging them. Consequently, nationalism is rapidly spreading, even in the United States, where the UN headquarters is located.

In response to these global issues, new ideas for a global market and global community have been proposed. However, without the establishment of a global public, the effective functioning of global private activities is difficult. Private interactions in markets and communities can be trusted and sustained only when they are built upon a solid institutional foundation ensured by a robust public authority. Ultimately, an effective response to global issues requires more than just the global economy and global community; it requires a global public authority. Who can create a global public authority and how? No one knows. This ignorance is the intellectual inheritance for the 21st-century social scientists.

24 Government Failure

Corruption and Privatization

Government intervention in the economy has been implemented to address market failures. Welfare states emerged to aid communities in need. Consequently, government administration has grown into a massive organization overseeing numerous aspects of society. However, as the scope of administration expanded, its limitations have become apparent. Administrations inherently lack the efficiency of markets. Bureaucracy, a cornerstone of administration, emphasizes procedures to curb the arbitrariness of public agencies, thereby limiting their capabilities. As administration enters into the realm of the economy, bureaucratic reliance on strict procedures stands in contrast to the efficiency-driven private enterprises. Paradoxically, the inefficiency of administration is considered to exacerbate the problems it intends to solve. By the mid-20th century, the term "government failure" began to spread.

Government failure can be broadly categorized into two main types. The first is corruption, where officials of government agencies, holding significant power in the economic area, seek unjust gains. The second is failure resulting from government incompetence. It is rare for government agencies to operate more efficiently than private enterprises. Government failure due to corruption is addressed by anti-corruption systems, while government failure due to incompetence is tackled through privatization.

Anti-corruption Acts

Serious government failure is more often associated with corruption than incompetence. Corruption is defined as "the abuse of public power for private gain." According to this definition, corruption occurs in the public area of administration and politics. The individuals providing private benefits to public officials mainly come from the private economic area. Therefore, corruption occurs at the boundary between the public and private areas. A typical example of corruption is when individuals in the private economic sector bribe public officials in the administrative area, and in return, officials grant favors to these individuals. "Abuse of public power for private gain" encapsulates the essence of corruption.

Corruption, occurring clandestinely in the corners of society, evolves differently depending on social cultures and practices. Michael Johnston studied various corruption styles in different countries and classified them into four types (Johnston

DOI: 10.4324/9781003464730-28

2005). The first type, "influence markets," refers to situations where markets wield significant financial power to influence politics and administration, as observed in the United States and Japan. The second type, "elite cartels," involves elites in political, economic, and administrative fields forming extensive networks to provide mutual benefits, as observed in Italy and South Korea. The third type, "oligarchs and clans," involves a few private groups controlling extensive public institutions, as seen in Russia and the Philippines. The fourth type, "official moguls," involves powerful leaders and their cohorts benefiting from their privilege, as observed in China and Indonesia.

Johnston's classification seems plausible, but it has also faced considerable criticism. In Korea, his classification gained significant traction, leading to the enactment of the "Improper Solicitation and Graft Act" in 2015 based on his theory. This law prohibits elites from providing each other with monetary support or treating each other to expensive meals, aiming to punish the corrupt connections among elites in society.

Privatization of Toll Goods

The failures resulting from incompetence in government call for a shift in management approach, from public to private. There is a growing demand for the dissolution of state-owned enterprises created to intervene in the market. However, completely dismantling all state-owned enterprises is not feasible, as there is no guarantee that private enterprises can efficiently assume the roles performed by these entities. Under these circumstances, theoretical criteria are needed to determine which public enterprises can be dismantled.

Emanuel S. Savas, in his 1987 book, *Privatization: The Key to Better Government*, provided compelling guidelines. He suggested that public enterprises dealing with "toll goods" could be effectively privatized. Traditional scholars argued that goods showing excludability and rivalry should be managed by the private sector, while goods characterized by non-excludability and non-rivalry should be handled by the government. However, Savas focused on goods with non-rivalry but excludability characteristics, which he referred to as toll goods.

> Unlike common-pool goods, toll goods can be supplied by the marketplace. Because exclusion is readily possible, users will pay and therefore suppliers will supply the goods, theoretically in the quantity and quality demanded by the users.
>
> (Savas 1987, p. 47)

Highways exemplify toll goods. Toll booths on highways collect fees, and vehicles that do not pay cannot use the highway, showcasing the characteristic of excludability. However, one vehicle's usage of the highway does not preclude others from using it, demonstrating non-rivalry. Electricity, gas, and water are also examples of toll goods. Households are billed based on electricity consumption, and electricity can be cut off for households that do not pay their fees, demonstrating perfect excludability. Additionally, electricity exhibits non-rivalry, as one household's consumption does not affect availability to others.

Savas advocated for the privatization of toll goods, involving the transfer of ownership from the government to the private sector. This represents a call for the government to withdraw from certain sectors of the economy. Private companies, due to their ability to collect fees for toll goods based on excludability, can effectively assume the roles previously held by the government.

Telecommunication companies initially had to install telephone networks at considerable cost to provide services, leading many countries to establish telephone companies through government investment. As the information society emerged, there was a growing consensus that competition should be introduced into the telephone market. It was believed that through competition among private companies, the traditional telephone market could expand to include internet and mobile communication services. According to the logic of Savas, telecommunication services are considered "toll goods." The usage of telephones by some people does not limit the usage by others, and telecommunication companies can block access for those who do not pay fees. Therefore, many countries have privatized telecommunications companies.

Privatization has been implemented as a response to government inefficiency and corruption. However, corruption can also infiltrate the privatization process itself. Acemoglu and Robinson illustrate this with the example of the privatization of the Mexican telephone company:

> In Mexico, Carlos Slim did not make his money by innovation ... His major coup was the acquisition of Telmex, the Mexican telecommunications monopoly that was privatized in 1990 ... Even though Slim did not submit the highest bid, a consortium led by him won the auction. Instead of paying for the shares right away, Slim managed to delay payment, using the dividends of Telmex itself to pay for the stock.
>
> (Acemoglu and Robinson 2012, p. 39)

Thus, privatization, initially aimed at combating inefficiency and corruption, can paradoxically exacerbate corruption. The authority to privatize large state-owned enterprises increases the potential for corruption during the privatization process. These concerns form the basis of much of the opposition to privatization.

If you overlay the classification of public goods, private goods, commons, and toll goods onto the four realms of society, you can directly understand their meanings and positions. Public goods, characterized by non-excludability and non-rivalry, belong to the administrative realm. Private goods, exhibiting both rivalry

Table 24.1 Two-by-two typology of goods: rivalry and excludability dimensions

	Non-excludability	*Excludability*
Non-rivalry	Public goods	Toll goods
Rivalry	Commons	Private goods

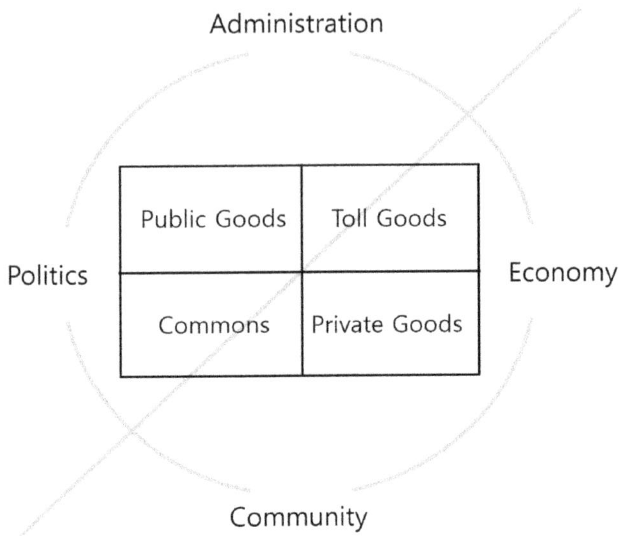

Figure 24.1 Location of public goods, private goods, commons, and toll goods in the four realms of society.

and excludability, fall within the private sector of the economic realm. Commons, marked by rivalry but non-excludability, straddle the boundary between administration and community. Toll goods, characterized by non-rivalry but excludability, are situated at the boundary between the administration and the economy. That is why toll goods are often discussed as the most suitable candidates for privatization.

Privatization of Public Service

Sometimes, even core functions of the administrative realm are subject to privatization. One of the biggest controversies arises with private prisons. Prisons are facilities where individuals convicted of crimes by the courts are detained and isolated from society by administrative authorities. Private prisons emerged in the late 20th century. In the UK and Australia, close to 15% of prisoners are housed in private prisons, while in the United States, around 8% of prisoners are accommodated in private facilities. There are many debates surrounding private prisons. While some argue that private prisons are more efficient than public prisons, studies have found no evidence to support this claim. Private prisons, operated for profit, often do not employ an adequate number of guards and have a higher risk of illegal dealings with inmates. There are even allegations that private prisons lobby judges to extend prisoners' sentences to receive more government subsidies.

Private companies also participate in the function of protecting citizens from crime through policing activities. Private police have been around much longer than private prisons. Thousands of years ago, China had "security companies (鏢局)," which provided protection services for merchants traveling long distances by employing professional warriors. Currently, in the United States, private security officers outnumber public policemen. According to the US Bureau of Labor Statistics, in 2022, there were 1,124,890 private security guards compared to 655,890 public police officers, nearly 2:1. While public police serve both the rich and the poor, private police exist solely for the security of the wealthy. The fact that private police outnumber public police by twofold implies, from a mathematical perspective, that the security of the wealthy is several times higher than that of the poor.

With recent advancements in information technology, unmanned private security services are rapidly increasing. Unmanned security systems typically conduct remote surveillance during normal times but dispatch private police when intruders are detected. The fees for unmanned security systems have decreased to a level that even ordinary households can afford. However, these fees remain beyond the reach of the poor, leading to issues of security inequality. Unmanned security systems, like private police, exacerbate security inequality by diverting criminals toward impoverished neighborhoods, resulting in deteriorating security in those areas and creating disparities in crime rates. Wealthy neighborhoods become increasingly safer, while poorer neighborhoods become more dangerous.

25 Government Failure

NPM and NG

As government failures became apparent throughout society, the scope of administration began to shrink. Administration was no longer seen as a panacea for all problems; instead, administrations themselves became the subject of treatment. As the 20th century drew to a close, administrative reform became a prominent issue in developed countries.

Government failure does not end with privatization; it extends to reforms within the government itself. The core of internal government reform lies in downsizing government organizations, advocating for the transformation of large governments into smaller ones. From an economic perspective, there is an emphasis on innovation in government organizations, demanding the introduction of market competition principles into government structures, known as "new public management (NPM)." Government services in the realm of communities are also subject to innovation, with a central focus on expanding community participation, termed "new governance (NG)."

New Public Management

Discussion on "government failure" broadened to encompass government reform, giving rise to the "New Public Management (NPM)" movement. Whereas privatization called for the reduction of administrative involvement in the economic sector, NPM took it a step further by advocating for the infusion of economic principles into administration. It contended that the efficiency of administration should be bolstered by integrating competitive mechanisms from the economic sector.

In the 1980s, led by Margaret Thatcher in the UK, there was a global push for government innovation aimed at streamlining operations. Some proponents argued that the services provided by public servants should be monetarily quantified, while others encouraged public servants to adopt a customer-oriented approach similar to businesses. Furthermore, there were proposals to foster competitive attitudes among public servants, similar to those found in the business world. This involved establishing detailed performance indicators for public servants and implementing peer-assessment systems. These measures were central to the NPM movement.

In 1992, David Osborne and Ted Gaebler's "*Reinventing Government*" outlined the direction for advancing NPM. Their propositions were actively embraced by the American government and were even adopted as principles for reforming

DOI: 10.4324/9781003464730-29

the federal government. The principles of NPM they proposed include a catalytic government, competitive government, results-oriented government, anticipatory government, and market-oriented government (Osborne and Gaebler 1992). They sought to enhance the practical feasibility of NPM by combining the principles of market competition with community empowerment.

> Much of what we have discussed in this book could be summed up under the rubric of market-oriented government: not only systems change, but competition, customer choice, accountability for results, and of course public enterprise. But market mechanisms are only half the equation. Markets are impersonal. Markets are unforgiving. Even the most carefully structured markets tend to create inequitable outcomes. That is why we have also stressed the other half of the equation: the empowerment of communities. To complement the efficiency and effectiveness of market mechanisms, we need the warmth and caring of families and neighborhoods and communities.
>
> (Osborne and Gaebler 1992, p. 309)

At first, NPM was widely accepted as an innovative approach to remodel administration in the likeness of the business. Many scholars in public administration were eager to adopt NPM. However, as NPM didn't harmonize with the core principles of administration, disillusionment among scholars grew. Critics accused NPM of secularizing and tarnishing the sanctity of administration. They argued that transforming citizens into "customers" conditioned their worthiness for service based on their financial status, undermining the foundational values of administration.

Concurrently with NPM, the concept of "small government" took a prominent role in government innovation. The idea of governance as a minimal state conveys a preference for less government intervention. Previously, in addressing market

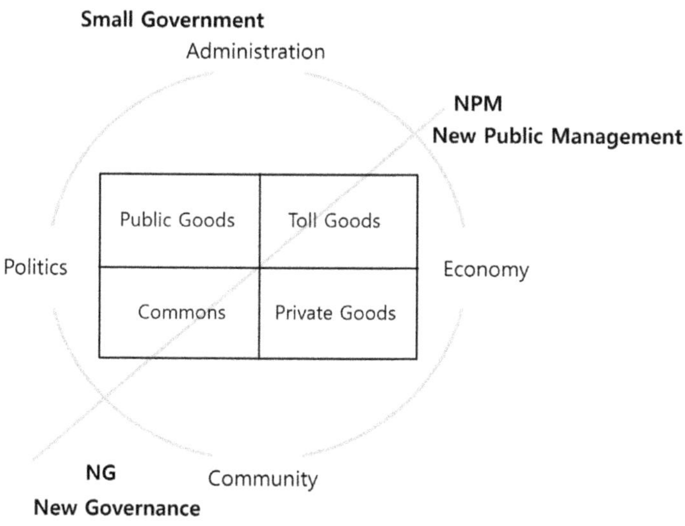

Figure 25.1 Location of small government, new public management, and new governance in the four realms of society.

and community failures, administrations had adopted a big government approach. However, as awareness of government failure grew, "small government" began to supplant "big government". A small government, composed of fewer civil servants, was seen as bringing vitality to the economy while using less budget. Most politicians became vocal proponents of the small government ideology.

New Governance

Elinor Ostrom's concept of self-governance revolutionized perceptions of communities. Until the mid-20th century, communities were viewed as weak organizations reliant on government support. However, as distrust in government grew, the proactive role of communities began to be emphasized. There was a growing recognition of the need for active community participation in the provision of government services. With increasing calls for government downsizing, the demand for active community participation has extended into the movement of "new governance (NG)" or "collaborative governance".

The advent of NG has dual origins. The first is rooted in the theory of self-governance, which opposes the tragedy of the commons. The former considers communities as autonomous entities deserving of trust, while the latter views them as self-interested actors. The second origin is the practical constraint imposed by the concept of small government. In small government settings, administrations lack sufficient personnel for service delivery, necessitating the assistance from communities.

How do communities participate in new governance? An important characteristic of communities is their networks. Community networks, which are widely spread among members, are emotionally intimate and intellectually rich, with high levels of trust. Communities utilize their diverse networks to identify those in need and relay this information to the government. Additionally, by participating in the process of service delivery, communities enhance the effectiveness and credibility of government program. Community networks serve as platforms that link the government to those members in need. Through such participation, governments come to understand communities, and communities can trust the administration. In the 21st century, communities are increasingly seen as partners collaborating with the administration, rather than entities under its control. This is why new governance is referred to as collaborative governance.

Social Capital

Professor Robert Putnam viewed the networks of communities as essential social capital. He defined social capital as "social networks and the norms of reciprocity and trustworthiness that arise from them," emphasizing the networks and reciprocal trust within communities (Putnam 2000, p. 19). Social capital allows community members to trust each other, enabling communities to skip complex and expensive procedures and engage in transactions based on this trust. Communities with high social capital tend to thrive economically and politically.

> Stocks of social capital, such as trust, norms, and networks, tend to be self-reinforcing and cumulative. Virtuous circles result in social equilibria with high levels of cooperation, trust, reciprocity, civic engagement, and collective well-being.
>
> (Putnam 1993, p. 177)

Professor Putnam believed that social capital would promote cooperation and complementary relationships between local communities and the nation. Putnam concludes his book "*Making Democracy Work*" with the following sentence:

> Building social capital will not be easy, but it is the key to making democracy work.
>
> (Putnam 1993, p. 185)

However, in "*Bowling Alone*," published in 2000, Putnam expresses concerns about the decline of social capital. He observed that an increasing number of Americans are bowling alone, symbolizing a sharp decline in civic organizations and participation in American society (Putnam 2000). As civic organizations disappear from local communities, people become increasingly isolated. Putnam cites the proliferation of household appliances as a significant factor contributing to this phenomenon. People who used to attend baseball and football games together in stadiums now prefer to watch television alone at home. As the number of people living alone increases, the vitality of civic organizations declines, and their absence confines more people to their homes.

Such phenomena are also observed in Asia. Urban residents in cities rarely interact with their neighbors. Those who are cut off from their neighbors live alone and die alone. This phenomenon, known as "lonely death," emerged in Japanese society in the 1980s and is referred to as "Kodokushi (孤独死)" in Japan. Japan's public broadcaster NHK reported that 32,000 elderly people nationwide died alone in 2009. Recently, lonely death has also emerged as a social issue in South Korea. In 2021, over 3,300 cases of "lonely death" were reported in South Korea. "Lonely death" literally refers to dying alone and the body being discovered long after death. It is a death where there is no one to share the pain, loneliness, or grief experienced during the dying process, and even the body is left abandoned. Lonely death is a death abandoned by society.

However, I do not believe that these indicators symbolize a decrease in social capital or community networks. Rather, they indicate a decline in traditional community networks. Young people are forming virtual communities through exchanges on the internet. Social Network Services (SNS) connected via smartphones create diverse communities with voluntary participation of individuals. As traditional networks decline, new IT communities are emerging. These emerging IT networks are rapidly increasing the power of communities. Nowadays, we are witnessing the explosive growth of invisible social capital on social networking services and the internet. Moreover, a new era of digital governance will emerge alongside the growth of IT communities. The future digital communities will exhibit new forms of social capital and new governance. This is a significant topic that 21st-century social scientists should observe.

26 Failure of Politics

Coup d'état vs. Non-violent Resistance

Politics, while being the smallest of the four realms of society, exerts remarkable influence. Moreover, political failures usually casue severe harm to other realms. Market failures and community failures are addressed by the administration. When administration fails, the economy steps in and assumes its roles. However, when politics fail, which realm can step in to take its place?

Coup d'état

What exactly does political failure entail? There are two potential interpretations. First, it refers to situations where the democratic system, especially the electoral system, fails to function properly, leading to loss of trust in the ruling group, thereby resulting in an unstable state in the realm of politics. Ruling groups that come into power through elections, which people doubt, can collapse overnight. Social distrust in the ruling group can lead to a state of uncertainty and instability in the whole society.

In times of severe political instability, military coups can occur to seize political power. This is commonly referred to as a "coup d'état" which translates from French to "stroke of state." According to the Merriam-Webster dictionary, a coup d'état means "sudden and violent overthrow or alteration of an existing government by a small group." However, Wikipedia defines it as "an illegal and overt attempt by a military organization or other government elites to unseat an incumbent leadership." I agree with Wikipedia's definition. As evident from Wikipedia's definition, a coup d'état is the political overthrow by administration. The military, being part of the administration, is responsible for executing coups, ultimately replacing politics with administration.

While coup forces overthrow political powers, they typically bring administration under their control. Those who seize power through a coup are typically military leaders or high-ranking government officials. While most coup forces restrict the activities of political organizations like parliaments, they do not usually curtail the activities of administrative organizations. Instead, they often assign new missions to existing administrative bodies. As administration supplants politics, overall political processes come to a halt, resulting in a prolonged period of administrative dictatorship.

DOI: 10.4324/9781003464730-30

The facilities that coup forces seize initially include broadcasting stations, telecommunication facilities, and major transportation networks. This is because these facilities are necessary for governing the country. It is crucial to seize control of broadcasting stations to explain the necessity of the coup to the citizens and to ensure that the success of the coup is accepted as an irreversible fact. Additionally, seizing telecommunication facilities is necessary to monitor any counter-coup efforts by opposing forces. Furthermore, controlling transportation networks is essential to block public agitation. In order to seize these facilities quickly, coup forces demand cooperation from the administration.

According to research by Powell and Thyne (2011), between 1950 and 2010, there were 457 coups in 94 countries. Coups have been most common in Africa and Latin America. Out of the 457 coups, nearly 50%, or 227, were successful. The region with the highest coup success rate is Asia, where out of 59 coups, 33 were successful, resulting in a success rate of 55.9%. This is remarkably high. In Europe, there were 12 coups, with only four being successful, resulting in a success rate of just 33%. Although not included in their study period, in October 1922, amidst the chaos and political turmoil caused by World War I, Benito Mussolini succeeded in securing power in Italy through the "March on Rome," a coup known for its bloodless success.

The fact that the success rate of coups is over 50% presents a tremendous temptation to military leaders. With just a small core of loyal troops, there is a 50% chance of seizing all the power in the country. This can lead to what is known as the "coup trap." The success of one coup can trigger a chain reaction of further coups. While the frequency of coups worldwide has decreased in the 21st century, they still occasionally emerge as a means of resolving political conflicts through force.

There is an opinion that the information and communication technology of the 21st century will inhibit coup attempts. This is because it is difficult to conduct a coup

Figure 26.1 Political failures leading to military coup d'état or non-violence civic movement.

covertly due to the widespread availability of information devices and platforms. As soon as coup forces mobilize tanks, citizens broadcast it in real-time on platforms like YouTube. Soldiers receiving sudden mobilization orders can also spread suspicious military movements through social media. In an environment where military mobilization cannot be done covertly due to the widespread monitoring enabled by information and communication technology, coups are nearly impossible. However, equally surprising is the possibility of modern information and communication technology to facilitate the swift mobilization of the military. Even more surprising is the possibility of AI (artificial intelligence) having the ability to mobilize the military and carry out a coup. Whether coups will cease or become more widespread in the 21st century remains another topic that future social scientists should carefully observe.

Non-violent Resistance

The second form of political failure occurs when the possibility of a change in power disappears. This happens when the electoral system favors the ruling forces and undermines the chances of a shift in power. In the absence of a change in power, corruption tends to flourish. A democracy that fails to facilitate a change in power becomes increasingly distorted. Members of the ruling class, assured of their continued hold on power, are more prone to corruption. In long-standing regimes where power changes rarely occur, coup attempts are less likely to happen. This is because political leaders who have successfully maintained power for a long time often have control over the military.

In this process, citizens lose trust in politics. They cannot trust ruling parties that are corrupt, nor can they trust opposition parties that are incompetent. Gradually, citizens put their trust in civic activists who encourage civil protests. Political parties that have no chance of gaining power often endorse civil protests. Ultimately, the community supplants politics and administration.

In South Korea, political instability led to two military coups in 1961 and 1979. The ruling powers that emerged from these coups enforced prolonged dictatorships, leading to the expulsion of many politicians from the political realm. Ousted politicians and intellectuals subsequently joined civil movements, and a collaborative effort toward democratization began to take shape. This movement involved individuals from various sectors, including the religious community, scholars, and civic activists. Ultimately, South Korea achieved a change in power in the late 20th century.

In the process of overcoming military dictatorships, South Korea fostered a culture of nonviolent protests epitomized by the candlelight protests (Kim and Kim 2005). These protests were primarily driven by civic organizations and religious individuals, with limited participation from politicians. The intention was to maintain the protests as a grassroots movement. The nonviolent protest proved to be a potent strategy, creating a virtuous cycle wherein increasing empathy and support for the peaceful protests bolstered their popularity. As more individuals joined the nonviolent protests, the likelihood of effecting change in power grew, leading to greater participation in civil resistance.

The epitome of nonviolent resistance can be found in the struggle led by Mahatma Gandhi, who liberated India from British rule. When Britain failed to fulfill its promise to grant independence to India after World War I, Gandhi initiated a campaign of noncooperation against the British. From 1919 until achieving independence in 1947, Gandhi urged all people to participate in resistance movements, which included boycotting British goods, refusing to pay taxes, and resigning from government positions. Gandhi's nonviolent resistance movement is known as "satyagraha" (truth-possession). When you hold onto truth, you cannot hold weapons of violence. Another movement by Gandhi was "aparigraha" (non-possession), meaning a life without possessions.

In the 1960s, Martin Luther King Jr. led the nonviolent resistance movement against racial discrimination in the United States. Reverend King's nonviolent movement was in contrast to Malcolm X's violent activism. Malcolm X, who turned to Islam, argued that using violent methods against white discrimination and oppression was justified. In response, Reverend King advocated for nonviolent resistance. He believed that nonviolent movements could undermine the moral foundation of white supremacy.

The nonviolent movement led by Martin Luther King Jr. has a historical connection to the nonviolent approach of Martin Luther from 440 years ago. In the 16th century, Martin Luther opposed the Catholic practice of indulgences and ignited a religious reform movement across Europe. Luther's courageous resistance led to religious reformation spreading throughout Europe. And resistance against the Roman Catholic Church escalated into struggles against nobility and kings, ultimately culminating in the German Peasants' War of 1524. Radical and militant religious reformers sought support from Martin Luther. However, Luther opposed the violent peasant uprising.

> For rebellion is not just simple murder; it is like a great fire, which attacks and devastates a whole land. Thus rebellion brings with it a land filled with murder and bloodshed; it makes widows and orphans, and turns everything upside down, like the worst disaster.
>
> (Martin Luther 1525)

Holding onto the nonviolent movement is not easy. Professor Lee, my mentor, was one of the leaders in the nonviolent democratization movement. Through him, I realized that the nonviolent movement was unpopular. Many politicians and students oppressed by the coup regime fell into radical thinking, advocating armed struggle, and even aligning with the North Korean regime. During hard times, radical thinking gains popularity. Advocates of nonviolence faced criticism from populist groups advocating violence, as well as oppression from the ruling powers. Upholding the nonviolent movement to the end required tremendous belief, patience, and sacrifice (Lee Moon-Young 2008).

27 Rule of Error

"Learning" is often the product of failure. Self-realized learning, in particular, emerges from personal experiences of failure, while traditional learning occurs through education in schools. Societal learning, which is realized by society as a whole, is achieved through harsh failures. There is a popular saying that "democracy thrives on blood." The failure of the existing political system has led to the shedding of countless lives. In order to prevent further innocent bloodshed, the political system has evolved to embrace democracy. However, this process of social learning is ongoing.

Learning does not immediately follow one or two failures. Numerous failures must be accumulated before one can gain true enlightenment. Often, the hard-earned enlightenment does not transition into societal learning. It requires numerous failures for the enlightenment of a minority to spread throughout society and establish itself as a social institution. Therefore, the history of societal learning is essentially the history of societal failures.

The concept that learning is achieved through failure is central to evolutionary theory. To embrace learning through failure, one must first overcome the fear of failure. Rather, an attitude that actively acknowledges failure is necessary. This principle is known as the "rule of error." When individuals openly acknowledge failure, they do not conceal their mistakes. Instead, learning occurs when experiences of failure are openly shared, leading to the extraction of valuable lessons.

In societies where failure is not allowed, individuals tend to conceal their failures. For instance, there was a time when the failure rate of research and development in a government research institute was reported as zero. This was because researchers who failed in their research were held accountable. Even if they had spent substantial resources on research that yielded no results, they would embellish their reports to make it appear as if they had achieved some level of success and would not document their failures. Subsequent researchers would then repeat past mistakes. In such a culture, the opportunity to learn from past failures is lost. The lack of remarkable performances in government research institutes cannot solely be attributed to the incompetence of researchers. Rather, it is the failure to acknowledge and learn from past failures that hinders progress. The problem lies not with the researchers themselves, but with the institutions and prevailing culture.

The inherent nature of human beings is limited. When people with limited abilities attempt something new, it often leads to failure. This process is commonly

DOI: 10.4324/9781003464730-31

Figure 27.1 Evolutionary rationality with the rule of error, and trial and error.

referred to as "trial and error." It means that if you try, you are likely to make errors. It is not wise to avoid unpromising trials that may lead to errors. What matters most is the ability to learn from those failures. This form of learning, which occurs through the "rule of error" and "trial and error," is known as "evolutionary rationality."

The four realms of society – market, community, politics, and administration – inevitably experience failure. However, failure is not a dead end. Instead, acknowledging failures in one realm allows for compensation by other realms. Through this process of failure and compensation, society as a whole learns. This is the dynamics of learning through failure. It may seem feeble at first, but gradually it overcomes failures. Importantly, no single realm of society can independently rectify its own failures. Instead, each realm compensates for the failures of others, supporting one another in the process. Society's progress is not achieved independently by each realm, but rather through collective support and cooperation. This is learning through failure as a whole society.

Three Kinds of Rationality

The concept of "rationality" discussed in the social sciences can be broadly categorized into three main perspectives. The first is institutional rationality, advocated by Max Weber, who viewed social development as a process of demystification and rationalization. In ancient societies, people lived immersed in numerous myths. They believed in countless gods, with each mountain, sea, tree, and insect having its own deity. Stars in the sky symbolized gods, and there were deities believed to protect kings of nations. As society transitioned into the medieval period, people gradually moved away from these myths and began to acquire rationality.

Bureaucracy, representing modern rationality, played a role in eliminating the mythic authority of kings. For Weber, bureaucracy represented an institutional rationality that demystified the authority of kings and ruling classes and provided a general and objective set of rules for all people (Weber 1922).

However, institutions do not encompass all forms of rationality. In the mid-20th century, Herbert Simon delved into the concept of "rationality in decision-making" (Simon 1947). How can individuals with limited rationality make satisfactory decisions? In exploring this question, Simon introduced the "searching process" to arrive at satisfactory choices. Constrained by information and time, human decision-makers cannot evaluate all alternatives and outcomes. Instead, they select suitable alternatives based on available information. This approach to decision-making incorporates the notion of "bounded rationality" or "limited rationality."

Before Simon, economics and policy studies operated under the assumption of optimal rationality. This assumed that decision-makers could obtain full information about all alternatives and outcomes and select the best alternative among them. Simon's concept of bounded rationality was a shock to the field of economics, which had built its theories on the premise of perfect rationality. Economists who embraced Simon's concept of bounded rationality went on to develop a discipline known as "behavioral economics." Simon's decision-making theory subsequently influenced policy studies and cognitive psychology, and even contributed to the development of artificial intelligence. Since the mid-20th century, social scientists and cognitive psychologists influenced by Herbert Simon have focused on rationality in decision-making.

However, for those who actually formulate and execute policies, the rationality of decision-making is at best "intended rationality." During the process of policy implementation and execution, entirely different issues emerge. Unforeseen problems may arise at this stage, leading to the discontinuation and failure of the policy. In such cases, what kind of rationality operates? The concept proposed for such situations is evolutionary rationality, which emphasizes learning from failure that occurs after the stage of decision-making.

Society for Evolutionary Rationality

In evolutionary rationality, failure is not concealed. Instead, it is considered as valuable experience necessary for learning. Failure is regarded as a precious asset. When the experiences of failure are shared among many people, societal learning takes place. Because failure is a valuable experience, those who fail should be remembered not as subjects of punishment but as subjects of learning. This is referred to as the "rule of error," which signifies tolerance towards failure.

On the contrary, there are societies that do not forgive those who fail. They are societies that reward successful individuals and punish those who fail. This principle is highlighted in ancient Chinese thought known as "legalism (法家)." Han Fei, a prominent philosopher of Chinese legalism, opposed Confucianism, which emphasized morality, compassion, and mercy. He advocated the principle of reward and punishment under the law without exceptions (Han Fei, BC 240).

Legalism, along with Confucianism, has been a governing philosophy in Asian countries for thousands of years. The spirit of legalism still lingers in various corners of modern Asian societies. It can be found not only in bureaucracies but also in corporate organizations. They believe that if employees who make mistakes during their duties are not punished, the entire organization will be at risk. This kind of legalism does not forgive failure.

Confucius opposed legalism due to its detrimental effects on the moral integrity of the people. He declared, "If the people are governed by laws, and controlled by punishment, they will seek to avoid punishment and will have no sense of shame" (Confucius, Around BC 500). This means that if the people are ruled by punishment, they will hide their failures to avoid punishment and will not feel ashamed of their failures.

In a society that does not forgive failure, one cannot expect evolutionary rationality. When the failure of subordinates is considered an organizational failure, leaders also face punishment. Leaders hide not only their own failures but also those of their subordinates. An even worse situation arises when leaders fail to acknowledge obvious failures and persist in issuing orders that have proven to be wrong. This is the paradox of legalism. A society that does not forgive failure will not only hide it but also firmly hold onto it. From concealed failures, not only does no learning arise, but erroneous learning also takes place.

In Asian countries heavily influenced by Legalism, there existed a culture that did not acknowledge failure. Particularly during World War II, the Japanese military was notorious for its refusal to admit failure. In the Battle of Imphal, General Renya Mutaguchi persisted in denying his failures despite repeated setbacks. As a result of his failure and refusal to acknowledge it, more than 130,000 soldiers died from starvation, disease, and exhaustion. Similarly, during the Pacific War, the Japanese Navy, which waged war against the United States, failed to learn from its mistakes. Often, the lack of learning from failure has been discussed as one of the major factors contributing to the defeat of the Japanese military.

Professor Hatamura Yotaro, astonished by the reluctance of modern Japanese companies to acknowledge failure, introduced the "study of failures." His books on the study of failures resonated greatly in both Japan and Korea. The first principle of failure studies is to acknowledge failure. The bigger mistake made by companies that do not acknowledge failure is their attempt to compensate for failure. Trying to reverse failure by borrowing money from acquaintances often leads to even greater failures. When failure occurs, the best approach, according to Hatamura Yotaro, is to acknowledge failure and cover yourself with a blanket to cry until the last tears (Hatamura Yotaro 2002).

In 20th-century Korean society, there was a strong aversion to failure. In such a culture, researchers shied away from creative endeavors that were prone to failure. They preferred research with guaranteed success, often imitating successful researches conducted abroad. Renowned Korean management scholar Professor Kim Linsu conceptualized this imitation as a viable strategy (Kim 1997). While other intellectuals in Korea felt ashamed of imitating the knowledge and technology of advanced countries, Professor Kim Linsu courageously treated imitation as a strategic concept. During a time of catching up with the advanced technology of developed countries, imitation was strategically important and proved to be effective.

As the 21st century began, South Korea needed to develop technologies ahead of foreign countries. In this situation, mere imitation was no longer effective. Experimental research became crucial. And Koreans began to realize the truth that experimental research is prone to failure. To encourage experimental research, tolerance towards failure, without punishment, needed to be acknowledged. The culture that forgives failure and even encourages it is the "rule of error."

One of the most representative examples of acknowledging failure and turning it into success was the strategic retreat of the Chinese Communist Party's Red Army after its defeat by the Nationalist Army. The Red Army embarked on the "Long March," spanning over 10,000 km from 1934 to 1935. It was not merely a strategic retreat from the Nationalist Army and their fellow countrymen but also an advance towards the Japanese forces in the north. By acknowledging failure while embarking on new challenges, they achieved unimaginable success. Edgar Snow, who accompanied the Long March, recorded:

> While the Red Army's March to the Northwest was unquestionably a strategic retreat ... they were advancing towards the anti-Japanese front, and this was a psychological factor of great importance ... In one sense, this mass migration was the biggest armed propaganda tour in history. The Reds passed through provinces populated by more than 200,000,000 people ... Millions of peasants have now seen the Red Army and heard it speak, and are no longer afraid of it.
>
> (Snow 1937, p. 217)

Evolutionary rationality emphasizes taking challenging actions. Error occurs only when action is taken. This action is not meticulously planned in advance; rather, it signifies experimental action that is prone to error. The term "trial," used by evolutionists, refers to adventurous action. The process of evolution is similar to that of experimentation. Experimental action often leads to failure, hence the term "trial and error."

Actions of those who do not know the future are also prone to failure. In this case, failures provide them with directions for future actions. Through this iterative process, failures gradually diminish. This is the essence of evolutionary rationality. Albert Einstein once said, "Anyone who has never made a mistake has never tried anything new." Without challenges, there are no errors, and without errors, there can be no learning. The essence of the "rule of error" is the encouragement of challenges and tolerance towards resulting failures.

28 Incrementalism vs. Revolutionism

When learning from failure, it is crucial that the failure is not too significant. When failures become unbearable, the fear of overwhelming responsibilities leads to the concealment of failures. Excessively significant failures tend to hinder the learning process. Maintaining failures on a small scale is advantageous for learning. Just like someone learning to ride a bicycle, they will fall several times. Through the failures of falling, they learn how to ride a bicycle. However, if they experience a major accident, such as colliding with a car while riding a bicycle, the learning process is interrupted. While failures lead to learning, significant failures halt the learning process itself.

Charles E. Lindblom applied this wisdom to policymaking. In 1959, he published a paper titled *The Science of Muddling Through* in the academic journal, Public Administration Review. Despite being written a long time ago, the title still feels fresh and poetic, reflecting the essence of politics and human nature. Lindblom suggests that the process of policymaking is akin to navigating through a mud puddle by pushing and pulling (Lindblom 1959). In a mud fight, one cannot leap freely. Instead, it is wise to move forward one step at a time. This gradual process of changing policies is called "incrementalism."

Karl Popper, who criticized the totalitarian ideologies that emerged in early 20th-century Europe, authored "*Open Society and Its Enemies*." In his book, Popper rejects the political idea of revolution. Arrogant intellectuals may believe they can reform society and eliminate social problems, but societal issues are not that simple. There are two ways to reform society: utopian engineering and piecemeal engineering. Utopian engineering assumes the existence of a blueprint of the ideal society. Any deviation from this utopian blueprint is seen as a target to be eliminated. In contrast, piecemeal engineering implies the partial and gradual improvement of society. Popper notes as follows:

> Piecemeal social experiments can be carried out under realistic conditions, in the midst of society, in spite of being on a small scale, that is to say, without revolutionizing the whole of society.
>
> (Popper 1947, Vol. I, p. 143)

While utopian engineers promise "social good," piecemeal engineers focus on addressing "social bad." The former advocate for radical reforms, whereas the latter advocates for moderate measures. Usually, the public becomes enthusiastic

DOI: 10.4324/9781003464730-32

about the passionate promises of utopian engineers, criticizing piecemeal engineers for being too passive. However, those who believe in rosy promises often fall into the trap of hidden darkness. Karl Popper articulates this as follows:

> But the attempt to make heaven on earth invariably produces hell. It leads to intolerance.
>
> (Popper 1947, Vol. II, p. 224)

Incrementalism involves gradually introducing policies for specific parts rather than the entire system. For instance, a policy could be implemented to exempt administrative regulations for innovative companies in a designated city. As the policy is partially implemented, discussions on the causes of any problems that arise take place, and adjustments are made to the scope of regulatory exemptions. This is how learning occurs. The incremental approach functions as an experiment. It does not assume perfection from the start and acknowledges the limitations of leaders. In the implementation of policies using the incremental approach, if problems arise, they are small enough to be honestly acknowledged. The "rule of error" operates, enabling learning to take place.

On the other hand, the revolutionary approach involves implementing the policy across the entire country without delay. The opposite idea to incrementalism is revolutionism. Advocates of revolutionism believe that their policy is inherently right and correct. They place trust in the rationality of the leader who proposed the ideologically excellent policy. They do not deem further learning necessary, as they believe in the infallibility of the leader. Loyalty in faithfully following the leader's goodwill is the only requirement.

Revolutionism aims to change the entire society rapidly. It dreams of utopia and promises it to the masses. According to Britannica, "utopia" was compounded by Thomas More from the Greek words for "ou (no)" and "topos (place)" and thus meant "nowhere." As the name suggests, utopia is a fictional place that does not exist anywhere in this world. More's utopia recommends having two slaves per household (More 1516). In the utopian world, those who commit crimes become slaves. The slave system not only ensures the comfortable life of the masters but also helps suppress crime in utopia. However, from the perspective of slaves, the utopia for the masters is their hell.

A utopia for some can be a dystopia for others. Moreover, the frightening aspect of utopia is that escape is not allowed. If escape were permitted, utopia could not be sustained. In reality, utopia for a few thrives on the dystopias of many. Recently,

Table 28.1 Premises and beliefs in incrementalism and revolutionism

Incrementalism	*Revolutionism*
Partial and gradual policy	Comprehensive and speedy policy
Emphasis on process and consensus	Emphasis on results and ideology
Accept the limitations of leaders	Assume the rationality of leaders
Accept learning from failure	Assume Infallibility without learning
Adaptation to reality	Denial of reality

a documentary film titled "Beyond Utopia," directed by Madeleine Gavin, has shocked and moved many people. It chronicles the stories of individuals who escaped from North Korea, which they believed to be their utopia. Their stories are real. While the mother successfully escaped, her young son remains trapped in a political prison camp. The tragedy of utopia continues to unfold before the eyes of many people today.

Most utopian zealots adhere to the "doctrine of uniformity." They impose their utopia on others and do not tolerate anyone advocating ideas different from their own utopia. This leads politically to "totalitarianism." Totalitarianism eliminates those who do not conform to its ideals through the use of violence. Jacques Ellul criticizes all forms of violence. Revolutionary idealists who claim to realize utopia argue for the inevitability of violence.

> Invariably, an idealism serves to justify the use of violence.
>
> (Ellul 1969, p. 115)

However, all violence is fury and madness. All violence begets more violence, and violence can only be sustained by violence, with temporary violence solidifying into permanent violence.

The most representative form of revolutionism is Stalinism, named after Stalin, who ruled the Soviet Union for over three decades. Stalin's rule, which began in 1927 after Lenin, was brutal. Countless people were literally killed. Stalin labeled those obstructing his rule as "opportunists" and "counter-revolutionary infiltrators," and sent them to forced labor camps or subjected them to summary trials. This period, known as the "Great Purge," saw the deaths of up to one million people in the early 1930s.

Stalin radically reformed the economy. He abolished Lenin's mild economic policy and pursued a fully planned economy, known as a command economy. He transformed privately owned factories into state-owned ones and mobilized all resources to foster industrialization. Similarly, privately owned farmland was converted into collective farms. Excess labor from farms was transferred to factories. Initially, the Soviet industry was deemed successful in achieving rapid modernization. However, a major famine occurred from 1930 to 1933, resulting in the death of at least five million people.

Lastly, there was a cult of personality surrounding Stalin himself. He was referred to in the media as the "Father of the Nation," many streets and areas were renamed after him, and his birthday was commemorated nationwide. Within the atmosphere of personal worship and oppressive rule under Stalin, there was no room for dissenting opinions on government policies. The policies proposed by Stalin never failed to receive unanimous support. However, this unanimity support did not signify wholehearted endorsement but rather pervasive fear.

In such situations, when signs of policy failure appear, administrative officials become bewildered. Unacceptable failures occur, extending throughout society. However, most of the time, policy failures are concealed. Intellectuals who attempt to expose such failures are imprisoned and executed, as they are deemed counter-revolutionaries. This revolutionary approach renders learning impossible. Hidden failures give birth to even greater failures, ultimately resulting in the collapse of the ruling power. However, the problem extends beyond the collapse of the ruling power. By the time the ruling power collapses, the entire society is already filled with failures.

Revolutionary minds are often blinded by their passion, leading to shortsightedness. However, there are instances where revolutionary ideas have been advocated with moderation. One such case is the religious reformation of the 16th century. During that period, Luther's assertions were inherently radical, yet he did not endorse revolutionary extremism. Bridget Heal evaluates Luther's Reformation as follows.

> The pace of reform must, Luther argued, be gradual. For all the subversive potential of his theological insights, moderation became a hallmark of Luther's Reformation as it developed.
>
> (Heal 2017)

If Luther had insisted on revolutionary extremism, the religious reformation in Europe would have unfolded differently, possibly resulting in more sacrifices and even failure. Two thousand five hundred years ago, Lao-tzu wrote the following in China.

> Those who rise on tiptoe cannot stand.
> Those who stride cannot walk.
> (Chapter 24, Lao-tzu Around BC 500)

Part V

Futures of Social Science

Social science evolves in tandem with the times. The social science of an agricultural society cannot be the same as that of an industrial society. Present-day social science has been shaped by the characteristics of industrial society. Now, as the world transitions from an industrial society to an information society, social science is set to undergo further transformations. In this section, I will put forward some preliminary thoughts that might provide insights into what this transformation could entail.

The key to future societal change lies in the revival of communities. In the economic sphere, the market economy based on money is giving way to the platform economy based on networks, with digital communities playing a central role. Online communities demand more horizontal relationships in administration and call for a deliberative process in politics. As society evolves, so do the individuals within it. The paradigm of intellectuals in future society is transitioning from verbal thinkers to visual thinkers.

DOI: 10.4324/9781003464730-33

29 New Economics

Network Externality

In the mid-1990s, a cadre of economists introduced a novel branch of economics called "network economics" (Shapiro and Varian 1998). This novel approach diverged significantly from traditional economics. While traditional economics concentrated on market mechanisms, network economics downplayed the significance of markets. Instead, these economists focused on an entirely different phenomenon: "network externality." They termed goods that generate network externality as "network goods." Notable examples of network goods include social networking services (SNS) such as Facebook, X (Twitter), and Instagram. The growth mechanics of these network goods starkly differ from traditional market mechanisms. The term "network goods" essentially refers to "goods that derive considerable value through networks." Why is Instagram popular? Because it has a large user base. By joining Instagram, individuals can connect with numerous other users. The value of Instagram is rooted in its "user network." The demand for Instagram is determined by the "size of its user base." When the user base is large, demand increases, leading to a greater allure for new users, which in turn expands the user base. This phenomenon is known as "network effects."

Three key aspects of network effects should be noted. Firstly, network effects engender a "positive feedback loop." While traditional market mechanisms operate through negative feedback loops that seek equilibrium in both demand and supply, network effects are characterized by positive feedback loops that deviate from equilibrium and tend to amplify over time. Positive feedback loops can lead to either a "virtuous circle" or a "vicious circle."

The success or failure of network goods depends on the "size of the user base." In the software market, there was a rivalry between Microsoft's MS Word and Corel Corporation's WordPerfect. WordPerfect was once a formidable competitor to MS Word, especially during the 1980s and early 1990s. However, as MS Word gained widespread adoption, WordPerfect's user base dwindled. MS Word's user base became extensive and pervasive. Documents created in MS Word could be easily shared and printed anywhere. Despite WordPerfect's affordability and superior performance, users were hesitant to switch due to its smaller user base. Consequently, while MS Word entered a "virtuous circle," WordPerfect slipped into a "vicious circle."

The second attribute of network effects to consider is that they operate "outside the market." The expansion of social networking services (SNS) is driven by the

DOI: 10.4324/9781003464730-34

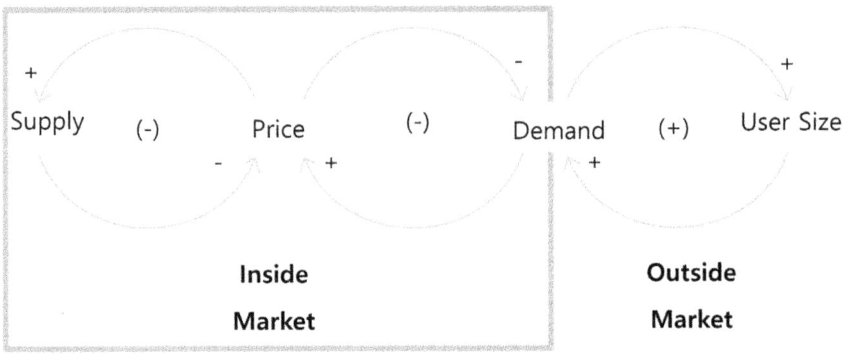

Figure 29.1 Network externality located outside the market.

"size of the user base," with the number of users serving as the pivotal factor. The "price" of using SNS is not crucial. Price does not impact the growth of network goods. Economists refer to this phenomenon as an "externality," as it exists outside the market. Hence, it is termed "network externality."

How much will network externality expand in this information age? In the industrial society, only a few goods displayed network externality. However, in the information society, nearly all goods and services can be classified as network goods. Mobile phones themselves qualify as network goods, and almost all applications running on mobile phones are network services. Computer software is also subject to the influence of network externalities. Even vehicles in modern times, with their connection to GPS and internet-based navigation systems, are susceptible to the power of network externalities.

An increasing number of goods and services are breaking free from market mechanism and coming under the influence of network externality. Will market functions persist in the information society? In an era where markets served as the cornerstone of the economy, any effects existing outside the market were labeled "externality" because of the market's centrality. However, in the information society, the market no longer holds such centrality. Hence, many scholars prefer the term "network effects" over "network externality" as there is no need to associate it with the market any longer.

Competition vs. Monopoly

The third hallmark of network effects is their "monopolistic" nature. In markets dominated by network effects, service providers often maintain a monopolistic stance. This is linked to the first characteristic; service providers who leverage positive feedback loops tend to emerge as dominant entities. In the IT sector of the information age, monopolistic corporations are easily identifiable. Microsoft with its Windows operating system, Google with YouTube, Facebook, and Instagram, all possess near-monopolistic statuses.

Monopolies were rare in the markets of industrial society. Economic textbooks from the industrial era regarded monopolies as market failures. Indeed, even in the United States, a stronghold of capitalism, monopolistic companies were subjected to disintegration. In 1911, the US Supreme Court mandated the breakup of Standard Oil, a Rockefeller-owned behemoth in the oil industry. Similarly, in 1982, the US government enforced the breakup of AT&T, the world's largest telecommunications company, on account of its monopoly. Monopolistic companies were seen as obstacles to market competition and as harmful to consumers. In industrial society, "competition" was celebrated as the highest virtue, while "monopoly" was condemned as a symbol of market failure.

The resource allocation mechanism of the market adheres to the principle of competition. However, there are cases where free competition suppresses competition. The market concentrates resources on a small number of highly competitive entities. Through the market competition mechanism, competitive companies acquire more resources and become more competitive. This is known as the "rich get richer" mechanism. It is the reason why big corporations emerge in capitalist societies. The market mechanism in capitalist societies enables the growth of capital through capital accumulation. However, capital-deficient companies lose to companies with abundant capital in market competition. While a few companies enjoy a virtuous cycle, many companies fall into a vicious cycle.

In the industrial age, such cycles were exceptional, but in the network economy, they are normal and even general. Economist Brian Arthur, who contributed to the formation of modern complexity theory, describes this as an "economy with increasing returns." He states as follows:

> Conventional economic theory is built on the assumption of diminishing returns … The parts of the economy that are knowledge-based, on the other hand, are largely subject to increasing returns. Products such as computers, pharmaceuticals, missiles, aircraft, automobiles, software, telecommunications equipment, or fiber optics are complicated to design and to manufacture. They require large initial investments in research, development, and tooling, but once sales begin, incremental production is relatively cheap.
>
> (Arthur 1990, pp. 92–93)

In the world of increasing returns, competition is limited. Established companies in the market can provide software to consumers without charging any money. It is almost impossible for new companies to enter the market.

In the information society, monopolies are no longer viewed with disdain. If the presence of monopolies is regarded as a market failure, then a majority of the information society's market should be deemed a failure. This presents a conundrum for scholars adhering to industrial-era economics. Some scholars persist in castigating dominant IT companies as malevolent entities that ought to be disassembled. It is crucial to acknowledge the rapid evolution of the times. A principle that social scientists must bear in mind is that "if theory and reality are at odds, then the theory is flawed." Many intellectuals berate reality for not conforming to their theoretical ideals. However, reality should not be assailed merely because it deviates from theory. Instead, theories that fail to explicate reality deserve criticism.

Platform Economy

As the network economy evolves, network externality is observed not only in the demand sector but also in the supply sector. It is a mechanism where the value increases as more suppliers gather. This is commonly referred to as the platform economy. Founded in 2009, Uber started as a ridesharing service company and quickly grew into a global enterprise. Uber serves as a matchmaker, connecting drivers and commuters. The network externality of Uber occurs in both the demand and supply sides. The more commuters use Uber and the more drivers join Uber, the more attractive Uber becomes.

Online food delivery applications also fall under the platform economy. The more customers ordering food and the more restaurants joining the platform, the higher the value of the food delivery platform. However, there is one additional economic agent involved here: the deliverers who transport the food. Between 2020 and 2022, during the COVID-19 pandemic when visiting public restaurants became difficult, food delivery platforms experienced explosive growth.

Uber is also viewed from the perspective of the sharing economy. Around 2010, the sharing economy gained prominence as a new business model, rapidly expanding to include various sectors such as office sharing, house sharing, and bike sharing. The usage time of vehicles or office spaces by owners is not extensive. The motto of the sharing economy is to maximize profits by allowing others to utilize assets during the owner's idle time. The sharing economy has garnered interest and support from many intellectuals.

However, I had a pessimistic view of the future of the sharing economy. Especially concerning office-sharing services, there are physical limitations. When more users seek to share offices, more may be rejected due to the physical constraints of space. This is true for the supply side of sharing economy as well; the more suppliers participate, the more idle time they face. Eventually, the network effects of the sharing economy unfold in a self-defeating manner.

The sharing economy and the network economy are distinct. The driving force behind the network economy is network externality or network effect. The platform economy generates network effects in both the demand and supply sectors. The presence of numerous users and diverse suppliers becomes the source of value. This reflects the nature of online communities, where people attract people. The new economy in the information society is transitioning from markets to communities.

What destiny awaits traditional economics in the information society? Hitherto, traditional economics has reigned supreme in the realm of social sciences, with economists monopolizing the prestige of the Nobel Prize. However, the crux of the matter lies in the fact that this economics is predicated upon market mechanisms. In the information society, where market dominance is substantially weakened, will traditional economics face obsolescence? This is the most pressing and significant question that social scientists must grapple with in the future.

30 Revival of Community

In agricultural societies, the cornerstone was farmland, while industrial societies revolved around factories. In contrast, the information society is structured around information networks. In agricultural society, family units engaged in farming were of paramount importance. The area of community, composed of families, villages, and kinship groups, held significant weight in agricultural society. On the other hand, industrial societies valued entrepreneurs who established factories and the laborers they employed. Merchants who marketed the products as well as consumers who bought them were also vital players. Consequently, industrial society was anchored in the economic domain. As society evolved from agricultural to industrial, the emphasis shifted from the community to the economy.

Iron Triangle in Industrial Society

In industrial society, the influence of communities was significantly diminished. Policy analysts introduced the concept of the "iron triangle," which highlights the strong interrelationships among three sectors: politics, administration, and the economy. Through standing committees in the National Assembly, close ties are formed among politicians, administrators, and business leaders. Within this framework, policies cutting corporate taxes are formulated by administrators, endorsed as legislation by politicians, and reciprocated by corporations supporting politicians and administrators with their profits. The iron triangle facilitates the implementation of policies, laws, and budgets that benefit businesses within the economic sector. Typically, communities are noticeably absent from the iron triangle, relegated to the periphery in industrial society.

According to C. Wright Mills' famous book *Power Elite*, elites from the economic, political, and military domains in the United States form higher circles and monopolize immense power. The power elites identified by Mills represent a formidable iron triangle of industrial society.

> In the structural sense, this triangle of power is the source of the interlocking directorate that is most important for the historical structure of the present … At the pinnacle of each of the three enlarged and centralized domains, there have arisen those higher circles which make up the economic, the political, and the military elites.
>
> (Mills 1956, pp. 12–13)

DOI: 10.4324/9781003464730-35

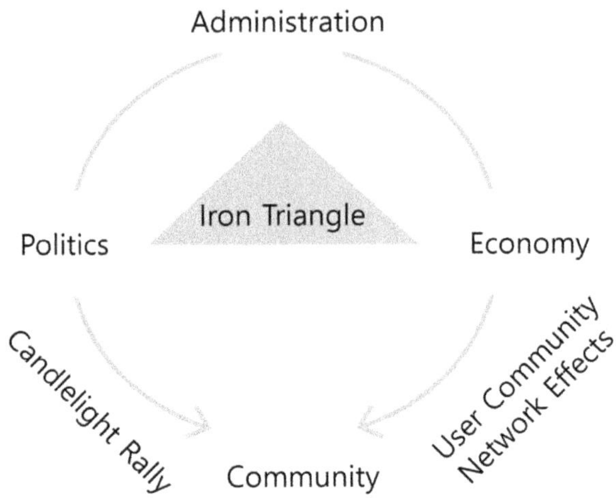

Figure 30.1 Iron triangle among economy, politics, and administration.

Power of Online Community

In the modern information society, market mechanisms no longer wield the same influence as they did in the industrial era. Instead, network effects, which extend beyond traditional market boundaries, are propelled by user communities. Communities are experiencing a resurgence in the form of social networks, facilitated by information networks and distinct from traditional familial, regional, or academic bonds. Through these networks, individuals share every aspect of their lives. As a result, the focal point of the economy is shifting from the market to the "community" in the information age.

A buzzword that epitomizes 21st-century Korean politics is the "Candlelight rally." This movement falls under the umbrella of community activism rather than traditional politics. It was sparked by a citizen's internet post suggesting a candlelit gathering to mourn for girls killed by an armored vehicle during military training, which quickly gained traction on online forums. The Candlelight rally thrives on positive feedback, as increasing participation leads to greater attention and further engagement. Subsequently, whenever social issues of concern arise in Korean society, Candlelight rallies have emerged. They have come to be accepted as channels for citizens to directly express their political opinions (Kim and Kim 2005).

The first Candlelight rally that ignited a political revolution took place in December 1989 in Timisoara, Romania. Laszlo Tokes, appointed as the Pastor of the church in Timisoara, openly criticized the dictator Nicolae Ceausescu, who had ruled Romania for 25 years. On December 15, 1989, the police attempted to arrest Pastor Tokes and his family, but hundreds of Christians and students in Timisoara formed a human chain to protect his house. As evening fell and darkness descended, concerned that participants might leave, 19-year-old Dan Gavra brought candles and distributed them to the participants. Lighting the candles, the crowd stayed all through the night – and the next night. This candlelight vigil ultimately led to the fall of the dictatorship, and Ceausescu and his wife were executed on December 25. Romania regained its freedom, just 10 days after the candles were lit.

As we transition into the information age, communities are evolving into online communities. Previously, membership in a community was largely restricted to those who were geographically close. Now, communities once tied to physical locations are migrating to cyberspace. In the early 21st century, the inception of online communities began with blogs hosted on websites. The term "blog" is a blend of "web" and "log," where individuals with shared interests visited these platforms to exchange greetings and share news. Over time, online communities expanded through platforms like Facebook and KakaoTalk, utilizing messenger services, as well as YouTube and TikTok, leveraging video-based platforms. By 2022, Facebook alone boasted over three billion monthly active users, indicating that more than half of the global population is part of online communities.

Online communities have played a significant role in revitalizing communities that have waned physically. Especially during the Covid-19 period from 2020 to 2022, there was a notable surge in the development of online communities. Students attended classes through online video conferences, and worship services, regardless of the congregation's size, were conducted online. Various performances also took place via online concerts. While not identical to gathering in the same physical space, nearly everyone experienced that online communities could serve as substitutes for physical ones.

Communities in the information age differ greatly from those in the industrial age. In the industrial era, communities were scattered across the societal landscape. However, in the information age, online communities are closely interconnected through information networks, facilitating real-time exchange of views and emotions. Online communities in the information age are tightly interconnected and wield significant capital, with more funds flowing in through funding and advertising on social networking services (SNS). Simultaneously, online communities evolve into centers of political movements and gatherings, capable of bypassing physical constraints to spread political messages and quickly gather supporters. In the information society, online communities expand their domains into the realms of economy and politics.

In agricultural society, the focal point was the community consisting of families and rural collectives engaged in agriculture. In the industrial society, the business in the realm of the economy took the central place of society. Nowadays, in the information society, the focal point is gravitating towards online communities that are intertwined through information networks and possess abundant economic and political resources. In the information society, all networks converge into communities. Through these networks of communities, political messages are disseminated, and economic activities are interconnected. Ultimately, communities are awakening from centuries of dormancy and moving from the periphery to the center of society.

31 New Relationship between Community and Administration

The relationship between administration and community has a long history. In fact, administration and community might have once been indistinguishable. In the beginning, Adam and Eve's household in the Garden of Eden essentially constituted a nation. The term "nation(國家)" in Chinese characters combines the words for "state(國)" and "house(家)." In agricultural society, administration resided near the community, while in industrial society, administration moved away from communities and aligned with corporations in the realm of economy. With the revival of communities as a potent focal point in the information society, it is imperative to redefine the relationship between administration and community. Administration must acknowledge and engage with the community as a driving force of the future society.

Administration does interact with communities every day and night. However, the interaction between administration and citizens remains somewhat strained. The administration cannot accommodate all residents' opinions, and citizens often find policies unsatisfactory. Both administration and citizens are aware of this situation, making their interactions perpetually strained.

In 2008, I visited Professor Chung's cottage along with Professor Yoon. As we were resting in the tranquil beauty of the forest, Professor Chung abruptly inquired about my recent thoughts. I will recount our conversation here.

Kim: I believe it's time for us to contemplate the essence of administration. In my opinion, the essence of administration is "waiting." This notion has resonated with me for a long time. Waiting is a ubiquitous approach in the public sector.

Chung: To me, the essence of administration is "meeting" – but not just any meeting, a heartfelt embracing. I believe that at the core of the concept of "humanity(仁)" in Confucianism is meeting. We need genuine, warm interactions between public officials and citizens, as well as between superiors and subordinates.

Yoon: The term that comes to my mind is "empty." Nowadays, when you visit public spaces, there seems to be an incessant compulsion to fill them with something. I think that leaving public spaces empty is imperative. This emptiness can broaden the spectrum of possibilities for future generations.

DOI: 10.4324/9781003464730-36

Following this dialogue, we delved deeper into the roles of "empty-wait-meet" within administration. In English, there are no precise counterparts for our concepts of "empty-wait-meet." Many scholars consider these concepts to be nonacademic terms. Even most politicians and administrators are oblivious to them. However, if you search for "empty-wait-meet" on internet platforms in the East Asian region, a plethora of information surfaces. This indicates that "empty, wait, and meet" are deeply ingrained in Asian culture.

To restore relationships between administration and communities in the future, we must recall the essence of their relationship. After thorough discussion, we concluded that "empty-wait-meet" represents the ancient archetype of their relations. Therefore, this could serve as a guiding principle to replace the iron triangle of the industrial age that alienated communities. It does not necessitate intricate theories. Simply conveying "empty, wait, and meet" to administration and communities is sufficient. To adhere to this guideline, administration and communities should keep open minds and tolerate each other. Meaningful interactions between administration and communities can be fostered in the future through this approach.

After discussing the concept of "empty-wait-meet," I began to ponder the origins of these ideas. The origin of "empty" was straightforward to pinpoint, as Professor Yoon has a penchant for Buddhism and Taoism. Additionally, Professor Chung, who stressed "meet," indicated that the Chinese character for "humanity(仁)" in Confucianism represents the meeting of two individuals. The concept of "meet" has roots in Confucianism's understanding of human relationships.

However, the origin of the concept of "wait" which I highlighted as significant posed a challenge. What was the genesis of the idea of waiting? Undoubtedly, my focus on waiting comes from the essence of administration, which is "queuing." While the objective aspect of administration is queuing, the subjective experience of queuing is waiting. But I thought there should be a deeper philosophical ground

Figure 31.1 Horizontal relationship between administration and the community: principle of empty-wait-meet.

for waiting. After several weeks of study, I found that Zhu Xi, the founder of Neo-Confucianism, encapsulated the philosophy of the "I Ching" with two Chinese characters "待對" meaning "waiting opposite." Most Eastern philosophers interpreted his words as emphasizing harmony with opposite people. However, what captivated me was the first character "待," which means "waiting." Men wait for women, and women wait for men. Allies wait for enemies, and enemies wait for allies. This is central to the philosophy of the "I Ching," which deals with the changes in the world. The core of the I Ching philosophy is "waiting opposite."

Integration of Eastern thoughts

Subsequently, I dedicated a significant amount of time to organizing Eastern thought. Through this process, I discovered that Eastern thought can be categorized into three dimensions: time, space, and humanity. I also realized that this categorization is linked to the concepts we discussed: "empty-wait-meet." Additionally, I found that these concepts are interconnected with another aspect of the Eastern worldview, which involves three elements and three behaviors. I compiled this into a table and named it "Three layers of Eastern thoughts and perspectives", which is described below.

The first layer pertains to heaven. Heaven's will is invisible, but, like the flow of time, it inevitably comes true. What people can do regarding the heaven is predicting. The rising of the sun is an inevitable law of heaven, and therefore, it can be predicted and waited for. The philosophy that deals with these ideas is the "I Ching."

The second layer belongs to Earth. The empty places on Earth are referred to as space. The mountains, rivers, flowers, and trees existing in these spaces are called nature. Nature moves naturally. It is natural for humans to do nothing. This philosophy is called Taoism. Taoism shares with Buddhism the concept of nothing (無).

The third layer deals with humans. The most significant relationships for individuals are those with other humans. Human relations are influenced by random accidents, which can lead to various outcomes. Random accidents may result in the development of love between individuals, but they can also escalate into conflicts among them. Confucianism established a set of rules and etiquettes to manage random accidents in human relations.

Table 31.1 Three layers of Eastern thoughts and perspectives

	Eastern thought	*Key concept*	*Three betweens*	*Three elements*	*Three behaviors*
Wait	I Ching	待對 Wait Opposite	時間 Time	天 Heaven	必然 Inevitable
Empty	Taoism	無爲 Do Nothing	空間 Space	地 Earth	自然 Natural
Meet	Confucianism	仁禮 Humanity	人間 People	人 Human	偶然 Accidental

It's noteworthy that Confucianism focuses solely on human relationships without paying attention to heaven and earth (Chung 2021), whereas Taoism disregards human society, and the "I Ching" pays little attention to the earth. Eastern thought is hierarchically compartmentalized – Confucianism focusing on human relationships, Taoism on the empty space of nature, and the "I Ching" on the time of heaven.

The "three-between" worldview of "time-space-people (時間-空間-人間)" is considered to have been developed by the Chinese. The Chinese character "間" means "between," picturing an open door. Fundamentally, "between" signifies a relationship itself. People exist in the vacant space that exists between walls. People act within the time period that lies between past, present, and future. People live within human relations that emerge between man and woman, between elder and young, and between superior and subordinate. With the "three-between" worldview, the Chinese have developed a culture of "guanxi(關係)" that emphasizes human relations of mutual respect and benefit, even in the realm of business.

The "three-element" worldview of "heaven-earth-human (天地人)" is believed to have originated in Korea. King Sejong, who created the Korean characters in the 15th century, designed the shapes of Korean characters according to the idea of "heaven-earth-human". This worldview has been deeply rooted and spread throughout Korean culture and philosophy.

The "three-behavior" worldview of "inevitable-natural-accidental (必然-自然-偶然)" is somewhat ambiguous in terms of its origin. It may be associated with Japanese culture, which emphasizes the virtuous meaning and beauty of behavior. However, no concrete evidence has been found to support this claim. In relation to this concept, I introduce students to a famous Japanese poem collected by Matsura Seizan in the 19th century. This poem encapsulates the different leadership styles of three warlords who unified Japan in the 16th century.

If a bird does not sing, just kill it.
If a bird does not sing, make it sing.
If a bird does not sing, wait it to sing.

"The bird that does not sing" refers to a soldier who refuses to fight in war. The first line refers to the legalistic strategy of Oda Nobunaga. His adherence to the legal punishment mirrors the inevitable behavior of the first layer. The second line refers to Toyotomi Hideyoshi, who used incentives to motivate soldiers to fight. His approach resembles Confucian efforts to manage accidental behavior of individuals. The third line refers to Tokugawa Ieyasu and illustrates his patient and strategic waiting until his soldiers are ready to fight. His strategy involves "doing nothing" until the soldiers naturally develop their will to fight.

Among the three strategies, the most superior is the waiting approach of Tokugawa Ieyasu, who became the first shogun of a completely unified Japan. The waiting approach is not weak but strong. Waiting is an effective attitude applied not only toward heaven but also to subordinates. Likewise, "empty-wait-meet" can be applied to all kinds of social relations, especially the relationship between administration and communities.

32 New Relationship between Community and Politics

The revival of communities transforms politics. The premise of politics is the silence of communities. Politics claims to represent the voice of the community because the community cannot speak for itself. This is the underlying premise of representative democracy. Now, armed with the internet, smartphones, and social media, communities can raise their own voices. Communities can directly convey their voices to the administration. Through the internet, citizens can vote on policy options in real time, often without incurring significant costs.

On the other hand, there has been accumulated dissatisfaction with traditional politics. Despite the emergence of numerous communities advocating various values in modern society, the political world is still dominated by a binary system of progressivism and conservatism. It is evident that politics cannot adequately represent the diverse values of communities in a numeric sense. Ross Ashby introduced the "law of requisite variety" in his cybernetics. He stated as follows:

> The law of requisite variety says that politics' capacity as a regulator cannot exceed politics' capacity as a channel of communication.
>
> (Ashby 1956, p. 211)

We can consider politics as a mechanism that regulates administration according to the values of the community. The law of requisite variety implies that politics cannot adequately represent the values of communities when the number of channels is less than the diversity of the communities.

Entering the 21st century, significant issues such as carbon emissions and climate change, nuclear power development, regulation of artificial intelligence, and global refugee acceptance have emerged. These issues defy classification within the traditional framework of progressivism and conservatism. Faced with these challenging issues, politics has lost its way in terms of determining which direction to take. Citizens of communities also hesitate regarding which party to vote for. Politics has become a massive barrier blocking communication between communities and administration, rather than serving as a channel for conveying the community's will to the administration.

In this situation, a change in politics was called for. The new mode of politics that emerged is deliberative democracy or discursive democracy, sometimes referred to as DD for short. DD involves careful but open discussion on public issues through

DOI: 10.4324/9781003464730-37

deliberative processes within the community. Unlike traditional representative democracy, where all political issues are delegated to the parliament through one-time elections, DD allows for ongoing dialogue and engagement within the community.

DD is different from direct democracy. While direct democracy presupposes the demise of representative democracy, DD coexists with the traditional indirect way of democracy. It is a method of entrusting policy issues that are difficult to address to the careful deliberation of the community. If direct democracy is seen as revolutionary reform, then DD can be regarded as incremental experimentation. Applying direct democracy to all public issues can lead to social chaos. The greater risk of direct democracy is the potential loss of control over administration. Unchecked administration, armed with formidable physical power and information, can easily control the masses. Therefore, DD is considered a safer approach to new democracy with rejuvenated communities.

Public Spheres of Habermas

The theoretical foundation of deliberative democracy is the "public sphere," emphasized by Jürgen Habermas. According to Habermas, the public sphere may be conceived above all "as the sphere of private people for public discourse against public authorities" (Habermas 1962, p. 27). He later defines it as follows.

> By the public sphere, we mean first of all a realm of our social life in which something approaching public opinion can be formed.
>
> (Habermas 1964, p. 49)

The "public sphere" refers to a communal space where individuals from the private area come together to discuss public issues and request new policies from the government, i.e., public authorities. The "public sphere" exists at the boundary between private and public areas. While Habermas often uses the term "bourgeois

Figure 32.1 Deliberative democracy with the public sphere in the realm of community.

public sphere" to describe the modern public sphere, it is closer to the "citizen public sphere" belonging to the community area rather than the economic area. His "public sphere" is a private assembly that exists within the community area while discussing public issues.

The "public sphere" takes place in the salons, coffee houses, or table parties of the town. Although its form and scale vary, all public spheres share three common institutional criteria (Habermas 1962, pp. 36–37). First, participants in the public sphere are equal. Individual status, wealth, or profession is not important. Second, there is no limit on areas of public concern. For example, there are no restrictions stating that issues such as abortion must be addressed by religious figures or that nuclear energy issues must be left to scientists' analysis. All public concerns can be raised. Third, the public sphere is open and inclusive to all people. Blocking specific types of people would lead to the loss of the publicness and result in a clique.

> The issues discussed became general not merely in their significance, but also in their accessibility; everyone had to be able to participate.
>
> (Habermas 1962, p. 37)

However, in modern society, the public sphere is shrinking. Habermas introduces C. W. Mills' discussion on the difference between "public" and "mass". In a "public" assembly, many people speak, there is a two-way discussion, it is connected to public action, and it possesses autonomy free from state interference. Conversely, in a "mass" meeting, the masses listen to the opinions of elites, messages are delivered in one direction, they are subject to state control, and they lose autonomy (Habermas 1962, p. 249). In modern mass media society where newspapers and broadcasting dominate the media landscape, the public sphere is shrinking. The emergence of the social-welfare state, in addition to the spread of mass media, further diminishes the role of the public sphere. The influence of mass media has stripped the public sphere of its role in raising public issues, while the social-welfare state has strengthened the control of state authorities over public concerns. Consequently, the role of the public sphere has been diminished.

To restore the role of the public sphere in modern society, Habermas proposed the "intraorganizational public sphere." He stated as follows.

> In contrast to this, under conditions of the large democratic social-welfare state, the communicative interconnectedness of a public can be brought about only in this way through a critical publicity brought to life within intraorganizational public spheres, the completely short-circuited circulation of quasi-public opinion must be linked to the informal domain of the hitherto nonpublic opinions.
>
> (Habermas 1962, pp. 249–250)

Habermas does not provide a specific outline for the "intraorganizational public sphere." Perhaps citizen groups in the community area could provide a small and autonomous public sphere. However, Habermas did not anticipate the unlimited power of communication networks provided by modern information technology. In the 21st century, social digital networks allow many people to engage in two-way discussions while maintaining autonomy free from state interference. Now, social networks surpass mass media in shaping public opinions. As this communicative power of communities deals with public issues, the restoration of the public sphere as envisioned by Habermas may occur.

Looking back over the past century, the central public sphere in Korean society has moved from churches to colleges, and then to internet forums. During the era of Japanese rule, the independence movement was primarily discussed in churches. As Korean society industrialized after the end of Japanese rule, the public sphere shifted to colleges, where free debate was ensured. With the emergence of the information society in the 21st century, sympathy for social minorities was primarily discussed and disseminated on internet forums. The Candlelight rally, which had a significant impact on politics, began on internet forums. As the location of public spheres shifted, the composition of participants also changed. In the early 20th century, the independence movement was led by Protestant Christians in churches, while democratization movements have been led by college students. In the 21st century, the Candlelight rallies spread among netizens sharing posts on internet forums.

Deliberative Wave

In 2020, the OECD published a report titled "*Innovative Citizen Participation and New Democratic Institutions – Catching the Deliberative Wave*," noting the global spread of deliberative democracy. They documented 282 cases of deliberative processes in OECD member countries observed from 1986 to 2019. Particularly since 2010, there has been a significant increase in citizen participation aimed at representative deliberative democracy.

> Across the globe, public authorities are increasingly using representative deliberative processes to involve citizens more directly in solving some of the most pressing policy challenges.
>
> (OECD 2020)

The OECD report summarizes three common characteristics of deliberative democracy that appear across various forms of citizen participation. First, deliberative processes are carefully designed and provided. This includes weighing different options carefully, which requires accurate and relevant information and a diversity of perspectives. Second, participants in deliberative processes must represent a wide cross-section of society. Finally, the process must have an impact on policymaking, meaning it was initiated by a public authority (OECD 2020).

The OECD report forecasts that deliberative democracy will continue to spread in the future. Particularly, it suggests that deliberative democracy can be effectively applied when public policy decisions are stalled due to value-driven dilemmas leading to political deadlock. Establishing a public sphere for discussing difficult choices, ensuring citizens' freedom of discussion and choice, and making all proceedings public are proposed. Politicians and administrators can not only escape from deadlock at a lower cost but also gain greater legitimacy to make hard choices.

In 2017, a national-level experiment on deliberative democracy was conducted in South Korea, focusing on whether to fulfill the presidential pledge to halt nuclear power generation. Particularly, the debate centered on the nuclear power plant construction project that had commenced a year earlier. On one side, there were arguments advocating for the cessation of nuclear power plant construction to mitigate the risks associated with nuclear energy. On the other hand, there were opinions supporting the continuation of construction, citing the substantial investment already made and the need for economic development in the local community. This conflict extended beyond the local community to the national level. Ultimately, conflicting viewpoints emerged between those advocating for the complete cessation of nuclear power generation and those arguing for the continued maintenance of nuclear power.

To resolve such conflicts, the government decided to utilize a deliberative democracy process. A group of 471 citizens was selected based on regional, occupational, and age demographics, and a Public Opinion Committee was formed. The citizen participants were provided with extensive information in various formats regarding arguments both for and against halting nuclear power generation. Over a period of two nights and three days, they engaged in intensive discussions, which were broadcast nationwide on public television. The process commenced on July 24, 2017, and lasted for about three months until October 20 of the same year, during which four rounds of surveys were conducted. After a long process of deliberation, 57.2% of the 471 participants in the final survey indicated their support for resuming the construction of nuclear plants. The President of South Korea promptly accepted the committee's recommendation while still adhering to his gradual nuclear phase-out policy.

The experiment of deliberative democracy left most citizens disappointed. Progressive citizens were disappointed with the policy direction drawn by the Public Opinion Committee. Conservative citizens, on the other hand, generally did not welcome the deliberative democracy process itself. In Korean society, there is a negative memory of the People's Court, which was utilized to execute landlords, officials, and their families without legal basis. Conservative citizens with these memories did not have positive expectations for the Public Opinion Committee. While conservative citizens doubted the rationality of the deliberative democracy process, progressive citizens were not satisfied with its outcomes. Since then, deliberative democracy has not received much attention in Korean society. A new deliberative democracy process is needed that satisfies both conservative and progressive perspectives. Perhaps the power of social digital networks in the information society will contribute to forming a new form of the public sphere with critical rationality.

33 New Wine in New Wineskin

Visual Thinkers

The first chapter of this book emphasizes society emerging beyond the individual human. In the last chapter of this book, I would like to return to the individual human being. In the information and communication society of the 21st century, a new kind of human is emerging. These new individuals, in turn, change society as a whole. One of the most important characteristics of the newly transformed individuals in the information society is their ability for visual thinking.

For thousands of years, intellectuals who have dominated human civilization have been proficient in language. Using Toynbee's terminology, these linguistic thinkers have played the role of the "creative minority," leading the development of human civilization. Now, these linguistic thinkers have become a "dominant minority" instead. They dominate not with creative thinking but with linguistic dogma. The slogans politicians shout, the legal dogma relied upon by jurists, and the fashionable catchphrases of business consultants are all closer to the brutal forces of the dominant minority. Society is now ruled by linguistic thinkers who no longer think creatively. In this day and age, visual thinkers are emerging, offering creative ideas and fulfilling the role of the "creative minority." Understanding this emerging "creative minority" may allow us to anticipate the future of a new civilization. As Jesus Christ said, "new wine must be put into new wineskins, and both are preserved" (Luke 5:38, NKJV).

As society rapidly transitions from agricultural to industrial, and presently to an informational epoch, the archetype of the intellectual is evolving accordingly. In agricultural societies, literacy was a hallmark of intellectuality. During the industrial era, technological proficiency was highly valued. In contemporary information societies, there is a paradigmatic shift redefining the concept of what constitutes an intellectual.

It is intriguing to note that the transition from an agricultural to an industrial society did not significantly alter the conception of intellectuals. Literacy remained the cornerstone of intellectualism, supplemented by the emergence of skilled technicians who were previously marginalized as craftsmen in agricultural societies. "Verbal thinking," characterized by proficiency in language and rhetoric, continued to be the dominant intellectual mode.

However, the advent of the information society has begun to transform the concept of intellectuals. This transformation stems from an epistemological shift in the modality of knowledge processing. Intellectuals in the information age are

DOI: 10.4324/9781003464730-38

increasingly characterized not by proficiency in "verbal thinking," but by mastery in "visual thinking." This marks a tectonic shift as the traditional association of intellectualism with eloquence and oratory, entrenched for several millennia, is supplanted by a focus on the ability to distill complex ideas into visual representations.

The turning point from verbal thinking to visual thinking emerged with the introduction of PowerPoint in the late 1990s. Originally launched as software for Macintosh computers in 1987, it expanded to the Windows system in 1990. The mode of intellectual activity is differentiated before and after PowerPoint. In the era before PowerPoint, social scientists conveyed their knowledge through speeches delivered in a manner akin to reading a text. However, following the advent of PowerPoint, knowledge dissemination by social scientists shifted from speeches to presentations. Presentations involve displaying images in front of an audience, serving as a powerful means of conveying knowledge. Even before PowerPoint, a few social scientists used overhead projectors for presentations. However, after PowerPoint, almost all intellectuals transmit their knowledge through presentations rather than speeches. From scholarly seminars and policy briefings for government officials to strategic meetings for corporate executives, political briefings for politicians, and labor union reports, nearly all intellectual communications are conducted through presentations. Those who insist on delivering speeches instead of presentations at such meetings are considered to lack socialization in the information society.

Verbal thinking entails processing thoughts through words and is associated with linear modes of cognition through reading and listening. It has long been the hallmark of human civilization. In contrast, visual thinking involves cognition through images and visual stimuli. The human eye, capable of "parallel processing," can assimilate a plethora of information simultaneously, unlike the ear's "sequential processing." Therefore, visual thinking facilitates the rapid assimilation of information.

In early human civilization, pictorial representations such as cave paintings served as the primary mode of information recording. However, with the emergence of writing, a significant civilizational transformation occurred, enabling the precise recording and transmission of knowledge. Writing quickly became the cornerstone of education and intellectual thought. This era can be aptly described as a "civilization of literacy," symbolized by the Chinese character for civilization (文明), which signifies "the enlightenment through the literacy."

Table 33.1 Differences between verbal thinking and visual thinking

Verbal thinking	*Visual thinking*
Language	Image
Ears	Eyes
Serial thinking	Parallel thinking
Vertical perspective	Horizontal perspective
Traditional intellectuals	Emerging intellectuals
Speech	Presentation

These distinctions have evolved into visual culture and oral culture within the realm of art. Visual culture has flourished through the works of painters and architects, while oral culture, or writing culture, has progressed through literature and music. Technological advancements have driven the evolution of these cultural forms. Revolutionary innovations that significantly advanced visual culture include photography and broadcasting. These technologies have democratized art culture, bringing it from the exclusive domain of a few to the everyday lives of ordinary people. Technological innovations that propelled oral culture include the printing revolution and recording technology. Gutenberg's printing revolution fostered widespread literacy, facilitating religious reformations. Visual culture and oral culture are not merely individual phenomena; they are formidable forces shaping the trajectory of human civilization.

The emergence of the information society is shaking the core of the "writing civilization." The widespread adoption of imaging technologies and the omnipresence of visual media have diminished the centrality of writing in information dissemination. The simplicity of vivid information conveyed through visual media has highlighted the limitations of language-based communication, making it seem somewhat outdated.

Social Relations of Visual Thinking

Within the context of verbal intellectualism, oratory has traditionally been a prominent medium for articulating thoughts. However, in contemporary times, formal speeches are largely reserved for heads of states and corporate leaders. Oratory, once a vital instrument for those in positions of power to guide and reprimand their subordinates, is waning in the information society. In an era that celebrates horizontal diversity, traditional speeches are perceived as outdated relics. The prevailing mode of knowledge dissemination now relies on presentations that utilize simple and vivid imagery. These presentations do not stifle free thinking but rather encourage creative thinking in a nonhierarchical setting.

While text fosters a linear and hierarchical mode of thought, diagrams encourage a more collaborative and horizontal way of thinking. Within the paradigm of verbal communication, when one person speaks, many others must listen passively. Verbal communication is fundamentally one-way and results in vertical relationships, where the speaker dictates and the listener complies. Such a paradigm often discourages alternative interpretations. In contrast, images and diagrams allow for diverse interpretations, fostering communication on equal footing. When presenting visual slides, individuals can focus on different parts of the slides as they wish. Visual thinking facilitates diverse interpretations and fosters an intellectual environment that is more egalitarian and emancipated.

Speech in verbal thinking serves as a mode of knowledge transmission that delivers teachings and commands from top to bottom, suitable for hierarchical organizations. In contrast, presentations in visual thinking are a mode of knowledge dissemination conducive to the free exchange of ideas in horizontal organizations. In hierarchical organizations, commands flow from top to bottom through written documents. In team organizations, however, ideas are shared through visual presentations.

According to Habermas' logic, verbal thinking corresponds to the mode of mass media, while visual thinking is suitable for the public sphere. If speech is the primary mode of communication in elections of representative democracy, visual thinking is appropriate for conducting deliberative discussions in the public sphere. Especially, the future public spheres will be vastly different from traditional ones. Lengthy speeches on public issues are no longer effective means of communication. Instead, images accompanied by simple catchphrases will become the natural mode of communication in online public spheres.

Language possesses the characteristic of serial processing. It is difficult for verbal thinking to process many words simultaneously. However, images have the characteristic of parallel processing. In fact, most images presuppose multiple existences. Light presupposes darkness, and the foreground presupposes the background. An image reveals its essence in relation to other images. Trees in the mountains, for example, reveal themselves in the context of their relationship with the soil below, the sky above, and the other trees nearby. While language exists alone, images coexist in plurality. When discussed verbally, disputes often arise. However, when discussed through images, a peaceful coexistence is easily found. Verbal thinking has been a suitable intellectual paradigm for hierarchical, unequal, and aristocratic societies. The paradigm of visual thinking is required for the transformation of the information society into a horizontal and egalitarian society.

Examining historical precedents, Confucianism, which flourished in East Asia, esteemed the written word and emphasized verbal thinking. Confucianism aligned with a respect for hierarchy, and written culture played a key role in perpetuating this hierarchical order. In contrast, Buddhism was skeptical of language. Buddhists believed that habitual reliance on language hindered the attainment of true enlightenment. Buddhism even coined the phrase "No place for words" to signify a rejection of language.

The teachings of Buddhism emphasize enlightenment that transcends language. One of the most well-known anecdotes is the "Flower Sermon." When Buddha gives a sermon in the mountains, he delivers a wordless sermon. He holds up a white flower and presents it to the audience. No one in the audience understands the meaning of the Flower Sermon except for one disciple who smiles. Buddha's teaching has been transmitted to his smiling disciple. In Asia, Buddha's "flower sermon" is referred to as "拈華示衆", which means "to hold up and present a flower to people." Buddha's Flower Sermon is akin to a presentation of visual thinking.

In Asia, there is a similar teaching conveyed through the proverb "百聞不如一見", which means "hearing something a hundred times isn't better than seeing it once." A similar adage in the West is "A picture is worth a thousand words," which is used as an important lesson in designing advertising in modern society. The public did not pay attention to repeated warnings about the crisis of the Earth due to climate change. However, with just one photograph of a single polar bear on a tiny iceberg, the public became aware of everything. Similarly, a photograph depicting the lifeless body of a refugee child on a beach became a catalyst for raising awareness of the refugee tragedy worldwide. A photograph of a student killed by a tear gas canister led to the resignation of South Korea's president twice. In 1960, Kim Ju-Yeol was killed by a tear gas canister, and in 1987, Lee Han-Yeol suffered the same fate. Photographs of their deaths led to the resignation of the two presidents.

In the information society, visual thinking blurs the lines between intellectuals and nonintellectuals. When engaging with visual content, such as analyzing images or enjoying movies, the distinction between the two groups is hardly noticeable. However, when dealing with textual content, such as reading and analyzing a movie script, the gap becomes evident. Typically, those who can delve deep into a script are considered intellectuals who are well-versed in language. In contrast, this distinction fades when dealing with visuals. Visual thinking is helping to break down barriers, reducing discrimination and inequalities that have previously separated intellectuals from non-intellectuals. In agricultural societies, a minority of royalty and bureaucrats dominated society, while in industrial societies, an elite class emerged. Now, those leading the information society are visual thinkers. For the first time in human history, ordinary people with remarkable abilities in visual thinking are emerging as leaders, constituting the majority of the population.

A future society where visual thinking is prevalent will look different from what we see now. In such a society, people will have a more equal footing due to their shared ability to think and communicate visually. This equality could foster a sense of mutual respect, encouraging individuals to value each other's contributions across various segments of society. Visual thinkers will transform vertical societies into horizontal ones and even create true public spheres for deliberative democracy. However, visual thinking technologies will be a double-edged sword. There will be much more failures than we anticipate in the future. The point to bear in mind is that failure shapes new societies. Failure, not success, is the driving force behind shaping the future of society.

References

Abrahamson, E., 1996, "Management Fashion," *Academy of Management Review*, Vol. 21, pp. 254–285

Acemoglu, D., A. Robinson, 2012, *Why Nations Fail: The Origins of Power, Prosperity, and Poverty*, Crown Business.

Arendt, Hanna, 1963, *Eichmann in Jerusalem - A Report on the Banality of Evil*, The Viking Press.

Arthur, B., 1990, "Positive Feedbacks in the Economy," *Scientific American*, February 1, pp. 92–99.

Ashby, W. Ross, 1956, *An Introduction to Cybernetics,* Chapman & Hall.

Beveridge, W., 1942, "Social Insurance and Allied Services," Report presented to British Parliament, London.

Berger, P. L., T. Luckmann, 1966, *The Social Construction of Reality - A Treatise in the Sociology of Knowledge*, Penguin Books

Buber, M., 1923, *I and Thou*, translated by Walter Kaufmann 1970, Charles Scribner's Sons.

Burrell, G., G. Morgan, 1979, *Sociological Paradigms and Organisational Analysis – Elements of the Sociology of Corporate Life*, Heinemann. Published by Routledge in 1985.

Chung, Sung-Ho, 2021, *Korean Public Administration and Desire of Confucius*, Korean Language, Communications Books.

Confucius, Around B. C. 500, *Confucian Analects*, translated by James Legge, Project Gutenberg.

Downs, A., 1972, "Up and Down with Ecology - the Issue-Attention Cycle," *Public Interest*, Vol. 28, pp. 38–50.

Durkheim, E., 1895, *The Rules of Sociological Method*, translated by W. D. Halls in 1982, The Free Press.

Elliott, R. N., 1938, *The Wave Principle*, published 2012 by Snowball Publishing.

Ellul, Jacques, 1969, *Violence: Reflections from a Christian Perspective,* Seabury.

Elster, J., 1979, *Ulysses and the Sirens: Studies in Rationality and Irrationality*, Cambridge University Press.

Engels, Frederick, 1847, *The Principles of Communism*, translated by Paul Sweezy.

Forrester, J. W., 1961, *Industrial Dynamics*, Productivity Press.

Forrester, J. W., 1971, *World Dynamics*, Wright-Allen Press.

George, Henry, 1879, *Progress and Poverty: An Inquiry into the Cause of Industrial Depressions and of Increase of Want with Increase of Wealth - The Remedy*, 6th printing in 1934, Kingsport Press.

Glaser, B., A. Strauss, 1967, *Discovery of Grounded Theory*, Aldine Atherton.

Graeber, D., 2018, *Bullshit Jobs - A Theory*, Allen Lane.

Habermas, Jürgen, 1962, *The Structural Transformation of the Public Sphere- An Inquiry into a Category of Bourgeois Society*, translated by Thomas Burger in 1991, The MIT Press.

Habermas, Jürgen, 1964, "The Public Sphere: An Encyclopedia Article (1964)," translated by Sara Lennox and Frank Lennox in 1974, *New German Critique*, No. 3, pp. 49–55.
Han Fei, Around B. C., 240, *Han Feizi (韓非子)*, Project Gutenberg.
Harari, Y. N., 2015, *Sapiens: A Brief History of Humankind*, Harper Collins.
Harari, Y. N., 2018, *21 Lessons for the 21st Century*, Spiegel & Grau.
Hardin, G., 1968, "The Tragedy of the Commons," *Science*, Vol. 162, No. 3859, pp. 1243–1248.
Hatamura, Yotaro (畑村洋太郎), 2002, *Principles of Study of Failures (失敗学の法則)*, 文藝春秋, translated in Korean language by Yoon in 2004.
Hayek, F. A., 1945, "The Use of Knowledge in Society," *The American Economic Review*, Vol. 35, No. 4, pp. 519–530.
Heal, B. M., 2017, "Martin Luther and the German Reformation," *History Today*, Vol. 67, No. 3,pp.28-36.
Hobbes, Thomas, 1651, *Leviathan*, London.
Honneth, A., 1995, *The Struggle for Recognition - The Moral Grammar of Social Conflicts*, translated by Joel Anderson, The MIT Press.
Hume, D., 1739, *A Treatise of Human Nature*, edited by David F. Norton and Mary J. Norton in 2007, Oxford University Press.
Johnston, M., 2005, *Syndromes of Corruption: Wealth, Power, and Democracy*, Cambridge University Press.
Kim, Doa-Hoon, Tae-Hoon Moon, Dong-Hwan Kim, 1999, *System Dynamics*, Korean Language, Daeyoung-Munhwasa.
Kim, Dong-Hwan, 2004, *Systems Thinking*, Korean Language, Sunhaksa.
Kim, Dong-Hwan, 2016, *Big Data is a bubble*, Korean Language, Seoul: Paper Road.
Kim, Dong-Hwan, 2018, "Big Data Policy as a Fashion: Autoethnography as Personal Testimony of a Scholar," Korean Language, *Korea Public Administration Review*, Vol. 52, No. 1, pp. 3–25.
Kim, Dong-Hwan, 2022, *Essence of Social Science*, Korean Language, BOOKOREA.
Kim, Dong-Hwan, Hun-Sik Kim, 2005, *Social Mechanism of the Candlelight Movement*, Korean Language, BOOKOREA.
Kim, Jin-Hong, 2002, *A Desert Becomes a Garden: The Autobiography of Kim Jin-Hong*, YBM/Sisa.
Kim, Linsu, 1997, *Imitation to Innovation: The Dynamics of Korea's Technological Learning*, Harvard Business Review Press.
Kim, Sung-Yeon, Dong-Hwan Kim, 1993, *System Simulation and Simulation Language*, Korean Language, Hongneung Publishing.
Lakoff, G., M. Johnson, 1980, *Metaphors We Live By*, The University of Chicago Press.
Lao-tzu, Around B. C., 500, "TAO TE CHING (道德經)," in *A Translation of Lao Tzu's TAO TE CHING and Wang Pi's Commentary*, edited by Paul J. Lin 1978, Center for Chinese Studies, The University of Michigan.
Lee, Moon-Young, 2008, *Courage of Timid Mind – The Minimal Principle To Follow*, Korean Language, Sam-In.
Lindblom, Charles E., 1959, "The Science of Muddling Through," *Public Administration Review*, Vol. 19, No. 2, pp. 79–88.
Locke, John, 1689a, *Two Treatises of Government*.
Locke, John, 1689b, *A Letter Concerning Toleration*.
Luo, Guanzhong, 1400, *Romance of the Three Kingdoms*, Chinese Text Project, https://ctext.org/sanguo-yanyi
Luther, Martin, 1525, *Against the Robbing and Murdering Hordes of Peasants*, translated by Charles M. Jacobs.
Malthus, T., 1798, *An Essay On The Principle Of Population*, published in 1998 by Electronic Scholarly Publishing Project.
Marx, Karl, 1867, *Capital- A Critique of Political Economy*, translated by Ernest Mandel, 1976, Penguin Books

Marx, Karl, Frederick Engels, 1848, *Manifesto of the Communist Party*, translated by Samuel Moore in cooperation with Frederick Engels.

May, T. C., 1988, *The Crypto Anarchist Manifesto.*

Meadows, D. H., D. L. Meadows, J. Randers, W. W. Behrens III, 1972, *Limits to Growth*, Potomac Associates Book.

Merton, R. K., 1968, *Social Theory and Social Structure*, The Free Press.

Mill, John Stuart, 1859, *On Liberty*, published 2001 by Batoche Books Kitchener.

Mills, C. W., 1956, *The Power Elite*, Oxford University Press.

Montesquieu, Charles de Secondat, 1748, *The Spirit of Laws*, translated by Thomas Nugent, published 2001 by Batoche Books Kitchener.

More, T., 1516, *Utopia*, published in New York 1912 by The Macmillan Company.

Myrdal, G., 1944, *An American Dilemma: The Negro Problem and Modern Democracy*, Harper & Brothers.

OECD, 2020, *Innovative Citizen Participation and New Democratic Institutions - Catching the Deliberative Wave*, OECD.

Okun, A. M., 1975, *Equality and Efficiency: The Big Tradeoff*, Brookings Institution Press.

Olson, Mancur, 1965, *The Logic of Collective Action – Public Goods and the Theory of Groups*, Harvard University Press.

Osborne, D., T. Gaebler, 1992, *Reinventing Government: How the Entrepreneurial Spirit is Transforming the Public Sector*, Addison-Wesley Publishing Company.

Ostrom, E., 1990, *Governing the Commons - The Evolution of Institutions for Collective Action*, Cambridge University Press.

Parkinson, C. N., 1957, *Parkinson's Law and Other Studies in Administration*, Houghton Mifflin Company.

Peters, B. G., 2015, *Advanced Introduction to Public Policy*, Edward Elgar Publishing.

Popper, Karl, 1947, *Open Societies and Its Enemies – Volume I. The Spell of Plato*, George Routledge & Sons, LTD.

Popper, Karl, 1947, *Open Societies and Its Enemies – Volume II. The High Tide of Prophecy: Hegel, Marx, and the Aftermath*, George Routledge & Sons, LTD.

Powell, J. M., C. L. Thyne, 2011, "Global Instances of Coups from 1950 to 2010: A New Dataset," *Journal of Peace Research*, Vol. 48, No. 2, pp. 249–259.

Proudhon, P. J., 1851, *General Idea of the Revolution in the Nineteenth Century*, translated by John B. Robinson, 1969, Haskell House Publishers.

Putnam, R. D., 1993, *Making Democracy Work*, Princeton University Press

Putnam, R. D., 2000, *Bowling Alone*, Simon & Schuster.

Putnam, H., 2004, *The Collapse of the Fact/Value Dichotomy, and Other Essays*, Harvard University Press.

Richardson, G., 1991, *Feedback Thought in Social Science and Systems Theory*, University of Pennsylvania Press.

Ricoeur, Paul, 1980, *Essays on Biblical Interpretation*, Fortress Press.

Rousseau, Jean-Jacques, 1754, *Discourse on the Origin of Inequality*, translated by G. D. H. Cole.

Sandel, Michael, 2013, *What Money Can't Buy: The Moral Limits of Markets*, Farrar, Straus and Giroux.

Savas, E. S., 1987, *Privatization - The Key to Better Government*, Chatham House Publishers.

Sawyer, R. K., 2005, *Social Emergence - Societies as Complex Systems*, Cambridge University Press.

Schelling, T., 1978, *Micromotives and Macrobehavior*, W. W. Norton.

Schneider, A., H. Ingram, 1993, "Social Construction of Target Populations: Implications for Politics and Policy," *American Political Science Review*, Vol. 87, No. 2, pp. 334–347.

Schumacher, E. F., 1973, *Small Is Beautiful: A Study of Economics as If People Mattered*, Blond & Briggs.

Schumpeter, J. A., 1939, *BUSINESS CYCLES: A Theoretical, Historical and Statistical Analysis of the Capitalist Process*, McGraw-Hill Book Company.

Senge, P. M., 1990, *The Fifth Discipline – The Art & Practice of The Learning Organization*, Random House.

Shapiro, C., H. R. Varian, 1998, *Information Rules: A Strategic Guide to the Network Economy*, Harvard Business Review Press.

Simon, H. A., 1947, *Administrative Behavior: A Study of Decision-Making Processes in Administrative Organization*, Macmillan.

Smith, Adam, 1776, *An Inquiry into the Nature and Causes of the Wealth of Nations*, 1976 edition. Oxford University Press.

Snow, E., 1937, *Red Star Over China*, published in 1944, Random House.

Spinoza, B., 1677, "Ethics," in *A Spinoza Reader – The Ethics and Other Works*, edited and translated by Edwin Curley, published in 1944, Princeton University Press.

Sowell, T., 2015, *Basic Economics – A Common Sense Guide to the Economy*, Basic Books.

Sterman, J., 2000, *Business Dynamics - Systems Thinking and Modeling for a Complex World*, Irwin/McGraw-Hill.

Tocqueville, Alexis de, 1840, *Democracy in America*, translated by Henry Reeve and published as 'A Penn State Electronic Classics Series Publication' in 2002, The Pennsylvania State University.

Tolstoy, Leo, 1882, *Confession*, translated by David Patterson in 1983, W. W. Norton & Company.

Toynbee, A., 1946, *A Study of History: Abridgement of Vol. I–VI*, abridged by D. C. Somervell, Oxford University Press.

Tversky, A., D. Kahneman, 1981, "The Framing of Decisions and the Psychology of Choice," *Science*. Vol. 211, No. 4481, pp. 453–458.

Weber, Max, 1904, *The Protestant Ethic and the Spirit of Capitalism*, translated by Talcott Parsons in 1930, Routledge.

Weber, Max, 1919, *Politics as a Vocation*, translated by C. Wright Mills in 1946, published in 2014 as Mouling Digital Edition.

Weber, Max, 1922, *Economy and Society*, edited by G. Roth and C. Wittich in 1968, 1978, University of California Press.

Weick, K. E., 1979, *The Social Psychology of Organizing*, McGraw-Hill.

Williamson, O. E., 1975, *Markets and Hierarchies - Analysis and Antitrust Implications*, Free Press.

Wilson, J. Q., J. J. Dilulio, 2008, *American Government - Institutions and Policies*, Houghton Mifflin Company.

Yoon, Gyun-Soo, Soh Young-Jin, Kim Dong-Hwan, Lee Chong-Bum, 2000, *Dilemma and Administration*, Korean Language, Nanam Publishing.

Zuckerberg, M., 2017, *Building Global Community*, posted in his Facebook account.

Index

Page numbers in **bold** indicate tables, while page numbers in *italics* indicate figures.

For Product Safety Concerns and Information please contact our EU representative GPSR@taylorandfrancis.com
Taylor & Francis Verlag GmbH, Kaufingerstraße 24, 80331 München, Germany

www.ingramcontent.com/pod-product-compliance
Ingram Content Group UK Ltd.
Pitfield, Milton Keynes, MK11 3LW, UK
UKHW020005200926
475702UK00015B/2491
9781032735450